INSIGHT GUIDES

ST PETERSBURG
smart guide

Discovery
CHANNEL

APA PUBLICATIONS
Part of the Langenscheidt Publishing Group

Contents

Areas

St Petersburg.....................4
Nevsky Prospekt 6
Palace Square to
    Liteiny Prospekt 8
The Admiralty to St
    Nicholas's Cathedral....10
Peter and Paul Fortress....12
Petrograd Side 14
Vasilievsky Island 16
Vladimirskaya, Liteiny
    and Smolny 18
Moskovsky Prospekt 20
Peterhof 22
Other Excursions 24

A–Z

Architecture 28
Ballet, Opera and
    Theatre 32
Banya 34
Bars and Pubs 36
Bridges 38
Cafés 40
Children 42
Churches 44
Environment 50
Essentials.......................52
Fashion 54
Festivals 56
Film 58
Food and Drink 60
History 64
Hotels 66

Below: Palace Square, home of the Alexander Column and the Winter Palace.

Left: St Isaac's Cathedral from across the Neva.

Atlas

Vaslilievsky Island, Peter and Paul Fortress and the Petrograd Side....**132**
Liteiny and Smolny........**134**
City Centre....................**136**
Vladimirskaya and Eastern Nevsky Prospekt......**138**

Inside Front Cover: City Locator
Inside Back Cover: St Petersburg Transport

Street Index: 140–41
General Index: 142–4

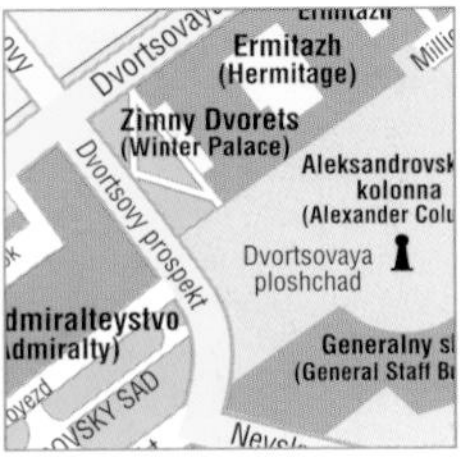

Language........................**74**
Literature........................**76**
Monuments....................**82**
Museums and Galleries....**86**
Music............................**100**
Nightlife........................**102**
Palaces and Houses......**106**
Parks and Gardens........**110**
Restaurants..................**114**
Shopping......................**122**
Sports..........................**124**
Transport......................**126**
Walks and Views..........**128**

Below: Vladimir Church icon.

St Petersburg

Russia's second city was for over 200 years the capital of the Russian empire. Built on a series of islands, its numerous rivers and canals are one of its most striking features, while its majestic architecture renders the city itself an open-air museum. Known as Russia's cultural capital, St Petersburg is thriving with museums and history, along with a vibrant and varied nightlife.

St Petersburg Fact and Figures

Population: **4.6 million**
Time zone: **GMT+3**
Currency: **Ruble**
Average salary: **16,000 rubles per month ($622)**
Number of bridges in the city: **308**
Number of islands in the city: **44, reduced by construction from the original 200 islands**
Number of names: **Four. Three official: St Petersburg (until 1914 and from 1991), Petrograd (1914–24), Leningrad (1924–91); and the unofficial nickname used by locals, 'Piter'**

The Granite City of Glory and Disaster – Anna Akhmatova

Founded in 1703 as a 'window onto Europe' by Peter the Great, St Petersburg stands proudly on the banks of the River Neva, a city of ornate palaces and glittering spires reflected in tranquil waterways. Dozens of architects from Western Europe helped to build it, with the result that St Petersburg does not resemble any other Russian city. It is often said that St Petersburg is a city built on bones, due to the number of Swedish prisoners of war and labourers who died building the city in the harsh, damp northern climate.

Though one of the most fascinating aspects of St Petersburg is undoubtedly its rich history – it has been the scene of revolutions, coups, mutinies, massacres, terror and a devastating 900-day siege – contemporary St Petersburg has far more to offer than historic buildings alone. It has over 170 museums, including the world-famous Hermitage museum, exploring the history, arts and culture of the city, as well as a plethora of theatres, jazz venues and a unique bar and club scene with something to cater for almost every kind of taste.

Divided by Water

The heart of the city is the side south of the Neva, where the city's main street, Nevsky Prospekt, and many of the most impressive sights are located. Across the Neva, Vasilievsky Island and another set of islands known collectively as the Petrograd Side both have their own distinct character and attractions.

Since the city was methodically planned just 300 years ago instead of developing naturally over many centuries like most cities of its size, St Petersburg is not difficult to navigate. The separate islands and the grid formed by the three streets radiating from the Admiralty – Nevsky Prospekt, Gorokhovaya Ulitsa and Voznesensky Prospekt – intersecting with the Canal Griboedova and Moika and Fontanka rivers divides the map into convenient areas.

The most popular time of year for visiting St Petersburg is during the city's celebrated White Nights from mid-May to mid-July, a magical and surreal period when there is no

Above: Peter the Great. **Below:** the Red Bridge over the Moika Canal.

real darkness, only a few hours of twilight a night. The phenomenon is the result of St Petersburg's northerly location.

Modern Abundance

The days of food shortages and mafia shoot-outs are long gone, and St Petersburg is now in many ways no different to any European metropolis. The enormous oil revenues the country has seen in recent years have had their impact on society, and the growing middle class is in evidence everywhere, from the sushi restaurants mushrooming around the city to the new shopping malls on the outskirts, where many foreign brands have become available for the first time in Russia.

Though property and commodity prices have soared during the last few years and continue to grow steadily, prices for public transport and basic goods remain considerably lower than in most Western European countries.

The northern capital continues to affirm its position as Russia's second city with the transfer of the Constitutional Court and Gazprom Neft – the oil division of Russia's state-owned energy behemoth and a welcomed taxpayer – to St Petersburg from Moscow. Both President Dmitry Medvedev and his predecessor Vladimir Putin are native Petersburgers, and the city is increasingly chosen to host the country's biggest international events.

Highlights

▲ The majestic **Palace Square** is home to the ornate Winter Palace, part of the colossal **Hermitage Museum**. ▶ **Nevsky Prospekt** is the city's main artery, a bustling thoroughfare lined with shops, palaces and churches.

▲ **Church on the Spilled Blood** is St Petersbug's most memorable church – a breathtaking sight with a dark, turbulent past.

▶ The historic **Peter and Paul Fortress** was founded by Peter the Great himself as the heart of his new city.

▲ Less than half an hour by boat, the summer retreat of the Tsars, **Peterhof**, is renowned for its fountains. ▶ A walk up to the dome of the magnificent **St Isaac's Cathedral** is well worth the climb.

Nevsky Prospekt

'*Nevsky Prospekt is deceptive at all hours of the day, but the worst time of all is at night... when the devil himself is abroad, kindling the street-lamps with one purpose only: to show everything in a false light*' – Nikolai Gogol. Nevsky Prospekt, which stretches 4.5km (3 miles) from the Admiralty building to the Alexander Nevsky Monastery *(Alexandro Nevkskaya Lavra)*, is St Petersburg's main street, the very heart of the city and a microcosm of life in Russia's second city. As depicted by Gogol in his short story entitled 'Nevsky Prospekt', at any time of the day or night Nevsky is thronged with people from all walks of life, from beseeching beggars to strolling couples.

Within Canal Griboedova

A walk along Nevsky starting from the Admiralty *(see p.10)* is the best way to get acquainted with the city. The first object of interest is a small plaque at No. 14 with a stencilled message in Russian, which translates as: '*Citizens! During artillery shelling, this side of the street is more dangerous.*'

The warning dates from the siege of Leningrad during World War II, when the Ger-

Left: Alexandriinsky Theatre.

mans regularly bombed the city. The significance of the siege for the city and continuing awareness of it is illustrated by the fact that flowers are still left beneath the plaque almost every day.

Two doors down on the same sunny side of the street is the **Literary Café**, which proudly markets itself as the place where Russia's greatest poet, Alexander Pushkin, met his second on his way to a fatal duel. As a café it is overpriced and best avoided, though the risk of dying from cholera after drinking a sip of water here, as Pyotr Tchaikovsky is reported to have done, no longer seems likely.

The first of the waterways to intersect Nevsky, the River Moika, is graced by the elaborate pink **Stroganov Palace** ①

on the right-hand side after the bridge, followed shortly by the imposing **Kazan Cathedral** ② *(Kazansky Sobor)*, flanked by monuments to Kutuzov and de Tollay.

On the left, the **Singer Building** ③ at No. 28 houses the city's favourite bookshop, **Dom Knigi** (House of Books). SEE ALSO ARCHITECTURE, P.31; CHURCHES, P.45; LITERATURE, P.81; MUSEUMS AND GALLERIES, P.86

Nevsky Prospekt was intended by Peter the Great to be one straight avenue from the Alexander Nevsky Monastery to the Admiralty. Building began on the road in 1711, starting from both points. When the teams met on the site of the current Ploshchad Vosstaniya, it became clear that miscalculations had been made, hence the significant bend in the avenue in that spot.

See Atlas Pages 136–139

Left: Anichkov Palace.

during which Lenin came there to read. The nearby **Catherine Garden** *(Yekaterinsky Sad)* is named after and dominated by a monument to the library's founder – Catherine the Great. Behind her looms the magnificent **Alexandriinsky Theatre** and the **Theatre Museum**.

SEE ALSO BALLET, OPERA AND THEATRE, P.32; CHURCHES, P.44, 45; MONUMENTS, P.82; PARKS AND GARDENS, P.112; SHOPPING, P.123

River Fontanka

The third waterway to intersect Nevsky is the River Fontanka – the original boundary of the city. It is spanned by the majestic **Anichkov Bridge** with its quartet of horse sculptures.

Two palaces face each other over the Fontanka – the austere white **Anichkov Palace** on the right before the bridge, and the superb **Beloselsky-Belozersky Palace** over the river.

There is little to see from here to where the famous avenue ends at **Ploshchad Alexandra Nevskovo** (Alexander Nevsky Square), where the **Alexander Nevsky Monastery** was built on the orders of Peter the Great on the spot where Prince Alexander Nevsky defeated the Swedes in 1240.

SEE ALSO ARCHITECTURE, P.31; BRIDGES, P.39; CHURCHES, P.44

Gostiny Dvor

The writer Alexandre Dumas called Nevksy a 'street of tolerance' due to its diverse range of places of worship. At Nos 32–34 stands the city's first Roman Catholic church, **St Catherine's** *(Katolicheskaya Tserkov Sviatoi Yekaterini)*, in front of which local artists sell paintings and draw caricatures, while the beautiful Wedgwood-style building at 40–42 is the **Armenian Apostles' Church** *(Armyanskaya Apostolskaya Pravoslavnaya Tserkov)*. The

red tower across the street marks the old **Duma** (city parliament) building, and was used in the past to warn Petersburgers of floods and fires, while the enormous yellow building to the left of it is the city's oldest and most central department store, **Gostiny Dvor** ④ (Merchants' Arcade), which stretches around an entire block.

Crossing Sadovaya Ulitsa, the light-blue **Russian National Library** stands on the right, bearing a plaque commemorating the years

Palace Square to Liteiny Prospekt

This area includes some of St Petersburg's most breathtaking sights, including the art collections and buildings of the Hermitage and Russian Museum and the Church on the Spilled Blood, as well as the contrasting open spaces of the Field of Mars and the Summer Gardens. It takes in St Petersburg's most famous square, Palace Square, scene of the 1905 Bloody Sunday massacre, as well as Arts Square, so named due to the multitude of theatres, museums and concert halls surrounding it.

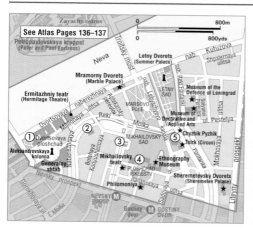

Following the Moika away from Palace Square, No. 12 on the embankment houses the **Pushkin Apartment Museum** ② *(Muzey-Kvartira Pushkina)*, where Russia's greatest poet lived and died. SEE ALSO BALLET, OPERA AND THEATRE, P.33; MONUMENTS, P.82; MUSEUMS AND GALLERIES, P.88, 89

Arts Square

One of St Petersburg's most popular and impressive attractions is the gaudy onion-domed **Church on the Spilled Blood** ③ *(Spas-na-Krovi)*, built on the spot where Alexander II was fatally wounded by a terrorist's bomb.

Across the road behind the church is a vast **souvenir market**, while the elaborate wrought-iron fence belongs to the **Mikhailovsky Gardens** *(Mikhailovsky Sad)*. The immense yellow classical building that backs onto the gardens is the **Mikhailovsky Palace** – the main branch of the **State Russian Museum** ④.

Its front faces onto **Ploshchad Iskusstv** (Arts Square), which centres around a monument to Alexander Pushkin. To the right of the Mikhailovsky Palace is the **Ethnography Museum**, while the opposite corner of the square (closest to the Canal-

Around Palace Square

Palace Square, St Petersburg's architectural centrepiece, is best approached by turning off Nevsky down Bolshaya Morskaya Ulitsa, which brings you under the arch of the **General Staff Building** *(Generalny Shtab)* to reveal the **Winter Palace** ① *(Zimny Dvorets)*, now home to the **Hermitage Museum**, in all its glory. In the centre of the square stands the **Alexander Column** *(Aleksandrovskaya Kolonna)*, which commemorates Russia's victory over Napoleon. The curved yellow General Staff Building was built for the ministries of for-

eign affairs and finance, but now houses part of the Hermitage's vast collection.

The street leading from the huge Atlantes holding up the New Hermitage, as the building immediately to the right of the Winter Palace is known, is called **Millionaya Ulitsa** (Millionaires' Street) after its well-to-do residents, and leads to the majestic **Marble Palace** *(Mramorny Dvorets)*, now a branch of the Russian Museum, at No. 5. The Hermitage complex continues along the embankment with a series of buildings joined by passageways, including the **Hermitage Theatre**.

Left: Church on the Spilled Blood.

tossing coins at the **Chyzhik Pyzhik** monument, while continuing along the Fontanka away from the Letny Sad will bring you to St Petersburg's **Circus** *(Tsirk)*.

Two more attractions in this area can be found on **Solyanoi Pereulok** (Salt Lane). The first is the superb, eclectic building at No. 13, housing the **Museum of Decorative and Applied Arts** – part of the college of the same name. The cannons outside No. 9 mark the **Defence of Leningrad Museum**, which offers moving insight into how the citizens who remained in the city lived and died during the 900-day siege. Finally, the impressive **Sheremetev Palace** *(Sheremetevsky Dvorets)* on

Griboedova) houses the **Mikhailovsky Theatre**.

Adding to the arts and cultural institutions around the square, the **St Petersburg Philharmonic** *(Philomoniya)* sits at the corner of Mikhailovskaya Ulitsa and Italianskaya Ulitsa. Culture aside, the square itself is a very pleasant spot to sit and enjoy an ice cream, contemplate the Pushkin statue and witness the city's goth population.
SEE ALSO BALLET, OPERA AND THEATRE, P. 33; CHURCHES, P.45; MUSEUMS AND GALLERIES, P.87, 91; MUSIC, P.100; PARKS AND GARDENS, P.112; SHOPPING, P.122

Open Spaces

Across the River Moika from the Mikhailovsky Sad is another green open space, the **Field of Mars** *(Marsovo Pole)*. Less formal than its neighbours, it is popular with sunbathers and dog-walkers.

The **Summer Gardens** *(Letny Sad)* across the road to the east (entrance from the Neva embankment or from Ulitsa Pestelya) are quite a contrast, with their classical statues.
SEE ALSO PARKS AND GARDENS, P.112, 113

Around the Fontanka

Crossing back over the Moika, the **Mikhailovsky Castle** ⑤, also known as the Engineers' Castle, is another branch of the Russian Museum, and the scene of the murder of Paul I.

Next to the bridge at the intersection of the Moika and Fontanka rivers, you are likely to see a crowd of people

the Fontanka conceals the more modest Fountain House, where the poet Anna Akhmatova spent much of her fascinating life. It now houses the **Anna Akhmatova Museum**.
SEE ALSO CHILDREN, P.42; MONUMENTS, P.83; MUSEUMS AND GALLERIES, P.86, 87, 88

According to local folklore, if you stare at the monument to Peter the Great outside the Engineers' Castle at exactly 3am during the White Nights, you will see the statue move. Especially if you have been roaming the streets drinking beer and champagne all night, one suspects.

Right: General Staff Building.

The Admiralty to
St Nicholas's Cathedral

The area southwest of Nevsky Prospekt is one of the most picturesque in the city. One of the best ways to see this area is by taking a boat trip along the scenic Canal Griboedova, passing under some charming bridges and taking in the city's most celebrated theatre, the Mariinsky, home to the renowned Kirov opera and ballet troupe. The area also includes several well-known landmarks: the Admiralty building crowned by its soaring spire, the city's biggest cathedral, St Isaac's, and the legendary Bronze Horseman.

Above: New Holland Arch.

From the Admiralty to Ploshchad Dekabristov

The **Admiralty** ① *(Admiralteistvo)* was built as a ship-yard fortress to designs by Peter the Great himself; the building that stands today was built a century later. It houses an academy for naval officers and engineers. To its south lies the **Alexandrovsky Garden**, whose benches around the majestic fountain are a popular spot with young cadets from the Admiralty and their girlfriends.

West along the embank-ment is **Ploshchad Dekabristov** (Decembrists' Square), dominated by the architectural marvel of the **Bronze Horse-man** ② *(Medny Vsadnik)* mon-ument to Peter the Great.

Erected by Catherine the Great, the Bronze Horseman received both its name and legendary status after Pushkin's eponymous poem. It is now the first photo stop for newlyweds leaving the nearby Wedding Palace.

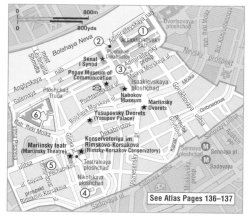

See Atlas Pages 136–137

The two matching buildings behind the Bronze Horseman are the **Senate** and **Synod**, designed by Rossi.
SEE ALSO ARCHITECTURE, P.30; MONUMENTS, P.82; PARKS AND GARDENS, P.111

St Isaac's Square

St Isaac's Cathedral ③ *(Isaakievsky Sobor)* is the largest church building in Russia and the dominant fea-ture of **Isaakievskaya Ploshchad** (St Isaac's Square). In the centre of the square stands an equestrian **Monument to Nicholas I**, while the **Mariinsky Dvorets** on the south side of the

square is home to St Peters-burg's legislative assembly.

Adjacent to the square, Bolshaya Morskaya and Malaya Morskaya ulitsas boast their own fair share of history. Malaya Morskaya was home to the the com-poser Pyotr Tchaikovsky (No.13) and the writer Nikolai Gogol (No.17), while No.47 Bolshaya Morskaya was the beloved childhood home of the writer Vladimir Nabokov, and now houses the **Nabokov Museum**.

Pochtamtskaya Ulitsa, as Malaya Morskaya becomes on the other side of the square, is named after the

Left: the Admiralty.

The Yusupov Palace was the scene of a murder in 1916, when Prince Felix Yusupov and his fellow conspirators decided to rid Russia of the infamous preacher Rasputin. Despite wild rumours about the holy man's sexual conquests, Nicholas II and his wife Alexandra adored Rasputin for his apparent ability to cure their haemophiliac son Alexei. The friendship damaged Alexandra's reputation irreparably, and when Rasputin's influence extended to appointing and dismissing ministers, the conspirators decided enough was enough. Having poisoned and shot Rasputin in the basement of the palace, they then pushed him through a hole in the ice on the Neva. The autopsy found that the cause of death was neither the poison nor the bullet wounds to the head – but drowning.

city's main post office (*Pochtamt*), which boasts an impressive Art Nouveau interior and is located at No.9. Just around the corner is the **Popov Museum of Communications**, one of St Petersburg's most hi-tech museums.
SEE ALSO CHURCHES, P.46; MONUMENTS P.84; MUSEUMS AND GALLERIES, P.92, 93

Theatre Square

From St Isaac's Square, it is a short walk along the River Moika or Ulitsa Dekabristov to **Teatralnaya Ploshchad** (Theatre Square), so named due to the fabulous green-and-white **Mariinsky Theatre** building. Facing the entrance to the theatre is the **Rimsky-Korsakov Conservatory**, in front of which stands a monument to the composer. This is the alma mater of many great composers and musicians, including Sergei Prokofiev

and Dmitry Shostakovich. The road that runs between the two buildings is named after another great Russian composer, Glinka, and leads to the stunning blue-and-gold two-storey **St Nicholas's Cathedral** ④ (*Nikolsky Sobor*). Just off Ulitsa Dekabristov on Ulitsa Lermontova is the city's main synagogue, the **Great Choral Synagogue** ⑤ (*Bolshaya Khoralnaya Synagoga*).

Walking back along the Moika will take you past **New Holland Island** ⑥ (*Novaya*

Gollandiya), built to store timber for shipbuilding, dominated by a large triumphal arch. The island is being redeveloped by British architect Norman Foster as a hotel and entertainment complex. Back along the Moika, the **Yusupov Palace** is well worth a visit for its opulent interiors.
SEE ALSO BALLET, OPERA AND THEATRE, P.33; CHURCHES, P.46, 47; MUSIC, P.100; PALACES AND HOUSES, P.106

Right: Lion Bridge.

Peter and Paul Fortress

The Peter and Paul Fortress occupies an entire island chosen by Peter the Great in 1703 as the site for the heart of his new city. The grounds are open daily and are an interesting walk in themselves, while one combined ticket provides entrance to all the buildings, except for the walk across the ramparts of the Gosudarev Bastion, for which tickets are sold separately. The fortress is an excellent way to get a feel for how St Petersburg was when it was founded, and the cathedral and panoramic view from the ramparts are particularly recommended. A trip to the fortress can take the best part of a day, depending on how thoroughly you explore the museums.

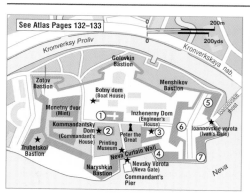

The Peter and Paul Cathedral

The **Peter and Paul Cathedral** ① *(Petropavlovsky Sobor)* was consecrated in 1732 and dominates the fortress island with its spire, which remains the tallest historic structure in the city.

The cathedral contains the tombs of all but two of the Russian Tsars from Peter the Great onwards, including those of Nicholas II, the Empress Alexandra Fyodorovna and three of their children, who were shot by the Bolsheviks in 1918. After lengthy tests conducted on remains discovered in a mineshaft in Yekaturinburg, Russia's last Tsar and his family were finally laid to rest here in 1998. In the same alcove of the cathedral lie the tombs of the family's doctor and three servants who were shot along with the imperial family.
SEE ALSO CHURCHES, P.47

Museums

Although it was built to defend the city, the Peter and Paul Fortress has never taken part in military combat. For much of its history it was used as a political prison,

> Every day at noon, the cannons of the Naryshkin Bastion fire a shot, a tradition dating back to the 18th century when few people had their own clocks. The practice, stopped after the revolution, was reintroduced in 1957.

resulting in its nickname of the Russian Bastille.

The first prisoner of the fortress's infamous **Trubetskoi Bastion** was Peter the Great's son Alexei, who was tortured to death there in 1718, while later prisoners included Dostoevsky, Trotsky and Chernyshevsky.

Now most of its buildings are given over to museums, the most interesting of which are the **History of St Petersburg and Petrograd 1703–1918** ② housed in the Kommandantsky Dom (Commandant's House), and the **Museum of Old St Petersburg** ③ housed in the Inzhenerny Dom (Engineer's House). The history of the complex itself is covered in the **History of the Peter and Paul Fortress Museum** ④ in the

Left: Peter and Paul Cathedral and its coat of arms.

to death were led to their place of execution, earning it the title 'Gates of Death'.

Separate tickets are sold at the base of the **Gosudarev Bastion** ⑦ to walk along the top of the ramparts, from where there is an unparalleled panoramic view of the opposite embankment, including the Hermitage buildings, Marble Palace, Strelka and much more.

Walks and Views

Near the cathedral is an unusual monument to the fortress's founding father, Peter the Great. Created by the sculptor Mikhail Shemiakin, it caused something of a furore when it was presented in 1991 due to the disproportionate size of the figure's head. It quickly became a beloved part of the fortress, however, and is popular with visitors, who like to sit on Peter's knee and have their photograph taken. Holding the figure's long, bony fingers is said to bring good luck.

The small Botny Dom (Boat House) now houses a ticket office and gift shop, but was originally built from 1762–6 to house the 'Grandfather of the Russian Navy' – the boat of Peter the Great. In 1940, the boat was moved to the Central Naval Museum (see p.96), where it can still be seen, while the one on display in the Botny Dom is a replica.

Nevsky Curtain Wall, while on a rather different theme, the Ioannovsky Ravelin houses the **Museum of Space Exploration and Rocket Technology** ⑤, dedicated to the history of space exploration in Russia and the Soviet Union, and the Pechatnya contains a **Printing Museum**. SEE ALSO MUSEUMS AND GALLERIES, P.93, 94

From April, when temperatures range from 0–8°C (32–46°F), the fortress beach attracts dozens of sun-craving Russians (right), who stand against the Neva Curtain Wall, often wearing little and assuming yoga-like poses, in the hope of catching some sun from the feeble spring rays. Braver still are the 'walruses' who in deepest winter break the Neva's ice to swim from the beach. Many are elderly people who swear these freezing dips are the secret of their longevity.

Ramparts, Gates and Bastions

The main entrance to the fortress is the **Petrovskie Vorota** ⑥ (Peter's Gate), built from 1714–18 by Domenici Trezzini. The wooden bas-relief depicting *The Magician Simon Cast Down by the Apostle* is an allegory of Peter the Great's victory over Charles XII of Sweden, while the arch is crowned by the symbol of imperial Russia, the double-headed eagle.

The **Nevsky Vorota** (Neva Gate) on the south side of the fortress was the exit through which prisoners condemned

13

Petrograd Side

The Petrograd Side comprises the land mass directly behind the Peter and Paul Fortress – known as the Kronverk – Aptekarsky Island and the three islands to the northwest – Kamenny, Yelaginsky and Krestovsky – known collectively as the Kirov Islands. The Kronverk is home to three museums commemorating the Bolshevik revolution and the original home of Peter the Great. Kamennoostrovsky Prospekt, with its stately buildings and multitude of shops and cafes, is like a second city centre, while the Kirov Islands have long been a favourite place for locals to walk and relax at weekends.

The Kronverk

The Kronverk is dominated by the **Artillery Museum** (Voenno Istorichesky Muzey Artillerii). To the west of it is the **Leningrad Zoo** (Zoologichesky Sad), which can be located by following the smell, while to its east, the Gorkovskaya metro station is surrounded by the small **Alexandrovsky Park**. On the other side of the semicircular Kronverkskaya Naberezhnaya is the **Sytny Rynok**, the city's oldest market. Following the twin minarets of the **Great Mosque** ① (Sobornaya Mechet) leads to the beautiful blue-domed building itself.

Beyond this is the **Kshessinskaya Mansion**, once the home of the ballerina Matilda Kshessinskaya and now home to the **Museum of Political History** ② and an exhibition on the ballerina herself.

A walk through Troitskaya Ploshchad with its small monument to those who suffered and died in the Soviet Gulags (labour camps) will bring you out onto the Petrovskaya Naberezhnaya, where the **Cabin of Peter the Great** ③ (Domik Petra I) is located. Peter lived in this modest wooden hut while the first structures of his new city were being built. Along the embank-

Matilda Kshessinskaya was famed for both her dancing and her romance with the future Tsar Nicholas II. According to rumour, an underground passage under the Neva connected the ballerina's house with the Winter Palace, enabling the young lovers to meet.

ment and around the corner is the famous cruiser **Avrora** ④, which fired the blank shot at the Winter Palace that signified the start of the 1917 October Revolution.

SEE ALSO CHILDREN, P.42; CHURCHES, P.48; FOOD AND DRINK, P.63; MUSEUMS AND GALLERIES, P.94, 95; PARKS AND GARDENS, P.111

Kamennoostrovsky Prospekt

A stroll down Kamennoostrovsky Prospekt takes in a number of sites, starting with the monument to Maxim Gorky outside the metro station named after the Soviet writer, who lived nearby at Kronverksky Prospekt 23. Heading north on Kamennoostrovsky Prospekt is the **Lenfilm Studios**, founded in 1918 as Russia's first film studio.

Further on is the **Kirov Museum** ⑤, dedicated to the Leningrad Communist Party

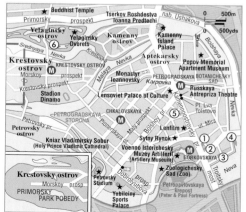

Left and below: Avrora and its crew.

Apartment celebrating the renowned opera singer, as well as the **Popov Memorial Apartment Museum**.
SEE ALSO PARKS AND GARDENS, P.111

Kirov Islands

The Kirov Islands remain the greenest, leafiest districts of the city. **Krestovsky Island** is usually the busiest, due to the fact it has its own metro station, providing easy access to the island's **Seaside Victory Park** *(Primorsky Park Pobedy)* and funfair. On the western tip of the island, a new state-of-the-art stadium is being built to replace the demolished Kirov Stadium.

Yelagin Island is devoted to the **Central Park of Culture and Leisure ⑥ (TsPKO).** A popular place to skate and cycle, the park's cultural focus is the **Yelaginsky Dvorets.** Rowing boats can be hired to enjoy the island's numerous lakes, and there is also a small zoo on the island.

Kamenny Island is home to the private dachas of the super-rich, the **Church of St John the Baptist** and **Kamenny Island Palace**, now a military sanatorium.

Along the road beyond Krestovsky Island, on the way to the resorts along the Gulf of Finland, is the colourful **Buddhist Temple**.
SEE ALSO CHURCHES, 48; PARKS AND GARDENS, P.112, 113

leader who lived here prior to his murder in 1934.

The romantic Tower House, home of the **Russkaya Antrepriza Theatre**, dominates Ploshchad Lva Tolstovo

Past Petrogradskaya metro is the **Lensoviet Palace of Culture**, a popular venue for concerts. Opposite is a monument to physicist Alexander Popov, generally accepted in Russia as the inventor of radio.
SEE ALSO FILM, P.59; MUSEUMS AND GALLERIES, P.95

Bolshoy Prospekt

Bolshoy Prospekt runs from Petrogradskaya metro to Sportivnaya metro, and is lined with stores and boutiques. Around Sportivnaya are several objects of interest, including the **Yubileiny Sports Palace** that gave the metro its name. The arena is now mainly used as a concert venue and contrasts sharply with the classical facade of the **Holy Prince Vladimir Cathedral** *(Kniaz*

Vladimirsky Sobor) opposite. On the other side of Bolshoy Prospekt is the **Petrovsky Stadium**, where FC Zenit, winners of the 2008 UEFA Cup, play their home games.
SEE ALSO CHURCHES, P.48; SPORTS, P.125

Aptekarsky Island

Aptekarsky Island, separated from the main island by the small River Karpovka, is a charmingly dilapidated district of crumbling facades and weeds. It is home to the city's **Botanical Gardens**, the soaring **TV Tower**, visible from all around the city, and the **Chaliapin Memorial**

Vasilievsky Island

Vasilievsky Ostrov was originally planned by Peter the Great to be the centre of the city – a network of canals modelled on Venice and Amsterdam. Though the ground eventually proved unsuitable for Peter's plan, the streets on the island still form a grid of geometrically straight lines, with three main prospects – *Maly* (Small), *Sredny* (Medium) and *Bolshoy* (Big) – intersecting rows of roads with numbers rather than names. Most of the island's objects of interest are located along a small stretch of the embankment and easy to incorporate into a stroll across the Neva from the Hermitage, while the other side of the island faces out onto the Gulf of Finland.

The Strelka

Walking over **Dvortsovy Most** (Palace Bridge) from the Hermitage will bring you to the **Strelka** ① (Spit) of Vasilievsky Island – the perfect departure point for a walk around the island.

The Strelka was originally the city's main port, and was developed into the architectural ensemble of the Stock Exchange, **Rostral Columns** and granite embankment by Thomas de Thomon at the beginning of the 19th century. The two magnificent columns flank the semicircular tip of the Strelka. When this was a working port, the large bowls crowning the columns were filled with oil and lit to enable them to serve as lighthouses, and on special occasions such as City Day (27 May) the columns are still lit – a truly majestic sight.

The stately classical building opposite the tip of the island was built to house the city's Stock Exchange, but since 1940 has contained the **Central Naval Museum** *(Voenno-Morskoy Muzey)*. During the summer months, a large floating fountain illumi-

Above: Egyptian Sphinx.

nated with changing hues is turned on in the Neva near the Strelka to add to the marvels of the White Nights and the opening of the bridges.

SEE ALSO MONUMENTS, P.85; MUSEUMS AND GALLERIES, P.96

Along the Embankment

Heading west along Universitetskaya Naberezhnaya from the Strelka, No.1 contains the superb **Zoology Museum** *(Zoologichesky Muzey)* – certain to be a hit with children – while its striking turquoise-and-white neighbour is the legendary **Kunstkamera** ② – the first public museum in Russia, and one of the city's most unusual collections – but not for the fainthearted.

Legend has it that Peter chose this site for a purpose-built museum to house his personal collection of rarities

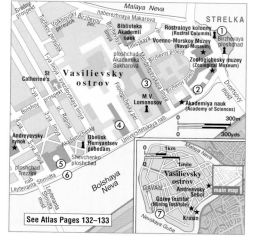

Left: Rostral Column.

flanked by impressive sculptures depicting the rape of Proserpine and Hercules fighting Antaeus.
SEE ALSO ARCHITECTURE, P.28, 29, 30; MONUMENTS, P.85; MUSEUMS AND GALLERIES, P.96, 97; PALACES AND HOUSES, P.106

Bolshoy Prospekt

If you are ready to venture further afield than the embankment, a walk along Vasilievsky Ostrov's main street, Bolshoy Prospekt, takes in the cheerful **St Andrew's Cathedral** (*Andreevsky Sobor*) on the corner with the 6th liniya, and the **Andreevsky Rynok** at No.16. At the very end of Bolshoy Prospekt is **Lenexpo** ⑦, the city's main trade and exhibition centre.
SEE ALSO CHURCHES, P.48

To the Sea

Though just two metro stops from Nevsky Prospekt, the area around Primorskaya metro could not seem more removed from the centre's cosmopolitan vibe. Walking southeast from Primorskaya along the River Smolenka will bring you to the overgrown **Smolensk Orthodox Cemetery** (*Smolenskoe Pravoslavnoe Kladbishche*), separated by the river from the **Smolensk Lutheran Cemetery**, while following the river northwest leads to the Gulf of Finland.

when he saw on this spot two pine trees whose branches had become so intertwined that it was impossible to distinguish them.

No.5 on the embankment houses the austere **Academy of Sciences** (*Akademiya Nauk*) built during the reign of Catherine the Great, while continuing the unbroken row of historic edifices is the long red building of the **Twelve Colleges** ③ (*Dvenadtsat Kollegii*) – built by Trezzini to house the 12 ministries founded by Peter the Great. The building now houses part of the St Petersburg State University.

Passing the monument to St Petersburg's most famous academician, Mikhail Lomonosov, the stately yellow building at No.15 is one of the oldest buildings in the city – the **Menshikovsky Palace** ④. The palace of Peter's best friend, Alexander Menshikov, was completed in 1714 and was the biggest and most luxurious building in the city, in stark contrast with Peter's simple tastes. The original interiors have now been recreated as a branch of the Hermitage Museum.

The small park after the palace contains an obelisk commemorating Field Marshal Rumyantsev, who led Russia to victory over the Turks in 1774.

The breathtaking facades continue with the **Academy of Fine Arts** ⑤ (*Akademiya Khudozhestv*), opposite which lie a graceful pair of **Egyptian Sphinxes** ⑥ dating from the 14th century BC.

Two final, less essential sights are located much further along the embankment – the prestigious **Mining Institute** on the corner of the embankment and 21st liniya, and the icebreaker *Krasin* moored in front of it. The former houses the **Mining Museum**, whose entrance is

The sloping walkways down to the water on the Strelka are another popular destination for newlyweds, who come here after their marriage ceremony to perform the tradition of breaking a champagne bottle on the wall to bring them happiness in their marriage.

Vladimirskaya, Liteiny and Smolny

The districts to the east of the Fontanka may be less awe-inspiring than the sweeping scale of the embankments and central squares, but they are no less interesting architecturally or historically and are home to some of the most fascinating museums, since many of the city's writers and artists lived in this area. Fewer tourists in this area allow you to get a feel for 'real' St Petersburg life. The area is also the city's culinary hub, embodied by Ulitsa Rubinshteina – one long street of restaurants offering every cuisine imaginable.

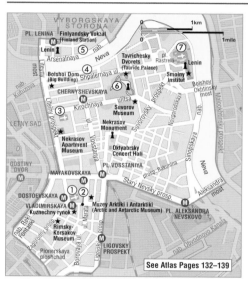

See Atlas Pages 132–139

Vladimirskaya

The focal point of the area around Vladimirskaya metro is the magnificent **Vladimir Cathedral** ① *(Vladimirsky Sobor)*. Following the line of *babushki* selling pickles, socks and vegetables outside the cathedral will lead you to **Kuznechny Rynok**, the best-quality fresh produce market in the city.

Vladimirskaya is often known as 'Dostoevsky's Petersburg' due to the fact that he lived in several apartments around here over many years. The one in which he died now houses the excellent **Dostoevsky Museum** ②.

The **Arctic and Antarctic Museum** *(Muzey Arktiki i Antarktiki)* is housed in a former church, while the **Rimsky-Korsakov Museum** is situated at the junction known as **Pyat Uglov** (Five Corners).

SEE ALSO CHURCHES, P.49; FOOD AND DRINK, P.63; MUSEUMS AND GALLERIES, P.97, 98

Liteiny

North of Nevsky, Vladimirsky Prospekt becomes Liteiny Prospekt. The Futurist poet Vladimir Mayakovsky is honoured by a monument halfway down the street that bears his name, while the writer, poet and publisher Nikolai Nekrasov is commemorated at the **Nekrasov Apartment Museum** on the corner of the street named after him and Liteiny Prospekt. At the other end of Ulitsa Nekrasova is a small garden with a large monument to the writer.

Continuing north along Liteiny Prospekt leads to the magnificent **Cathedral of the Transfiguration of Our Saviour** ③ *(Spaso-Preobrazhensky Sobor)*, surrounded by an ornate iron gate, while almost at the end of the prospekt (Nos 4–6) looms an immense and foreboding complex, which housed the local headquarters of the NKVD – the Soviet secret police. The **Bolshoy Dom** (Big Building), as it became known among residents, quickly became an object of dread and a symbol of the purges and arrests gripping Russia at that time. It now houses the FSB – the modern successor of the NKVD and KGB.

Left: Smolny Cathedral.

Smolny

The area around Cherny-shevskaya metro and along Suvorovsky Prospekt is one of the most tranquil parts of the centre. The **Tauride Gardens** ⑥ *(Tavrichesky Sad)* is a large, rambling park popular with pram-pushing mothers. Its north side contains the neoclassical **Tauride Palace** *(Tavrichesky Dvorets)*. Opposite the park on Kirochnaya Ulitsa is the **Suvorov Museum**. Walking down Shpalernaya Ulitsa will take you past a lone monument to Felix Dzerzhinsky, the founder of the Cheka (secret police) to the stunning architectural ensemble of Ploshchad Rastrelli and the Smolny complex, whose centrepiece – the **Smolny Cathedral** ⑦ – is another Baroque masterpiece by the architect.

The buildings encircling the cathedral are the Smolny Convent, while the **Smolny Institute** to the right was founded by Catherine the Great as a boarding school for young noblewomen. Lenin stands in front of the building, while amid the fountains and lilac bushes in the garden are busts of Marx and Engels.

SEE ALSO CHURCHES, P.49; MUSEUMS AND GALLERIES, P.98; PARKS AND GARDENS, P.113

There were rumours in the 1930s that the Bolshoy Dom had as many underground levels as it did above ground to house all the interrogation cells. This led to the chilling anecdote: *What is the tallest building in Leningrad?* *The administrative building on Liteiny. From its basement you can see all the way to Siberia.*

Appropriately enough, just a short walk from this symbol of Soviet terror is the unsettling **Monument to Victims of Political Repression** ④, in the form of Shemiakin's Sphinxes on Naberezhnaya Robespiera. Once in close proximity to the serene creatures, it becomes apparent that half of each Sphinx's face is an exposed skull. The site chosen for the monument was no accident. Directly opposite them on the other side of the Neva is the infamous **Kresty Prison** ⑤, where political prisoners were sent from the Bolshoy Dom.

Two memorials to Lenin can be found further west along the northern embankment from Kresty, at **Finland Station**, which has part of the train in which Lenin returned to Russia from Finland in 1917. The station's vast square is dominated by a statue to the Bolshevik leader.

SEE ALSO CHURCHES, P.48; MONUMENTS, P.84 MUSEUMS AND GALLERIES, P.97

Right: Smolny Institute.

Moskovsky Prospekt

Moskovsky Prospekt is the beginning of the road to Moscow, from where it gets its name. It is also the main road from the airport to the city centre, and is an awe-inspiring introduction to the city's grandeur, though with its immense Stalin-era ensembles, it is a world away from the imperial splendour of the historic centre. It is now considered to be one of the most desirable districts of the city in which to live, due to the proximity of numerous parks. The prospekt is too long to walk in its entirety, but buses 213, 350 and K3 travel the length of the prospekt, and the blue metro line runs directly beneath the street.

Sennaya Ploshchad

The prospect begins at Sennaya Ploshchad (Haymarket Square). Though it is not usually high on the average list of tourist attractions, Sennaya Ploshchad offers a fascinating glimpse of St Petersburg's

underworld, with its delirious drunks, street traders and the occasional scuttling rat. But don't let that put you off. Almost anything imaginable can be bought on or around Sennaya Ploshchad, and usually at a far lower price than in other districts of the city. During the Soviet Union the square was known as Ploshchad Mira (Peace Square), and in the centre of the square stands a semi-transparent **Peace Tower**, which features the word for peace written all over it in hundreds of different languages.

Heading south down the prospect, **Sennoy Rynok** ① at No. 4 is the cheapest market in the city. Shortly afterwards is the small **Yusupovsky Sad**, which is most attractive in the winter when its small lake freezes over.

At Tekhnologichesky Institut metro, if you look right you will see the deep-blue domes of the **Trinity Cathedral** *(Troitsky Sobor)* ②, which had just been restored when its roof caught fire in 2006, necessitating more major work, while a short walk the other way will bring you to **Vitebsky Vokzal** (Vitebsk Station) – the very first train station in Russia. Built to connect St Petersburg to the royal residences at Pavlovsk

Above: Victory Park.

and Tsarskoe Selo, it still has an air of faded grandeur to it.
SEE ALSO CHURCHES, P.49;
FOOD AND DRINK, P.63

Triumphal Arches

Frunzenskaya metro sits on the foreboding Obvodny Canal, which marks the industrial zone south of the city, where another two stations are located – Baltiisky Vokzal and Varshavsky Vokzal. The latter is no longer a functioning station, but has been turned into an upmarket shopping and entertainment centre called **Varshavsky Express** (Warsaw Express).

Slightly nearer to Moskovskaya Vorota metro is the **Novodevichy Monastyr**, where the artist Mikhail Vrubel is buried. Far more impressive are the pair of tri-

Left: Moscow Triumphal Arch.

in 1998. Nicknamed 'The Spider' and 'The Crab', it is a far cry from its classical counterpart on Nevsky Prospekt.

Continuing south, the almost edible-looking **Chesma Church** ⑥ *(Chesmenskaya Tserkov)* and palace on the left are built on the spot where Catherine the Great was told the news that the Russian navy had defeated the Turks at Chesme in 1770.

In 1936 it was decided by the city authorities to move the centre of Leningrad to the southern end of the prospekt, hence the plethora of Soviet architecture and symbols around Ploshchad Pobedy, most notably the immense **House of the Soviets** *(Dom Sovietov)*, which was to house the local government and party headquarters. Construction was interrupted by the outbreak of war in 1941, and the plans were never realised.

Finally, the vast monument at **Ploshchad Pobedy** ⑦ (Victory Square) commemorates the suffering and eventual victory of the city during the war and 900-day siege. The hall beneath the **Monument to the Heroic Defenders of Leningrad** is a museum.
SEE ALSO CHURCHES, P.49; MONUMENTS, P.83; MUSEUMS AND GALLERIES, P.99; PARKS AND GARDENS, P.113

The infamous haymarket area was the setting for *Crime and Punishment*. Dostoevsky lived on Grazhdanskaya Ulitsa, and housed his fictional antihero, the student Raskolnikov, there. During recent years the square, once notorious for its prostitutes and down-and-outs, has been dramatically prettified and property prices have shot up.

umphal arches in this area. The magnificent **Moscow Triumphal Arch** ③ *(Moskovskiye Vorota)*, located at the metro station of the same name, was modelled on the Brandenburg Gate. To the southeast of Baltiisky Vokzal (quite a walk away) is the smaller **Narva Triumphal Arch** ④ *(Narvskaya Triumfalnaya Vorota)*.
SEE ALSO MONUMENTS, P.84; SHOPPING, P.123

Right: apartments near Sennaya Ploshchad.

Victory Park

The area between Park Pobedy and Moskovskaya metro stations is the prospekt's most interesting. The former is adjacent to the very popular **Victory Park** ⑤ after which it is named. The smaller **Park of the Aviators** on the other side of the prospekt is less formal, and has an old fighter jet on a small island as its centrepiece.

Opposite the metro station is another branch of the **National Library** completed

Peterhof

The palace and park of Peterhof, 25km (15 miles) west of St Petersburg, is the oldest of the ring of imperial estates situated just outside the city. Often described as 'the Russian Versailles', it was built for Peter the Great (Peterhof translates as 'Peter's Yard' in German), who having visited the royal French residence on his extensive tour of Europe, returned home determined to build a seaside residence on the Gulf of Finland that would outdo all those of Europe. Peterhof's biggest attraction is the multitude of grandiose fountains, which work from late May to early October. A day trip to Peterhof is an excellent escape from the city.

Palaces and Museums

During World War II, Peterhof was occupied by the German army, and the palaces, fountains and grounds were almost completely destroyed. Though painstaking restoration work began immediately after the town was liberated, work on the fountains was only completed in 2000.

Peterhof contains several palaces, of which by far the grandest is the **Great Palace** ① *(Bolshoy Dvorets)*, which occupies a prime position in the Upper Garden, with its terraces overlooking the **Grand Cascade** ② and the Gulf of Finland. Beneath the cascade is the **Grotto**, for which separate tickets are sold on the terrace.

In the Lower Park, situated right on the seashore, is Peter the Great's **Monplaisir** ③ palace, built from 1714–23 in the practical Dutch style that Peter so admired. The Catherine Block, added by Rastrelli from 1747–54 for Elizabeth, takes its name from Catherine the Great, who departed from here on 28 June 1762 to go to St Petersburg and be declared Empress of All the Russias after she received news that the coup was under way.

The **Marly Palace** ④ and **Hermitage Pavilion** in the

Lower Park were both built in the early 1720s by Johann Friedrich Braunstein. The Hermitage was built for Peter to entertain his closest friends. The Marly Palace, which takes its name from the French royal hunting lodge Marly-le-Roi, was built on the orders of Peter for 'special guests', and now contains a museum devoted to Peter himself.

The **Cottage Palace** in the Alexandria Park was built from 1826–9 as a summer residence for Nicholas I and his family. It was designed by the Scottish architect Adam Menelaws in the pseudo-Gothic style. Along with its numerous palaces, Peterhof also contains an Imperial Yacht Museum and

Above: Grand Palace portraits.

a Bicycle Museum.
SEE ALSO PALACES AND HOUSES, P.109

Parks and Fountains

If you arrive by bus, before reaching the entrance to the

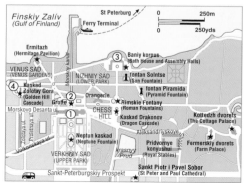

Finskiy Zalív
(Gulf of Finland)

St Peterburg
Ferry Terminal

0 ——— 250m
0 ——— 250yds

Ermitazh
(Hermitage Pavilion)

Baniy korpus
(Bath House and Assembly Halls)

VENUS SAD
(VENUS GARDENS)

③

NIZHNIY SAD
(LOWER PARK)

fontan Solntse
(Sun Fountain)

④ Kaskad
Zolotay Gora
(Golden Hill
Cascade)

②
Orangerie
Grotto

fontan Piramida
(Pyramid Fountain)

Rimskie Fontany
(Roman Fountains)

Morskovo Desanta ul.

①

CHESS
HILL

Kaskad Drakonov
(Dragon Cascade)

Kottedzh dvorets
(The Cottage Palace)

Aleksandriyskoye

Neptun kaskad
(Neptune Fountain)

Pridvornye
konyushui
(Royal Stables)

Fermerskiy dvorets
(Farm Palace)

VERKHNIY SAD
(UPPER PARK)

Krasnyy
Prud

Sankt Piotr i Pavel Sobor
(St Peter and Paul Cathedral)

Sankt-Peterburgskiy Prospekt

Left: one of Peterhof's
elaborate fountains.

highest in the park, reaching
a height of 20m (65ft).

A leisurely wander around
the Lower Park is perhaps
the easiest way to see its various fountains. Some of the
most delightful are the **Chess
Hill Cascade**, **Golden Hill
Cascade**, the **Roman Fountains** and the trick fountains
scattered between the latter
and Monplaisir, which turn on
when people sit under them,
or step on a nearby sensor,
such as the two in the garden
of Monplaisir commissioned
by Peter himself.

Getting There

Travel agents around the city
offer excursions to Peterhof
including transport by bus,
tickets to the park and
palace and a guided tour,
but at a vastly inflated price.
By far the most rewarding
way is to travel to Peterhof
the way Peter the Great
intended – by boat.

Hydrofoils leave every
15–30 minutes from the jetties on the Neva across from
the Hermitage and the Bronze
Horseman, and take 30 minutes to reach Peterhof. The
trains, buses and minibuses
(in descending order of comfort) that leave from Baltiisky
Station are cheaper but less
enjoyable options.

The fountains operate daily from
the last week of May to the first
week of October from 11am to
5pm (6pm at weekends). Every
year a special ceremony marks
the opening and closing of the
fountains. During the summer
months open-air concerts and
performances are held in the
grounds, including as part of the
Palaces of St Petersburg festival.

Upper Garden you will pass
the **Peter and Paul Cathedral**
(Sankt Piotr i Pavel Sobor),
which in sharp contrast with
its namesake in the city is built
in the Russian Orthodox style.

The Upper Garden to the
south of the palace is perhaps the part most reminiscent of Versailles, but its five
fountains are only a taste of
the splendour of the Lower
Park, which is home to more
than 150 fountains and four
cascades, the most impressive of which is the magnificent Grand Cascade
descending from the terrace
of the palace to the Lower
Park. Its centrepiece is the
Samson Fountain, which has
become a symbol of Peterhof
itself. The image of Samson
rending open the jaws of the
lion is an allegory of the
Russian victory over Sweden,
whose heraldry featured a
lion, at the battle of Poltava
on 27 June (St Samson's Day)
in 1709. The jets of the Samson Fountain are also the

Right: the Grand Cascade.

Other Excursions

Peterhof is just one of many recommended day trips from St Petersburg. The other imperial residences to the south and west of the city include Tsarskoe Selo (Pushkin) with its magnificent Catherine Palace and legendary Amber Room, and Pavlovsk and Gatchina with their wild, rambling parks. To the northwest of the city, the string of villages with their sandy beaches along the Gulf of Finland are popular picnic and sunbathing destinations in warm weather, and some have their own cultural attractions to offer, such as the holiday homes of artists and poets. All are easily accessible by train or minibus.

Tsarskoe Selo

Tsarskoe Selo, 25km (15 miles) from St Petersburg, means Tsars' Village. While the palace and park have been restored their pre-revolutionary name, the town itself is called Pushkin in commemoration of Russia's most beloved poet, who graduated from the town's **Lyceum**. A statue of the poet stands outside the school, which has been restored to look as it did in Pushkin's day.

The main attraction is **Catherine Palace**, yet another example of Rastrelli magnificence. Its famed **Amber Room** was recreated in time for the 300th anniversary of St Petersburg, after over 20 years of work. The surrounding park includes a formal landscaped garden as well as a large pond and pavilions in various states of disrepair.

The **Alexander Palace** and its park contrast with the splendour of Catherine Palace, which only serves to make them all the more appealing. The facade of the palace is peeling and the grounds unkempt, giving the place a melancholy aura, wistful for the past. This was the favourite residence of the last tsar and his wife, and now contains a moving exhibition in the right wing portraying the everyday life and objects of Russia's last royal family.

SEE ALSO PALACES AND HOUSES, P.107, 108; PARKS AND GARDENS, P.110, 111

Pavlovsk

Pavlovsk was founded in 1777 on land given by Catherine the Great to her son Paul (Pavel in Russian). It is just 5km (3 miles) from Pushkin, so can be combined into one trip for the particularly energetic.

Pavlovsk was so badly damaged during the Nazi

The **Amber Room** was created by Rastrelli in 1775, using panels inset with amber – a gift from Frederick of Prussia to Peter the Great. After Germany attacked in 1941, Soviet curators attempted to dismantle the Amber Room for storage, but found that the amber had become fragile and brittle. They then tried to disguise the panels behind ordinary wallpaper, but after the Nazis occupied Pushkin, the room was lost and has never been recovered. It is generally believed that the Nazis took it to Königsberg (now Kaliningrad), and a recent book by Catherine Scott-Clark and Adrian Levy concluded that the room was lost when Red Army soldiers torched Königsberg Castle, but versions persist that it was buried underneath a lake or in an old mine.

Left: Catherine Palace's Royal Chapel.

from Finlandsky Station. **Solnechnoye**'s highlight is its sandy beach and shallow water – a popular swimming spot with locals.

Repino is named after the artist Repin, one of the leading members of the Peredvizhniki (Wanderers) movement. His house, **Penaty**, is now a museum dedicated to his life and work. Finally, the village of **Komarova** is where Anna Akhmatova is buried, a fact commemorated by a memorial to the great poet.

SEE ALSO MUSEUMS AND GALLERIES, P.99

To get to Pushkin, take a train from Vitebsky Station to Detskoe Selo (the name of the station in Pushkin), from where you can walk to the palace or catch a bus (371 or 382). Alternatively, from outside Moskovskaya metro take minibus 342, 286, 287, 545 or 347. The journey time is around 45 minutes.

To get to Pavlovsk, take a train from Vitebsky Station to Pavlovsk (35 minutes), or take minibus 286 or 299 from Moskovskaya metro (one hour).

Gatchina can be reached by train from Baltiisky Station, or by bus and minibus 431 from Moskovskaya metro (about 45 minutes).

---

occupation that it took 26 years to restore, but its Great Palace has been fully reconstructed. The palace is less ostentatious than the Catherine Palace or Peterhof, but its human scale and smaller number of tourists add to its appeal.

The park is the largest of all the imperial residences. Divided by the River Slavyanka, it is a hilly, sprawling expanse of woods, ponds, bridges and pavilions. If all the walking has helped work up an appetite, the **Podvorye** restaurant near the station is renowned for its traditional fare.

SEE ALSO PALACES AND HOUSES, P.109; PARKS AND GARDENS, P.110; RESTAURANTS, P.121

Gatchina

Gatchina is further from the city than other estates –

45km (28 miles) to the south. Its park is the wildest and most romantic of them all and is especially beautiful in the autumn. Most of the palace has now been restored.

SEE ALSO PALACES AND HOUSES, P.108; PARKS AND GARDENS, P.110

Along the Gulf of Finland

Along the coast to the north of St Petersburg is a series of resort villages containing sanatoria where the elite used to spend their holidays. All can be reached by train

Right: sunset over the Gulf of Finland.

A–Z

In the following section St Petersburg's attractions and services are organised by theme, under alphabetical headings. Items that link to another theme are cross-referenced. All sights that fall within the atlas section at the end of the book are given a page number and grid reference.

Architecture 28
Ballet, Opera and Theatre 32
Banya 34
Bars and Pubs 36
Bridges 38
Cafés 40
Children 42
Churches 44
Environment 50
Essentials 52
Fashion 54
Festivals 56
Film 58
Food and Drink 60
History 64
Hotels 66
Language 74
Literature 76
Monuments 82
Museums and Galleries 86
Music 100
Nightlife 102
Palaces and Houses 106
Parks and Gardens 110
Restaurants 114
Shopping 122
Sports 124
Transport 126
Walks and Views 128

Architecture

St Petersburg is home to so many breath-taking architectural compositions that it is often described as an open-air museum. Its historic centre, where many of the city's most majestic and beautiful buildings are located, is a UNESCO World Heritage Site. Many foreign architects have contributed to the classical appearance of the city, which lacks the Soviet skyscrapers of Moscow – just one example of how the history of St Petersburg can be traced in its architecture. Some of the key buildings by notable architects are detailed below, organised by era.

Petrine Baroque

The first architects invited by Peter the Great to build his new capital on the Neva included Italian **Domenico Trezzini**, who was responsible for the city's initial planning and appearance from 1703–34. His heritage includes:

Alexander Nevsky Monastery
Nab. Reki Monastyrki 1; tel: 274 1702; www.lavra.spb.ru; 6am–9pm; M: Ploschad Alexandra Nevskovo; map p.139 D4
SEE ALSO CHURCHES, P.44

Peter and Paul Cathedral (1712–33)
Peter and Paul Fortress; tel: 238

> In the early days of the city's existence, Peter I banned the construction of stone buildings in every part of Russia with the exception of his new city, in order to attract stonemasons to the city and ensure its fast development.

0751; www.spbmuseum.ru; 10am–6pm; admission charge; M: Gorkovskaya; map p.132 C3
SEE ALSO CHURCHES, P.47

Twelve Colleges (1722–42)
Universitetskaya Nab. 7; not open to the public; map p.132 A4
The 400m (1,300ft) long building was originally built to house the 12 ministries founded by Peter the Great as part of his administrative reforms, and is now part of St Petersburg State University.

On Peter's orders, more renowned architects were brought from abroad, including the French architect and engineer Jean-Baptiste Le Blond, who designed the park at Peterhof and the interior of Peter the Great's Summer Palace, and the Italian sculptor Bartolomeo Carlo Rastrelli, who designed the interior of Monplaisir and many of the fountains and cascades at Peterhof. The style of this first generation of foreign architects became known as Petrine Baroque.

Elizabethan Extravagance

Under Peter's daughter Elizabeth, who reigned from 1741–62, the prevailing style of architecture was Baroque, led by **Bartolomeo Francesco Rastrelli** and Savva Chevinsky. Rastrelli's masterpieces include:

Left: the Winter Palace.

Left: corner of the General Staff Building.

Classicism school counted Jean-Baptiste Vallin de la Mothe and Antonio Rinaldi among its adherents, while the later, more restrained style towards the end of the century was practised by Ivan Starov and Giacomo Quarenghi.

De la Mothe created:

The Academy of Fine Arts (1764–88)
Universitetskaya Nab. 17; tel: 323 6496; www.rah.ru; Wed–Sun 11am–6pm; M: Vasilieostrovskaya
The Academy contains a museum displaying work by its teachers and students, as well as an exhibit in the history of Russian architecture.

The Arch of New Holland Island (1770s–1780s)
Nab. Admiralteiskovo Kanala; M: Sennaya Ploshchad; map p.136 A3

Gostiny Dvor (1760)
Nevsky Prospekt 35; tel: 710 5408; www.bgd.ru; M: Gostiny Dvor; map p.137 D2
SEE ALSO SHOPPING, P.123

Rinaldi is most famous for:

The Marble Palace (1768–85)
Millionaya Ulitsa 5/1; tel: 595 4248; www.rusmuseum.ru; Mon 10am–5pm, Wed–Sun 10am–6pm; M: Nevsky Prospekt/ Gorkovskaya; map p.133 D3

The Catherine Palace, Pushkin (1748–56)
Sadovaya Ulitsa 7, Pushkin; tel: 465 2024; www.tzar.ru; Wed–Mon 10am–6pm; admission charge; see Other Excursions, p.25, for details on how to get there
SEE ALSO PALACES AND HOUSES, P.108

Smolny Cathedral (1748–64)
Ploshchad Rastrelli 3; tel: 271 7632/314 2168; http://eng. cathedral.ru/smolny; Thur–Tue, winter 11am–6pm, summer 10am–8pm; admission charge; M: Chernyshevskaya or No. 5 trolleybus; map p.135 E3
SEE ALSO CHURCHES, P.49

The Stroganov Palace (1748)
Nevsky Prospekt 17; tel: 571 8238; www.rusmuseum.ru; Wed–Mon 10am–6pm; admission charge; M: Nevsky Prospekt; map p.137 C2
SEE ALSO MUSEUMS AND GALLERIES, P.86

The Winter Palace (1754–62)
Dvortsovaya Nab. 38; tel: 571 3420; www.hermitagemuseum. org; Tue–Sat 10.30am–6pm, Sun until 5pm; admission charge; M: Nevsky Prospekt; map p.136 B1
SEE ALSO MUSEUMS AND GALLERIES, P.89

The Age of Classicism

Catherine the Great did not like the ornate Baroque style that Elizabeth loved so much. During her reign (1762–96) the city took on a far more austere, classical appearance. Architecture during this period is split between two styles – early Classicism (1860s and 70s) and late Classicism (1780s to the 1800s). The early

Right: St Peterburg's buildings are loaded with intricate details.

Quarenghi's numerous architectural monuments include:

The Academy of Sciences (1784–7)
Universitetskaya Nab. 5; not open to the public; map p.132 B4

The Alexander Palace, Pushkin (1792–6)
Sadovaya Ulitsa 7, Pushkin; tel: 465 2024; www.tzar.ru; Wed–Mon 10am–6pm
SEE ALSO PALACES, P.107

The Hermitage Theatre (1783–7)
Dvortsovaya Nab. 34; tel: 579 0226; M: Nevsky Prospekt; map p.132 C4
SEE ALSO BALLET, OPERA AND THEATRE, P.33

The Yusupov Palace (1830s)
Nab. Reki Moiki 94; tel: 332 1991; www.yusupov-palace.ru; daily 11am–5pm; admission charge; M: Sadovaya; map p.136 A3
SEE ALSO PALACES AND HOUSES, P.106

High Classicism

The new century brought with it the arrival of High Classicism (1800–30). The chief architects in the city during this period included Jean-François Thomas de Thomon, Andrei Voronikhin, Andreyan Zakharov and Carlo Rossi, who created some of the city's biggest and most awe-inspiring ensembles.

Thomas de Thomon was responsible for redeveloping the Spit of Vasilievsky Island after it ceased to be a working port, including the addition of the Rostral Columns and the Stock Exchange building, which now houses the Naval Museum.

Central Naval Museum (1805–16)
Birzhevaya Ploshchad 4; tel: 328 2501; www.museum.navy.ru; Wed–Sun 11am–6pm; M: Gorkovskaya; map p.132 B4
SEE ALSO MUSEUMS AND GALLERIES, P.96

Voronikhin built:

Kazan Cathedral (1801–11)
Kazanskaya Ploshchad 2; tel: 570 4582; 9am–8pm; M: Nevsky Prospekt; map p.137 C2
SEE ALSO CHURCHES, P.45

The Mining Institute (1806–9)
22nd Liniya, Vasilievsky Island; not open to visitors

Zakharov was responsible for turning the old Admiralty shipyard into a classical masterpiece that would also become a symbol of the city.

The Admiralty (1806–19)
Admiralty Prospekt 1; not open to visitors; map p.136 B1

Rossi holds a special place in the history of the city's architecture, not least for his creation of the General Arch on Palace Square (1819–29). He also designed the matching Synod and Senate buildings on Ploshchad Dekabristov (not open to the public), and the National Library on the corner of Nevsky Prospekt and Sadovaya Ulitsa (1796–1834). You can go in the latter, but only if you register as a member first, which may be tricky if you don't speak Russian. His other masterpieces include:

Alexandriinsky Theatre (1828–32)
Ploshchad Ostrovskovo 6; tel: 312 1545; www.alexandriinsky.ru; M: Gostiny Dvor; map p.137 D2
SEE ALSO BALLET, OPERA AND THEATRE, P.32

> As well as buildings and arches, Rossi also designed a street of perfect proportions. Ulitsa Rossi *(left)* runs from behind the Alexandriinsky Theatre to Ploshchad Lomonosova. The width of the street (22m/72ft) is exactly equal to the height of its buildings, which have identical facades, and the street is exactly 10 times as long as it is wide.

The Mikhailovsky Palace (1819–25)

Inzhenernaya Ulitsa 4; tel: 595 4248; www.rusmuseum.ru; Mon 10am–5pm, Tue–Wed 10am–6pm; M: Nevsky Prospekt; map p.137 D1
SEE ALSO MUSEUMS AND GALLERIES, P.91

The Appearance of Eclecticism

The second half of the 19th century saw architects Andrei Stakenschneider and Auguste de Montferrand using a combination of styles and influences in their iconic buildings.

Stakenschneider's legacy to the city includes:

The Beloselsky–Belozersky Palace (1847–8)

Nevsky Prospekt 41; tel: 315 5236; http://beloselskiy-palace.pokypai.ru; excursions by advance booking; M: Mayakovskaya; map p.137 E2
This extravaganza is as opulent inside as it is out. Classical music concerts are also held regularly in the palace.

Mariinsky Palace (1839–44)

Isaakievskaya Ploshchad 6; not open to the public; map p.136 B3
Home to the city's Legislative Assembly.

Nikolaevsky Palace (1853–61)

Ploshchad Truda 4; tel: 312 5500; bus: 3, 22, 27

Right: the steps of Kazan Cathedral.

If you go to a performance of the Feel Yourself Russian folk show, you'll get a good look at the palace's main hall and staircase.

Montferrand's epic masterpieces include:

St Isaac's Cathedral (1818–58)

Isaakievskaya Ploshchad; tel: 315 9732; www.cathedral.ru; Thur–Tue 10am–10pm; admission charge; tickets for the colonnade (Thur–Tue 10am–4pm) are sold separately; map p.136 B2
SEE ALSO CHURCHES, P.46

Style Moderne

The turn of the century saw the emergence of Style Moderne, the form of Art Nouveau popular in Russia at that time. Along with Fyodor Lidval's iconic Hotel Astoria on St Isaac's Square, the following buildings made waves at the time:

Singer Building (1902–4)

Nevsky Prospekt 28; tel: 448 2355; www.spbdk.ru; 9am–midnight; M: Nevsky Prospektl; map p.137 C2
Designed by Suzor, the building that is now a beloved symbol of the city and houses the bookshop **Dom Knigi** was much criticised when it was first built for spoiling the classical facade of the surrounding buildings.

The **Yeliseevsky** shop at Nevsky Prospekt 56 (not in use at the time of writing) was met with similar dismay when it was unveiled in 1903. Designed as a purpose-built shop for the Yeliseevsky merchant brothers, the large glass windows were considered to be vulgar and out of place on the city's elegant main thoroughfare. Like the Singer Building, it is now considered to be one of the finest buildings in the city.
SEE ALSO LITERATURE, P.81

Contemporary Challenges

Current objects of controversy include the new Stock Exchange building completed in 2008 and the *bête noire* of city preservationists, the planned Okhta-Center, known informally as the Gazprom Tower. Plans to build a 396m (1,300ft) glass skyscraper on the bank of the Neva directly opposite Smolny Cathedral have caused outcry among some residents, who say it will ruin the city's historic skyline. The plans have also caused UNESCO to review the city centre's World Heritage Site status. Despite the protests, it seems certain that construction will go ahead. Only time will tell whether the tower will remain a source of discontent, or whether it too will one day become a beloved symbol of the city.

Ballet, Opera and Theatre

St Petersburg is not known as Russia's cultural capital without reason. The likes of Anna Pavlova, Fyodor Chaliapin, Vaslav Nijinsky and other stars of the performing arts have all graced the stages of the city's numerous theatres, and theatre-going remains a strong tradition. Plays are performed in Russian only, and operas are usually performed in the original language with Russian subtitles on a screen, but a traditional Russian ballet such as *Swan Lake*, *The Nutcracker* or *Sleeping Beauty* needs no explanation.

Tickets

Tickets for theatre performances can be bought at the venues themselves, or any of the many box offices around the city. The main one is located at Nevsky Prospekt 42; tel: 571 3183; www.bileter. ru; 10am–8pm; M: Nevsky Prospekt; map p.137 D2.

Performances nearly always begin at 7pm in Russia, but do check your tickets.

Be aware that some of the theatre troupes, including the Mariinsky and Mikhailovsky, go on tour during the summer months, so these theatres are closed from mid-July–mid-September.

Theatre Etiquette

Russians tend to dress smartly for the theatre, and it is rare to see people in jeans, especially women. In the interval, join the crush and head for the bar to down a swift glass of champagne and caviar sandwich – it's all part of the experience.

Foreigner prices

Unfortunately, theatre tickets are one of the things for

Above and right: ticket booths cater for all art events.

which foreigners still have to pay far more – up to 20 times – than Russians do. Unless you fancy getting a Russian to buy the tickets for you, then embarking on a heart-pounding mission of making yourself look as much like a Russian and trying to make it past the sharp-eyed *babushki* on the ticket check, there is not much you can do except pay. If you decide on the former option, dress smartly, but not too stylishly, and march through as confidently as possible – like the Russians. If you are caught, act the confused tourist and

pay the difference in ticket prices at the ticket desk.

Venues

Alexandriinsky Theatre
Ploshchad Ostrovskovo 6;
tel: 312 1545;
www.alexandriinsky.ru;
M: Gostiny Dvor; map p.137 D2
If you understand Russian, this is one of the city's best drama theatres, founded in 1756, with a repertoire of Russian classics as well as contemporary and foreign plays.

Right: performance at the Hermitage Theatre.

Left: performance at the Mariinsky Theatre.

popular theatre. Under the baton of its artistic director, the renowned Valery Gergiev, the troupe enjoys success all around the world. The theatre's lush imperial interior includes a Tsar's box.

Mikhailovksy Theatre
Ploshchad Iskusstv 1; tel: 595 4305; www.mikhailovsky.ru; M: Nevsky Prospekt; map p.137 D1
Also known as the Mussorgsky, this theatre is a slightly smaller version of the Mariinsky. Tickets here tend to be cheaper, and the performances are in no way inferior to those at the city's most famous theatre.

Nikolaevsky Dvorets
Ploshchad Truda 4; tel: 312 5500; www.folkshow.ru; bus: 3, 22, 27; map p.136 A2
The Feel Yourself Russian folk show is another performance that needs no translation. Far less tacky than the posters suggest, the show includes a traditional male peasant choir along with the obligatory balalaikas and Cossack dancing. The ticket price includes a glass of champagne upon arrival and snacks, champagne, wine and vodka during the interval.

If you fancy combining ballet and circus, go and see the Mikhailovsky Theatre's version of *Spartacus*, which features a live tiger on stage (in a cage, of course). This seemed just too outrageous to one of the British critics reviewing the performance when it went on tour to London, who decided that the rumours of a tiger couldn't possibly have any truth in them.

Hermitage Theatre
Dvortsovaya Nab. 34; tel: 579 0226; M: Nevsky Prospekt;

map p.132 C4
This small but delightful theatre was where the Russian royals used to enjoy private performances by the city's stars. The theatre's repertoire is limited, and tickets tend to be pricey, but the intimate atmosphere of the historic theatre is almost worth it.

Mariinsky Theatre
Teatralnaya Ploshchad 1; tel: 326 4141; www.mariinsky.ru; M: Sadovaya; map p.136 A4
Known as the Kirov during the Soviet era, the Mariinsky is the city's most famous and

Banya

Being whipped with birch leaves in the banya (Russian sauna) is an essential Russian experience, but not one you'd expect to receive back home. Visiting the banya is a very old tradition dating from at least the 6th century that bears many similarities to Scandinavian customs of building saunas. A trip to the banya, whether in rustic country style or as a modern city indulgence, is a hygiene routine and social event all rolled into one: the banya is hailed as a cure for tired muscles, circulation problems, bronchitis, flu, and just about any other ailment. It is also a good way to get warm during a long, cold winter.

Bare Necessities

Traditionally, a banya is a small wooden hut with a stove, located beside a body of water. After sitting in the heat and beating each other with sprigs of leaves until you can no longer bear the heat, you should run outside and either roll in the snow (if it is winter) or plunge into the lake or river if there is no snow. All of this should be done naked.

If you are lucky enough to go to an out-of-town banya, for example at someone's dacha, you will find that little

has changed, except that in the absence of a river or lake, you simply throw buckets of freezing water over each other in the anteroom.

However, there are also many banya facilities in the city – many Russians continue to visit the banya once a week.

Extreme Exfoliation

The beating is a major part of the experience. The sprigs of leaves used to beat each other are called *venniki*, and can be made from a variety

of leaves, each of which have their own properties. Birch leaves are said to be good for respiratory ailments, while oak leaves are said to be good for the skin. Lime leaves are recommended for relieving headaches and colds. Nettles (yes, really) are recommended for soothing muscles worn out by physical exercise.

Before commencing the whipping, the *vennik* is dipped in water to soak the leaves, then warmed on the stove before being shaken

Left: twigs are used for a rather painful exfoliation.

Russian women take a great deal of time and effort over their appearance, and make-up is a huge industry – along with cosmetic surgery. For buying cosmetics, the best place is the chain of Rive Gauche shops, which have everything you could possible need and more.
Rive Gauche
Passazh, Nevsky Prosepkt 48; tel: 570 5791; www.rive gauche.ru; M: Gostiny Dvor; map p.137 D2

These baths are very popular, especially with groups of young people. Facilities include a café, pool tables and private banyas.
Mytninskaya Banya
Mytninskaya Ulitsa 17–19; tel: 271 7119; 24 hours; M: Ploshchad Vosstaniya; map p.139 C2
This traditional banya has been refurbished and, like a growing number around the city, now includes a private banya that can be rented out by groups as well as the main section which has the standard sauna and cold plunge pool.

For more traditional forms of pampering, the beauty salons and spas at the Grand Hotel Europe, Astoria and other five-star hotels are open to non-guests. *(See Hotels, p.66–73.)* Beauty salons are a huge industry in St Petersburg, and there is no shortage of them around the city, but the beauticians may well not speak English, so if your waxing vocab is not up to scratch, it's probably best to stick to those at the hotels.

gently in the air to incorporate steam. Then one person lies face down on the bench while another person thrashes them from head to toe with the *vennik* (master whippers use two *venniki*, one in each hand.) The experience is extremely invigorating, and is said to be a good way of exfoliating the skin.

Banya Etiquette

Unless you have rented a private banya with a mixed group of friends, there are separate banyas for men and women, and swimming costumes are not required.

It is usual to cover your head while in the banya to stop the heat from over-whelming you. Special felt hats exist for precisely this purpose, or you can simply tie a headscarf around your hair. You can usually buy *venniki* and rent hats etc at the banya itself, though it's a good idea to take your own flip-flops if possible.

Drinking alcohol before, during or immediately after visiting the banya is not recommended by doctors, which does not stop many Russians from doing so.

Some banyas double as brothels, and while the establishments listed here are respectable, it is not unusual for parties of men to rent out a private banya and bring some paid female company along with them.

City Banyas

Kazachye Bani
Bolshoi Kazachy Pereulok 11; tel: 315 0734; 24 hours; M: Tekhnologichesky Institut

Left: cooling off the traditional way. **Right:** vetting the *venniki*.

Bars and Pubs

There is not a strong tradition of bars as such in Russia – in the Soviet Union drinking was either done at home, in a very basic kind of vodka bar known as a *rumochnaya*, or in a similar kind of beer bar known as a *pivnaya*. As a result, most of the city's bars tend to be either glamorous New Russian affairs where people go mainly to be seen, or the ubiquitous Irish and English pubs, of which St Petersburg has more than its fair share. The following places make a good starting point for warming up for the city's rich tapestry of clubs, *see Nightlife, p.102–105*.

Nevsky Prospekt

The Office

Kazanskaya Ulitsa 5; tel: 571 5428; www.mollies.ru; Mon–Thur noon–2am, Fri–Sat noon–3am, Sun noon–1am; M: Gostiny Dvor; map p.137 C2
The Office is an English-style pub handily located just behind the Kazan Cathedral – look out for the red phone box outside –

offering a range of pricey beers from around the world as well as Russian beer on tap. It doesn't tend to get as hot and busy as Mollie's *(see right)*, which is owned by the same people, making it a good choice for a relaxed drink.

The Other Side

Bolshaya Konushennaya Ulitsa 1; tel: 312 9554; www.theotherside.ru; daily noon–1am, Fri–Sat until 3am; M: Nevsky Prospekt; map p.137 C2
The American-owned 'gastro bar and refuge' The Other Side is hospitable and welcoming, making it a big hit with expats of all nationalities as well as Russians. The abundance of seating makes it a great place for a catch-up with friends, though when there is live music at weekends, conversation can be difficult. The menu has something to satisfy almost every craving for foreign food, from bagels to hummus to falafel.

Left and right: vodka is a popular drink whether neat or in cocktails.

The Soviet-era *rumochnayas* can still be found around the city, and are mostly full of alcoholics. If you are feeling brave enough to experience a *rumochnaya* first-hand, there are several around Ploshchad Vosstaniya, including one at 4aya Sovietskaya Ulitsa 10; 7am–11pm. With opening times like those, you can even knock down a shot or two before breakfast.

Palace Square to Liteiny Prospekt

SevenSkyBar

Italianskaya Ulitsa 15; tel: 449 9432; www.sevenskybar.ru; daily noon–2am, Fri–Sat until 6am; M: Nevsky Prospekt; map p.137 D2
A swanky bar located on the top floor of Grand Palace shopping centre (take the lift to the fifth floor). It has good views of the surrounding skyline, and despite its glamorous clientele, has reasonably priced Mediterranean and Asian food and dangerously good cocktails.

Tribunal Bar

Ulitsa Karavannaya 26; tel: 314 2423; 9pm–6am; M: Gostiny

fasts and a relaxed atmosphere. In summer, the beer garden overlooking the River Fontanka is the perfect place to enjoy a pint.

Liverpool
Ulitsa Mayakovskovo 16; tel: 579 2054; www.liverpool.ru; daily noon–1am, Fri–Sat until 3am; M: Mayakovskaya; map p.138 A2

This Beatles-themed bar at one time played only the Fab Four, but the owners have now relented, and live music of other genres can also be heard in the evenings. It has a wide range of beers, pub food and pool tables – somewhat of a rarity in St Petersburg's pubs and bars.

Mollie's Irish Pub
Ulitsa Rubinshteina 36; tel: 570 3768; www.mollies.ru; Mon–Thur noon–2am, Fri–Sat noon–3am, Sun noon–1am; M: Vladimirskaya; map p.137 E3

Mollie's was the first Irish pub in St Petersburg and remains extremely popular with both Russians and foreigners – both expats and tourists. It can get a little too rowdy to be able to have a decent chat at weekends, but is a good place to come for a pre-dinner drink before visiting one of the hordes of restaurants on Ulitsa Rubinshteina.

Dvor; map p.137 E2

If you like a bit of entertainment with your beer, namely scantily clad women dancing on the bar in front of you, then Tribunal is the place for you. There is an entrance charge on Fridays and Saturdays.

The Admiralty to St Nicholas's Cathedral

The Shamrock
Ulitsa Dekabristov 27; tel: 570 4625; www.shamrockpub.spb; 9am–2am; M: Sadovaya; map p.136 A3

The Shamrock is a lively Irish pub near the Mariinsky Theatre offering Guinness, good pub grub and frequent live performances by folk bands. It's not as large as some of its counterparts, so at weekends you may be pushed to find a seat, but it has a fun, lively atmosphere and a welcoming crowd.

Vladimirskaya, Liteiny and Smolny

Dickens
Nab. Reki Fontanki 108; tel: 380 7888; Sun–Tue 8am–1am, Wed–Thur 8am–2am, Fri–Sat 8am–3am; M: Sadovaya; map p.137 C4

Dickens is a smart, spacious two-storey pub offering international beers, good break-

Bridges

There are 315 bridges of varying sizes and designs over the many waterways in St Petersburg's historic centre alone. One of the favourite sights of locals and visitors alike is the raising of the bridges along the Neva in summer, especially during the magical White Nights. The best way to see the city's multitude of beautiful bridges is to take a boat trip around the rivers and canals – the following crossings are just some of the highlights. Boat trips leave from regular landing spots along the canals, and from in front of the Hermitage. Don't forget to make it back to 'your' island before the bridges open.

Bridges over the River Neva

There are nine bridges over the Neva, which are most impressive due to their size and majesty. They may lack the charm and ornamentation of the bridges over the smaller waterways, but are a spectacular sight in the summer when parts of each bridge raise up to allow the ships through. This is also a sight best seen from the water – boats depart at 1am from the Anichkov Bridge for

Legend has it that the sculptor Klodt became so exasperated with the Tsar, who kept giving away the sculptures commissioned for the bridge and ordering new ones, that in the groin of the final horse (the one closest to the white Anichkov Palace), he carved a face that resembled that of the Tsar.

the Neva to watch the opening of the first few bridges. Occasionally, films are projected onto the two halves of Dvortsovy Bridge during the White Nights.

The Moika

The bridge over the Moika on the corner of Palace Square is called the **Pevchesky (Choral) Bridge**, due to the proximity of the State Capella. Built after the Tsar's Chancellor fell into the river off the ferry that previously operated in this spot, it was originally called the **Zhyolty (Yellow) Bridge** due to the colour it was painted.

Left: *going under the Blue Bridge on the Moika Canal.*

by Pyotr Klodt in the 1840s. During the siege the horse sculptures were removed and buried in the grounds of the nearby Pioneers' Palace (Anichkov Palace) to keep them safe from German artillery fire.

The **Egipetsky (Egyptian) Bridge** on Lermontovsky Prospekt was originally a more ornate structure, but collapsed in January 1905 while a cavalry squadron was crossing it. The current bridge was completed in 1955, and the sphinxes that adorn each end are all that remain of the original bridge.

Three other bridges along the Moika are still known by the colour of their paintwork. The **Green Bridge** is where Nevsky Prospekt traverses the Moika, the bridge over the Moika aligned with Gorokhovaya Ulitsa is known as the **Red Bridge**, and the **Siny (Blue) Bridge**, which comprises part of St Isaac's Square, is the widest bridge in the city at 97.3m (320ft).

On the right bank of the Moika next to the Blue Bridge is a water gauge carved into the granite embankment. Markings on the gauge record both the current level of the water and the heights reached during the catastrophic floods of 1824, 1903, 1955 and 1967.

The romantic-sounding **Potseluev Bridge** (Bridge of Kisses) near New Holland Island, contrary to popular belief, takes it name from a bar that was formerly located next to the bridge, in the house of a merchant named Potseluev.

Left: *Engineer's Bridge.*

Canal Griboedova

Some of the most charming bridges in the city span the tree-lined Canal Griboedova. One of the most beloved by locals and visitors alike is the **Bankovsky (Bank) Bridge** behind Kazan Cathedral, named due to its location next to the gates of a building that was originally a bank and now houses the University of Finance and Economics. The footbridge is decorated with four griffin sculptures with gold wings. In mythology, griffins guarded treasure, and so the creatures were chosen to adorn the bridge beside the bank.

The **Lviny (Lion) Bridge** near the Mariinsky Theatre takes its name from its four majestic white lion sculptures. Like the Bankovsky Bridge, it is a one-span suspension bridge.

River Fontanka

The most famous bridge over the Fontanka is the **Anichkov Bridge** on Nevsky Prospekt, with its four magnificent horse sculptures known as the Horse Tamers, sculpted

From mid-April to mid-October, the bridges along the Neva open up at night to let through large ships, which is a popular sight with tourists, but not so popular with people who need to get home from the historic centre to one of the islands. If you miss the bridges, you have a few options: try to catch Blagoveshensky Bridge when it closes briefly, to let through other tardy islanders; take a 20+km (12-mile) detour to go over the Bolshoy Obukhovsky Bridge, which doesn't open, or stay out until the metro opens and the bridges close again at around 5am. Bridge opening times (like most things in Russia, subject to change):

Dvortsovy: 01.25–04.55
Blagoveshensky: 01.25–02.45, 03.10–05.00
Troitsky: 01.35–04.50
Liteiny: 01.40–04.45
Birzhevoi: 02.00–04.55
Tuchkov: 02.00–02.55, 03.35–04.55
Alexandra Nevskovo: 02.20–05.10

Cafés

There is certainly no shortage of places to stop and get a drink or a bite to eat around the centre of St Petersburg, but too often they can turn out to be an overpriced tourist trap serving very ordinary food, which is a shame when Russia's rich culinary heritage and tea tradition have so much to offer. It is often worth wandering a few steps off Nevsky Prospekt, which is lined with characterless coffee-shop chains, to find something with more substance. The following cafés and tea houses are ideal for breakfast, lunch, afternoon tea or just a relaxing cup of coffee.

Nevsky Prospekt

Abrikosov
Nevsky Prospekt 40; tel: 312 2457; 9am–11pm; M: Nevsky Prospekt; map p.137 D2
Abrikosov is an attractive little café decorated with mirrors and wallpaper depicting Chinese themes. Its location halfway down Nevsky is excellent, but do watch out for bag thieves.

Literary Café
Nevsky Prospekt 18; tel: 312 6057; no web; 11am–1am; M: Nevsky Prospekt; map p.137 C2
The Literary Cafe milks its status as the site of Pushkin's last meal for all it is worth. A wax model of the doomed poet sitting at a desk graces the small entrance to the cafe where he stopped on the way to his fatal duel, while a plaque draws attention to the stairs he trod.

Mocco Club
Nevsky Prospekt 27; tel: 312 1080; 9am–11pm; M: Gostiny Dvor; map p.137 D2
Despite its name, Mocco is a café, and one of the best places on Nevsky to refuel; given its prime location between Kazan Cathedral

Starbucks clones like Shokoladnitsa and Coffee House are appearing faster than mushrooms after the rain around St Petersburg, but are generally best avoided as they are vastly overpriced and inferior to the selection of cafés described here. If you want to experience quite how bad service in Russia used to be, visiting the Shokoladnitsa café on the first floor of Dom Knigi in the Singer Building is like taking a trip back to the '90s.

and Gostiny Dvor, it has surprisingly reasonable prices and free Wi-fi.

Teremok
Nevsky Prospekt 60; tel: 314 2701; www.teremok.ru; 10am–10pm; M: Gostiny Dvor; map p.137 D2
For fast food in a Russian style, visit one of the 35 Teremok pancake outlets around the city. You can choose from a range of fillings including ham and cheese, red caviar, chocolate and banana, and condensed milk – far nicer than it sounds. (Other central branches include Nevsky Prospekt

106, 7th Liniya 42 on Vasilievsky Island, and two on Sennaya Ploshchad.)

Palace Square to Liteiny Prospekt

James Cook
Shvedsky Pereulok 2; tel: 312 3200; 9am–2pm; M: Nevsky Prospekt; map p.137 C1
James Cook is both a bar and café – the café part on the left is a wonderful retreat from bad weather and any other setbacks. It's not cheap, but the divine cakes are worth every ruble, and the surroundings are so comfortable you might find it difficult to leave. (There is also a branch on the Petrograd Side, at Kamennoostrovsky Prospekt 45; tel: 347 6581.)

The Admiralty to St Nicholas's Cathedral

Zoom
Gorokhovaya Ulitsa 22; tel: 448 5001; http://cafezoom.ru; 9am–midnight; M: Sadovaya/ Gostiny Dvor; map p.136 C3
Zoom is a real gem, with its friendly staff, ridiculously

Right: St Petersburg's short summer is fully embraced.

Left: most cafés are decorated to provide cosiness in winter.

Stolle

Ulitsa Vosstaniya 32; 1st Liniya of Vasilievsky Island 50; Dekabristov 33 and 19; and Konushenny Pereulok 1; www.stolle.ru; tel: 312 1862 (Konushenny Pereulok branch); 9am–9pm. Stolle, famed around St Petersburg for its inexpensive traditional Russian pies, has become so popular that is has just expanded its small chain of cafés to Moscow and Yekaterinburg. The classic cabbage pie is an essential Russian dining experience, and the full range includes salmon, spring onion and egg, rabbit and mushroom, and an assortment of sweet fruit pies. Whole Stolle pies are now often bought instead of the ubiquitous sponge cakes with whipped cream and neon icing that traditionally graced a Russian birthday-party table – you can even order pies to be delivered to your home.

cheap but good meals, constantly changing artwork and library of books and magazines. It is very popular with the young crowd, and it can be difficult to get a table at lunchtimes.

Vladimirskaya, Liteiny and Smolny

Blinny Domik (Pancake House)
Kolokolnaya Ulitsa 8; tel: 315 9915; 10.30am–midnight; M: Vladimirskaya; map p.138 A3
For traditional Russian pancakes (blini) in a less plastic, fast-food environment than Teremok (see left), the famed Blinny Domik cannot fail to satisfy. Its wooden, cosy interior is warm and welcoming, as are the staff.

Along with various pancake fillings, the menu also offers traditional Russian soups and salads. A glass of sweet Russian myod or honey beer is the perfect way to wash down any of the above.

Chainny Dom (Tea House)
Ulitsa Rubinshteina 24; tel: 571 2784; 11am–2am; M: Vladimirskaya; map p.137 E3
The beckoning wicker armchairs, sprawling floor cushions and silk fabrics of the tiny Tea House can be impossible for passers-by to resist, inviting them to come in, relax, choose from a whole host of teas and smoke a hookah pipe. But places are limited, so you may have to wait.

Children

Generally speaking, Russia may not seem the most child-friendly destination, and facilities do lag behind most of Western Europe. Nevertheless, there are plenty of places and attractions to keep children of all ages busy and happy during a trip to St Petersburg. Along with the city's numerous parks, some of which have small amusement parks, the following is a list of attractions that are particularly interesting or enjoyable for children. Tickets for all these attractions can be purchased at the venues themselves or at any of the numerous theatre box offices along Nevsky and all around the city.

Circus on the Fontanka

Nab. Reki Fontanki 3; tel: 570 5198; www.circus.spb.ru; performances at 7pm; admission charge; M: Nevsky Prospekt; map p.137 E1

If bears riding motorbikes and roller-skating is your thing, the circus is the place for you. At Russia's oldest circus, the repertoire includes a variety of shows, including an impressive water show that features a swimming pool in place of the stage, and a less-than-impressed crocodile. The circus is also recommended for adults, though possibly not for PETA/RSPCA activists.

Dolphinarium

Konstantinovsky Prospekt 19; tel: 235 4631; www.dolphinarium.ru; admission charge; M: Krestovsky Ostrov

Kids and adults alike will be thrilled as trainers ride the dolphins like surfboards and dolphins perform synchronised swimming moves and paint pictures, accompanied by the occasional sea lion. Performances are at noon,

Kids are also likely to enjoy the **Kunstkamera**, the **Zoology Museum** and **Arctic and Antarctic Museum** (see Museums and Galleries, p.96, 97). Older kids may like the stomach-churning rides at Divo Ostrov – the amusement park on Krestovsky Ostrov – but be warned: they are not for the fainthearted. Health and safety in Russia is practically non-existent compared to the US and most Western European countries.

2pm, 4pm and 6pm, though they vary depending on the day – there are three performances per day at weekends, and one most weekdays. For an exact timetable, see the website (Russian only) or ask at the ticket office.

Leningrad Zoo

Alexandrovsky Park 1; tel: 232 8260; www.spbzoo.ru; 10am–7pm; admission charge; M: Gorkovskaya; map p.132 B2

The cramped, smelly Leningrad Zoo is one of the

Left: puppies for sale.

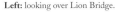

Left: looking over Lion Bridge.

An increasing number of restaurants around the city now have children's rooms, most notably **Tres Amigos** *(see p.120)*, **Russkaya Rybalka** *(see p.121)* and **Stroganoff Steak House** *(see p.117)*, which has a supervisor and a special children's toilet.

Puppet Theatre

Nevsky Prospekt 52; tel: 571 2156; performances three days a week at 11am and 2pm; admission charge; M: Nevsky Prospekt; map p.137 C2
Marionette performances of Russian fairy tales and other children's stories.

Waterville Aqua Park

Ulitsa Korablestroitelei 14 (Hotel Pribaltiiskaya); tel: 324 4700; www.waterville.ru; 11am–11pm; admission charge, free for children under four; M: Primorskaya
Waterville, located in the Hotel Pribaltiiskaya on the seashore, is another guaranteed success with children, with its many slides and Pirate Bar. If there are children in your party too young to enjoy the water park, there is a supervised children's room for children from 2–12. If possible, you should take your own flip-flops.

smallest in Russia, and there are plans to build a much larger, more modern facility out of town, but in the meantime, the zoo remains a popular attraction with local families. In 2008, two new polar bear cubs – Pyotr and Krasin – became the latest addition to its collection of the usual beasts, reptiles and birds, and were an instant hit. There are also several small fairground rides to keep children amused.

Oceanarium

Ulitsa Marata 86; tel: 448 0077; www.planeta-neptun.ru; 10am–9pm; admission charge; M: Pushkinskaya
Russia's first oceanarium is a guaranteed hit with kids, with its 4,500 species of fish and sea creatures, including five species of sharks, sea horses, coral reef and other wonders of the deep. A shark show takes place daily at 7pm, except for Mondays, which is

Right: visiting the circus is a Russian tradition, but animal treatment is not what you'd expect elsewhere.

Above: the Puppet Theatre.

presumably the sharks' day off. The Oceanarium is the perfect place to take children on a rainy day, and will also keep adults enthralled.

43

Churches

There are awe-inspiring churches and cathedrals on every second corner in St Petersburg. Unlike the Orthodox 'onion domes' of Moscow, most of the churches in the northern capital are built in a classical style, with the notable exception of the Church on the Spilled Blood, which was modelled on St Basil's on Red Square but has even more exaggerated textures on its domes. When entering an Orthodox Russian church, women should cover their heads with a scarf or similar, and during a service it is considered disrespectful to look in directions other than the altar.

Nevsky Prospekt

Alexander Nevsky Monastery (Alexandro-Nevkskaya Lavra)
Nab. Reki Monastyrki 1; tel: 274 1702; www.lavra.spb.ru; 6am–9pm, services daily 7am, 10am and 5pm; M: Ploshchad Alexandra Nevskovo; map p.139 D4
The Alexander Nevsky Monastery, or Lavra as it is called in Russian, was founded by Peter the Great in 1710 in honour of Prince Alexander Nevsky, who defeated the Swedes in the battle of Poltava in 1240. The monastery was planned as the spiritual centre of the new Russian capital. The original

As the most important religious centre of the city, the etiquette in Alexander Nevsky Monastery is particularly strict. Women should wear long skirts rather than trousers if possible, and obvious make-up such as lipstick is considered inappropriate.

designs were the work of Domenico Trezzini, but the focal point of the monastery is the classical Trinity Cathedral, designed by Ivan Starov and built from 1776–90. The three cemeteries on the grounds of the monastery contain the graves of many famous writers,

composers and artists, including Dostoevsky, Tchaikovsky and Rimsky-Korsakov, along with many of the architects who helped to build St Petersburg, such as Starov, Quarenghi, Voronikhin and Rossi.

Armenian Apostles' Church (Armyanskaya Apostolskaya Pravoslavnaya Tserkov)
Nevsky Prospekt 40–42; tel: 350 5301/570 4108; services Sat 6pm; M: Nevsky Prospekt; map p.137 D2
The beautiful neoclassical Armenian Church was built in 1780 by Yury Felten. Closed in the 1930s like so many other religious buildings under the Communists, it was used as a workshop for some years, but reopened as a functioning church in 1993. Legend has it that the construction of the church was financed by an Armenian businessman, Yokhim Lazarev, who raised the money by selling a single Persian diamond to Catheri-

Left: a long wait at the Alexander Nevsky Monastery.

Left: Kazan Cathedral.

with statues along its parapet, a high dome and arched portal, it demonstrates the transition from Baroque architecture to Classicism.

SS Peter and Paul Lutheran Church (Evangelichesko-Luteranskaya Tserkov)
Nevsky Prospekt 22–24; tel: 571 2423; www.elkras.ru; free; bilingual service Sun 10.30am; M: Nevsky Prospekt; map p.137 C2

The first German-Lutheran church on Nevsky was built as early as 1730, but the current building was designed by Alexander Briullov using elements of Roman architecture and completed in 1838. Converted into a swimming pool (a fate shared by many religious buildings) during the Soviet era, it has now been restored to its original purpose.

Palace Square to Liteiny Prospekt

Church on the Spilled Blood (Spas-na-Krovi)
Nab. Kanal Griboedova 2b; tel: 315 1636; www.cathedral.ru; Thur–Tue, winter 11am–7pm, summer 10am–8pm; admission charge; M: Nevsky Prospekt; map p.137 D1

Visiting a church service is highly recommended, not least to hear the superb choirs. The best choirs are those of the Alexander Nevsky Monastery *(left)*, the Cathedral of the Transfiguration of Our Saviour *(see p.48)*, and the outstanding male choir of St Nicholas's Cathedral *(see p.47)*.

ine the Great, who gave it to her lover, Grigory Orlov.

Kazan Cathedral (Kazansky Sobor)
Kazanskaya Ploshchad 2; tel: 570 4528; 9am–8pm, services daily 10am, 6pm; free; M: Nevsky Prospekt; map p.137 C2

On the order of Paul I, who had visited Rome before ascending the throne, Kazan Cathedral was built to resemble St Peter's. Completed in 1811 by Andrei Voronikhin, it takes its name from the icon of the Mother of God discovered by Ivan the Terrible's soldiers during a storm in Kazan. (The icon is now in the Prince Vladimir Cathedral on the Petrograd Side.) The bronze door of the portico is a copy of the 'Gates of Paradise' in the Baptistery of Florence, and the four bronze statues of St John the Baptist, St Andrew the First Called, St Vladimir Equal of the Apostles and St Alexander Nevsky were intended to draw allegorical parallels between the Orthodox Church and early Christianity. In front of the cathedral stand statues of the heroes of the Napoleonic Wars, Field Marshal Kutuzov and Michael Barclay de Tolly. The former, who was Commander-in-Chief of the Russian army in the 1812 war, is buried inside the cathedral.

St Catherine's Roman Catholic Church (Katolicheskaya Tserkov Sviatoi Yekaterini)
Nevsky Prospekt 32–34; tel: 571 5795; 8am–8pm, mass daily 8.30am and 7pm, mass in English Sun 9.30am; free; M: Nevsky Prospekt; map p.137 D2

St Catherine's was built by Jean-Baptiste Vallin de la Mothe and Antonio Rinaldi from 1763–83. Decorated

Right: Russian churches lack pews; the standing crowd comes and goes during the service.

45

The Cathedral of the Resurrection of Christ is more commonly known as the Church on the Spilled Blood, due to the story behind its construction. It was built on the orders of Alexander III on the site where his father, Tsar Alexander II, was fatally wounded by a terrorist's bomb on 1 March 1881. The church was conceived not only as a place of worship, but as a tribute to the assassinated Tsar and as a work of art and architectural monument. Designed by Alfred Parland, a Russian architect of English descent, in a traditional Orthodox style, it borrowed elements from churches in Moscow and Yaroslavl dating back to the 17th century, and took 24 years to build.

The cathedral's interior is decorated with precious stones from around the former Russian empire, and 6,000 sq m (64,500 sq ft) of intricate mosaics, including 134 mosaic arms of Russian cities and provinces that donated funds for the church's construction to atone for the crime of regicide. A jasper canopy and flowers mark the spot where the Tsar's blood stained the pavement – the embankment of the canal was expanded to allow the cathedral to be built around the exact spot where he was wounded. The intricate exterior features decorative arched gables and elaborate window surrounds and is crowned by five domes and a bell tower.

The Admiralty to St Nicholas's Cathedral

Great Choral Synagogue (Bolshaya Khoralnaya Synagoga)
Lermontovsky Prospekt 2; tel: 740 1952; www.jewish petersburg.ru; Sun–Fri, winter 10am–6pm, summer 9am–6pm, except Jewish holidays, services Sat 10am–noon; free (guided tours available if booked in advance – admission charge applies); M: Sadovaya; map p.136 A3

The city's main synagogue – the second-largest in Europe – not only has a spectacular exterior and beautiful Moorish interiors, but also includes

a restaurant and shop offering kosher food. Inside there is an exhibition on the history of the synagogue, which was completed in 1893.

St Isaac's Cathedral (Isaakievsky Sobor)
Isaakievskaya Ploshchad; tel: 315 9732; www.cathedral.ru; Thur–Tue 10am–10pm; admission charge; tickets for the colonnade (Thur–Tue 10am–4pm) are sold separately; map p.136 B2

St Isaac's Cathedral is named in honour of St Isaac of Dalmatia, whose feast day is on 30 May – the birthday of Peter the Great. Designed by the French architect Auguste de Montferrand in 1818, it took over 40 years to complete. At 101.5m (333ft) high, it is the biggest church in the country. Its four porticoes are decorated with 72 monolithic granite columns, while different kinds of rare stones, marble and mosaics adorn the

Several times during the Soviet era, the Church on the Spilled Blood was almost demolished; it was saved by the outbreak of World War II and other factors. Though the threat was never carried out, the church suffered serious neglect and damage, and was in critical condition when it was finally decided to make it into a museum in 1971. The church was painstakingly restored, and finally opened its doors again to the public in 1997. Look out for the damaged granite panel along the bottom of the cathedral on the side closest to Nevsky Prospekt. It was left unrestored as a reminder of the damage inflicted on the city by German artillery during the siege of Leningrad from 1941–4.

During the siege, all the priceless works of art that had been evacuated from the palaces at Pushkin, Peterhof and the other former royal residences were kept in the basement of St Isaac's Cathedral. Legend has it that an aged former artillery officer suggested the basement as the safest place, on the basis that the Germans would use the dome of the building as a point of orientation, and would therefore be unlikely to bomb it. During air attacks, the cathedral was indeed known as 'reference point No. 1' by Luftwaffe bombers, and escaped harm for the duration of the war.

interior, along with 150 paintings, including on the ceilings and inside the main dome. During the Soviet era, when religion was banned, the church was turned into a museum of religion. It was consecrated again in 1990, and now functions as both a museum and a working church – services are now held on religious holidays.

On a clear day, the view from the top of the colonnade – accompanied by stirring music and a recorded commentary in Russian – is well worth the climb up the 262 steps.

St Nicholas's Cathedral (Nikolsky Sobor)
Nikolskaya Ploshchad 1; tel: 714 0862; 6.30am–8pm, services daily 7am, 10am, 6pm; free; M: Sadovaya; map p.136 A4

The magnificent two-storey St Nicholas's Cathedral, also known as the Naval Cathedral, is named in honour of the patron saint of Russia and of sailors, and was built to bless Peter the Great's maritime city. Designed by

Savva Chevakinsky, it was completed in 1762 in the lavish Baroque style. The Upper Church is the more impressive of the two floors, with streaming sunlight reflecting off the heavily gilded interior. The two-tiered iconostasis is particularly elaborate. The cathedral contains many precious icons, including one of St Nicholas, as well as several plaques commemorating Russian sailors and submariners lost at sea. The cathedral is famed for the architectural ensemble formed together with its separate four-tiered bell tower against the backdrop of the Kriukov Canal.

Peter and Paul Fortress
Peter and Paul Cathedral (Petropavlovsky Sobor)
Tel: 238 0751; www.spb museum.ru; 10am–6pm; admission charge; M: Gorkovskaya; map p.132 C3

The Peter and Paul Cathedral, designed by Domenico Trezzini, was consecrated on 27 June 1732, and was built on the site of a former wooden church founded in 1703, the same year as the fortress. The 122.5m (402ft) spire of the church can be seen from all over the city, and the angel that crowns the spire, blessing the city, is itself a symbol of the city.

The main decorative features of the cathedral are its elaborate carved iconostasis and ornate lectern, reached by a small spiral staircase. All the tsars from Peter the Great except for two (Peter II and Ivan VI) are buried in the cathedral – Peter's tomb is marked by a bust of the city's founder. In July 1998, the remains of Nicholas II,

Right: St Isaac's dome.

47

his wife Alexandra and three of their five children were buried in the Catherine Chapel of the cathedral amid a solemn ceremony, along with the remains of the family's doctor and three servants shot together with Russia's last royal family by the Bolsheviks in 1918.

Petrograd Side

Buddhist Temple (Buddiisky Khram)

Primorsky Prospekt 91; tel: 430 9740; www.dazan.spb.ru; 10am–7pm; free; M: Staraya Derevnya

The brightly coloured Buddhist Temple was built from 1909–15, despite strong opposition from the Russian Orthodox Church, making it the first Buddhist Temple in Europe. The temple is open to visitors, but headwear should be removed before entry, and you should avoid turning your back to the altar.

Great Mosque (Sobornaya Mechet)

Kronverksky Prospekt 7; tel: 233 9819; 10am–7pm; free; M: Gorkovskaya; map p.133 C2

St Petersburg's stunning mosque, which is modelled on the 15th-century Gur Emir Mausoleum in Samarkand, was the largest mosque in Europe when it opened in 1913. It is open to non-Muslims, but both women and men should be dressed conservatively, and shoes should be removed at the entrance.

Holy Prince Vladimir Cathedral (Kniaz Vladimirsky Sobor)

> If you are visiting the city during Orthodox Easter (which does not usually coincide with Catholic Easter), you will have the chance to witness the most important festival on the Orthodox calendar. Masses are held in the evening all over the city, and many of the churches, especially Kazan Cathedral, are packed out. At midnight, the doors of the church are opened, and the priest leads the congregation in a procession around the church. It's an amazing sight, but the number of people standing packed together and holding flickering candles in a closed church may inspire unease in the health-and-safety-conscious.

Blokhina Ulitsa 26; tel: 232 7625; free; M: Sportivnaya; map p.132 A2

The Cathedral of Prince Vladimir, built from 1740–89 to designs by Mikhail Zemtsov, Antonio Rinaldi and Ivan Starov, combines both Baroque and classical elements. It contains the miracle-working Kazan icon of the Mother of God dating from the 16th century.

Vasilievsky Island

St Andrew's Cathedral (Andreevsky Sobor)

6th Liniya 11; tel: 323 3418; 9am–7pm; free; M: Vasilieostrovskaya

St Andrew's was built in the 1760s and has been fully renovated. It has a particularly beautiful Baroque iconostasis.

Vladimirskaya, Liteiny and Smolny

Cathedral of the Transfiguration of Our Saviour (Spaso-Preobrazhensky Sobor)

Preobrazhenskaya Ploshchad; tel: 272 3672; services daily 10am, 6pm; M: Chernyshevskaya; map p.134 A4

Left: Vladimir Cathedral.

The classical cathedral takes its name from the prestigious Preobrazhensky military regiment, in whose honour it was built by Vasily Stasov in 1829 to replace an earlier Baroque edifice that had burnt down. The fence surrounding it incorporates Turkish cannons captured by victorious Russian forces. The cathedral contains icons that belonged to Peter the Great and his sister Natalya.

Smolny Cathedral (Smolny Sobor)

Ploshchad Rastrelli 3; tel: 271 7632/314 2168; http://eng. cathedral.ru/smolny; Thur–Tue, winter 11am–6pm, summer 10am–8pm; admission charge; M: Chernyshevskaya or No. 5 trolleybus; map p.135 E3

Before Rastrelli's stunning creation stood here, the site contained a tar yard – *smola* in Russian means tar. Peter's daughter Elizabeth ordered the building of a cathedral and convent here, and commissioned her favourite architect Rastrelli to build it. It was built from 1748–64, but the original plans had to be modified somewhat due to financial considerations. In 1764, Catherine the Great founded a school for noble girls next to the convent, followed a year later by a school for middle-class girls – the first two educational establishments for girls in Russia. The cathedral was closed by the Bolsheviks in 1923, and reopened as a concert and exhibition hall in 1990. It regularly hosts concerts of choral music and large-scale exhibitions, and in the summer months the viewing platform of the cathedral's belfry is open.

Vladimir Cathedral (Vladimirsky Sobor)

Vladimirsky Prospekt 20; tel: 312 1938; 9am–8pm, services Mon–Fri 9am–6pm, Sun 11am; M: Vladimirskaya; map p.137 E3

Named after the ruler who converted mediaeval Rus to Christianity in 988, Vladimir Cathedral is a striking example of 18th-century Russian Baroque architecture and, like St Nicholas's, is divided into two floors. It is now once again a working church, having been turned into an ambulance station under the Communists.

Moskovsky Prospekt

Chesma Church (Chesmenskaya Tserkov)

Ulitsa Lensoveta 12; tel: 373 6114; Tue–Sun 9am–7pm, services daily 10am, Fri–Sun 6pm; M: Moskovskaya

The Brighton-rock-style Chesme Church was built from 1777–80 to commemorate the victory of the Russian fleet over the Turks off Chesme in 1770 – it is built on the spot where Catherine the Great was standing when she was told the good news by a messenger. Its striking appearance combines elements of romantic Orientalism with Gothic motifs. During the Soviet era it was turned into a museum about the battle, but has now been returned to the Church.

Trinity Cathedral (Troitsky Sobor)

Izmailovsky Prospekt 7a; tel: 251 8927; Mon–Sat 9am–7pm, Sun and holidays 8am–8pm, services Fri–Sun and holidays 5pm; free; M: Tekhnologichesky Institut

The distinctive deep-blue, star-studded dome of the Trinity Cathedral makes it one of the most beautiful in the city. It was built from 1828–35 to designs by Stasov, in honour of the Izmailovsky Life Guards Regiment. In 2006, restoration work on the domes was almost complete when the scaffolding caught fire, causing the central dome to collapse and gravely damaging another of the cupolas; renovation work had to be started all over again.

Right: Chesma Church.

Environment

Sadly, St Petersburg's environment is not yet one of its most attractive features. In a country with so many natural resources, leading a green lifestyle is not yet a priority for most, and many ordinary Russians struggling to make ends meet are concerned with economy over ecology. However, the northern capital is far less polluted than Moscow, and efforts are being made in the right direction. Young people are increasingly aware of the long-term consequences of their lifestyles, and there is hope that St Petersburg and Russia as a whole will become more environmentally friendly during the next decade.

Taming the Sea

Traditionally, St Petersburg's biggest environmental problem has been flooding – the city has suffered several catastrophic floods during its 300-year history, not to mention hundreds of less severe ones. A flood barrier was begun in 1979 but has been beset with financial and environmental problems; it is, however, once

The most enjoyable and productive ways to see the city are also the greenest: walking and cycling. For details of organised walking and cycling tours, *see Walks and Views, p.128–9*.

again under construction, though as previously, the completion date continues to be postponed.

The quality of the water in the Neva and the Gulf of Finland is very poor, and tap water should not be drunk unless boiled first. It is not unusual for water from the hot tap to be visibly brown. Environment officials from Finland and the Baltic States have complained that their efforts to protect the eco-structure of the Baltic Sea on which St Petersburg stands

parks, squares and beaches (Russia has a less than perfect record on littering, too) and returning them to bottle depositories in exchange for a few kopecks.

Environmental Activists

The environmental groups Bellona and Greenpeace and the local branch of the liberal political party Yabloko are active in the city and campaign regularly to improve the state of the city's ecology. Some of the issues they tackle include the reprocessing and storage of nuclear waste in Russia from Germany, the Netherlands and other countries, which arrives by sea to St Petersburg before being transported by train to Siberia and other parts of the country.

are thwarted by the toxins and other pollutants poured into it by St Petersburg's numerous industrial plants. Officially, hardly any of the water in the resorts along the gulf is safe to swim in, though this does not deter the locals.

Green Transport

In the Soviet Union, cars were a rarity on Nevsky Prospekt, and were generally the preserve of high-ranking Party officials. Any visitor to the city will see at once how times have changed. In 2008, there were 50 percent more car-owners than the year before, and unsurprisingly, this is reflected in the increasing number of traffic jams. However, much of the city's public transport system is relatively green, such as its extensive tram and trolley-bus network. In proportion with the growing traffic jams, more and more young Russians are starting to

cycle around the city, though there are as yet no cycle lanes, and given the somewhat reckless nature of Russian driving, this is only really recommended for those with nerves of steel and a good helmet.

For long-distance travel across the vast expanse of Russia – the largest country in the world – the train is still the most common method of transport. As well as being greener, it is considerably cheaper (and many might say, safer) than internal flights, and Russians usually make the most of anything from an overnight train journey to Moscow to a seven-day epic to Baikal, coming prepared with alcohol, vast quantities of food and even the occasional musical instrument.

Recycling

Recycling is something of an alien concept to Russians, and the closest thing to it that you are likely to see is pensioners and homeless people collecting empty beer bottles from

One of the quirky aspects of life in Russia is the central heating system, which is controlled by the local government, who decide when to turn it on and off. Once it is turned on for the winter (usually late September, depending on the weather that year), radiators blaze at full blast and cannot be regulated, often necessitating the opening of windows for the minority who have modern double-glazed windows. The same flat rate is paid by everyone for heating bills. Once it is turned off (around April), should May be chilly (as it often can be), out come the electric heaters.

With the growth of the economy and improving infrastructure, it can only be hoped that the city will eventually go over to a more modern, efficient system.

Essentials

Gone are the days when a tourist needs to be daunted by a trip to Russia. During the last few years, the St Petersburg government has made a concerted effort to make the city more tourist-friendly, and it has paid off. Signs in English direct tourists to the nearest places of interest, metros and consulates, the number of Tourist Information Offices has doubled, and the Tourist Angels were a particularly thoughtful addition. However, visas are still required by visitors from most countries, and it is best to start the application process at least a month before you plan to visit Russia.

Embassies and Consulates

Australian Consulate
Italianskaya Ulitsa 1; tel: 315 1100; M: Nevsky Prospekt; map p.137 D2

UK Consulate
Ploshchad Proletarskoi Diktatury 5; tel: 320 3200; M: Chernyshevskaya; map p.135 D3

US Consulate
Furshtatskaya Ulitsa 15; tel: 331 2600; M: Chernyshevskaya; map p.134 A3

Emergency Numbers

Fire 01
Police 02
Ambulance 03
Police helpline for foreigners 578 3094 (9.30am–6.15pm)

Gay and Lesbian

Homosexuality was illegal until not so long ago in Russia, and most Russians are to varying degrees homophobic, so gay travellers are advised to avoid public displays of affection. Gay nightclubs are raided by the police (with no reason given), but foreigners are unlikely to be arrested. A useful website for gay listings is www.gay.ru/english.

Above: postbox.

Health

There are several private, Western-standard clinics with English-speaking doctors:

American Medical Clinic
Nab. Reki Moiki 78; tel: 740 2090; www.amclinic.ru; 24 hours; M: Sadovaya; map p.136 B3

Euromed
Suvorovsky Prospekt 60; tel: 327 0301; www.euromed.ru; 24 hours; M: Chernyshevskaya; map p.135 D3

MEDEM International Clinic and Hospital
Ulitsa Marata 6; tel: 336 3333; www.medem.ru; 24 hours; M: Mayakovskaya; map p.138 A3

Information

All tourist information offices are open daily 10am–7pm:

If you need to send anything large or of value avoid the Russian post. There are courier services around the city, including DHL (Nevsky Prospekt 10; tel: 326 6400; www.dhl.ru; M: Nevsky Prospekt; map p.136 C2) and Westpost (Nevsky Prospekt 86; tel: 336 6352; www.westpost.ru; M: Mayakovskaya; map p.138 A2). If you don't like the look of their steep rates, pack some sandwiches and a thermos and head for the Central Post Office (Pochtamtskaya 9; tel: 315 8022; www.spbpost.ru; M: Sennaya Ploshchad; map p.136 A2). You may have to wait for several hours, but at least the Art Nouveau interior is nice to look at.

Sadovaya Ulitsa 14; tel: 310 8262; M: Gostiny Dvor; map p.137 D2
Dvortsovaya Ploshchad (near the Hermitage); tel: 982 8253; M: Nevsky Prospekt; map p.136 C1
Ploshchad Rastrelli (in front of Smolny Cathedral); tel: 310 2822; M: Chernyshevskaya; map p.135 D3
Tourist helpline: 300 3333; www.visit-petersburg.com

Left: a staged photo on Nevsky Prospekt.

Avoiding drinking tap water. It contains some nasty parasites and heavy metals, but it is fine for brushing your teeth.

Tourist Angels. Identifiable by their red baseball caps and jackets, which read, 'Can I Help?' the young people stand in pairs along Nevsky near the major tourist attractions. They speak several languages, and can help if you have any problems or queries.

Visa Information

All visitors require a visa to enter (and leave!) the Russian Federation. To get a visa, you must have an official invitation from a hotel, place of study or other establishment. If you are staying in a hotel, they will almost certainly arrange your invitation for you. If you are staying with friends or relatives, the easiest way to get an invitation is through the website www.visaable.com.

When you have your invitation, send it to the Russian embassy in your country along with the fee, your passport, a photograph, and completed application form (for Britain, these now have to be filled in online). Check the latest requirements and fees on the website of your consulate. Tourist visas are valid for 30 days.

When you arrive in Russia, you MUST register your visa within three working days of your arrival. The hotel or agency that arranged your invitation will take care of this. It is also important not to lose the small white immigration form that you fill in upon arrival, as you will need it to leave the country.

Internet Cafés

Cafemax
Nevsky Prospekt 90; tel: 273 6655; www.cafemax.ru; 24 hours; M: Mayakovskaya; map p.138 A2
There is also a branch of Cafemax in the Hermitage.
Quo Vadis
Nevsky Prospekt 76; tel: 333 0708; www.quovadis.ru; 9am–11pm; M: Mayakovskaya; map p.138 A2

Media

The city's English-language newspaper, **The St Petersburg Times**, comes out on Tuesdays and Fridays and is a free and reliable source of local news and events. The monthly **St Petersburg in Your Pocket** is another invaluable source of information, from train timetables to how to connect your laptop to the internet using a phone card.

Money

The currency in Russia is the ruble. Exchange rates can be checked before departure at xe.com. ATMs can be found along Nevsky Prospekt, in all major hotels and most metros.

Post and Telephones

The Russian post is notoriously slow; it will take at least two weeks for a postcard to reach Western Europe. Stamps can be bought at post offices and posted at any of the blue postboxes.

The best option for calling home is to buy a card from Yevroset, Ultra or any phone shop around the city. Calls abroad can cost from as little as 1 ruble per minute.

Tourist Angels

The city has introduced an ingenious new service – the

St Petersburg has its share of petty crime. Watch for pickpockets on the metro and along Nevsky, and for Romany women and children around tourist attractions. The latter are liable to surround tourists in large groups, taking their valuables in the process. Unfortunately, the police are very corrupt and should be avoided if possible. They have the right to stop anyone and ask for documents (you should carry a copy of your passport at all times).

53

Fashion

If during the Soviet era, Russians were not renowned for their style and class, they are certainly trying to make up for it now. The penchant for tight nylon clothes for women and ill-fitting leather jackets on men is declining, though still very much in evidence. The large number of designer shops around St Petersburg is quite remarkable, especially considering the ratio of the prices, which tend to be considerably higher than in the rest of Europe, to the average monthly wage of 16,000 rubles ($602). The city also has its share of local designers. *See also Shopping, p.122–3.*

Local Scene

St Petersburg's fashion queen is **Tatiana Parfionova**, who has a boutique on Nevsky, though little of it can be considered wearable by anyone other than the most daring. Her collections are a regular sight at the **Defile na Neve** (Defile on the Neva), a twice-yearly fashion show held in April and October. Other local designers regularly featured in the event include **Irina Tantsurina** and **Liliya Kiselenko**. See www.defilenaneve. ru/en for more information.

Russian women tend to dress smartly – trainers and indeed any shoes without heels are a rare sight. This remains true even in the winter months, when girls continue to wear miniskirts and confidently navigate the ice and snow in stiletto-heeled boots. Make-up is a huge industry in Russia, as is fur.

Local Outlets

Evgenia Ostrovskaya
Varshavsky Express; Nab. Obvodnovo Kanala 118; tel: 333 1090; 10am–10pm; M: Baltiiskaya
Evgenia Ostrovskaya's

Alternative cultures such as punks in the '80s were repressed by the Soviet authorities, but today the city is home to an explosion of emos. Along with the city's goth population, they often hang out on Ploshchad Isskusstv and Manezhnaya Ploshchad near Dom Kino. In a recent case of déjà vu, there has been a state attack on such subcultures, with government warnings being sent around schools advising teachers to be on the lookout for such students, as they are likely to be 'extremist' and 'suicidal'.

designs are bold and elegant, using contrasting blocks of colour. If you're looking to impress at a job interview or inspire respect in your colleagues, this is the place for you.

Sultana Frantsuzova
Kamennoostrovsky Prospekt 40; tel: 448 5276; 10am–8pm; M: Petrogradskaya; also at Varshavsky Express and Mega Dybenko
Sultana Frantsuzova's pseudo-Victorian collections are all about velvet, lace, high-collared blouses and

bows. If you can pull off this look without looking too much like the stereotype of a librarian, it's worth checking out her designs.

Tatiana Parfionova
Nevsky Prospekt 51; tel: 713 1415; www.parfionova.ru; 10am–7pm; M: Gostiny Dvor; map p.138 A2

Western Designers

If Western designers are your thing, then you will find plenty of opportunities for retail therapy in St Petersburg. Collections are not always the latest, however, and usually cost at least 20 percent more than they do in Western Europe.

Babochka
Nevsky Prospekt 36; tel: 324 3229; 11am–9pm; M: Nevsky Prospekt; map p.137 D2
This boutique by the Grand Hotel Europe is small and stylish.

Burberry
Grand Palace shopping centre; Italianskaya Ulitsa 15; tel: 449 9427; 11am–9pm; M: Gostiny Dvor; map p.137 D2

Right: Parfionova and Defile na Neve.

Left: Defile na Neve.

High-Street Shopping

If your bank balance does not match that of a New Russian, the city's shopping centres offer everything imaginable in the way of clothes, shoes, accessories and underwear.

Mega Dybenko
Murmanskoye Shosse, Vsevolozhsky district; tel: 933 7450; www.megamall.ru; 10am–10pm; M. Ulitsa Dybenko
It's even bigger than its name suggests. Along with Russian brands, it has Marks & Spencer, Topshop, Berksha and much, much more. To get there, take the metro to Ulitsa Dybenko and then get the free Mega bus from outside the metro station.

Sennaya
Ulitsa Yefimova 3; tel: 740 4624; www.sennaya.ru; 11am–9pm; M: Sadovaya; map p.137 C4
Sennaya is not as big as Mega, but is much nearer to the centre and still has a varied assortment of both men's and women's shops.

Varshavsky Express
Nab. Obvodkovo Kanala 118; tel: 333 1020; www.vokzala.net; 10am–10pm; M: Baltiiskaya
The converted Warsaw train station focuses on more expensive names such as Sultana Frantsuzova and Karen Millen.

The easiest way to obtain a ticket to **Defile na Neve** (they are generally distributed among industry professionals) is to buy an item of clothing from the Defile boutique at Nab. Kanala Griboedova 27; tel: 571 9010; 11am–8pm; M: Nevsky Prospekt; map p.137 C2.

Haute Couture Gallery
Gostiny Dvor (first floor); Nevsky Prospekt 35; tel: 314 9687; 11am–10pm; M: Gostiny Dvor; map p.137 D2
The section of Gostiny Dvor running parallel to Nevsky is given over to clothes and accessories by every designer you can imagine.

Vanity Opera
Kazanskaya Ulitsa 3; tel: 438 5548; 11am–10pm; M: Nevsky Prospekt; map p.137 C2
This glass giant next to Kazan Cathedral has all the usual suspects, such as Dior, Louis Vuitton and Gucci.

Versace
Rossi Pavilion, Nevsky Prospekt 39; tel: 314 1492; 11am–9pm; M: Gostiny Dvor; map p.137 D2
The brand is housed in the grand Rossi Pavilion adorned with classical statues that stands on Nevsky Prospekt near the Catherine Garden.

Festivals

There is always something going on in Russia's cultural capital, be it music, film or fashion – not to mention a glorious seven public holidays per year, plus 10 days off at the beginning of the year for Russia's most celebrated holiday. The most popular time for tourists to visit the city is in June, at the height of the White Nights, but the number of tourists in winter is also increasing thanks to projects such as the White Days programme, which promotes the other side of St Petersburg – its beautiful white winter and the mulled wine and Christmas markets that accompany it.

Festivals

JANUARY

New Year is the biggest celebration of the year in Russia, and to give revellers time to recover from drinking all that champagne, throwing all those fireworks and wandering the snowy streets until midday on the 1st, most offices are closed until the 9th or 10th. Many take the opportunity to go skiing or skating, and many more use it to continue partying. **Orthodox Christmas** is celebrated on 7th, but is only observed by churchgoers at special services. Then, on the 13th, just as everyone has gone back to work, the **Old New Year** is celebrated (New Year accord-

Maslenitsa (Shrovetide) is celebrated in late March or early April – the exact dates depend on those of Orthodox Easter. It is marked by a week of eating as many *blini* (pancakes) as possible, culminating in a celebration on Krestovsky Ostrov and other parks, featuring a straw doll representing winter being burnt on a bonfire, and men trying to climb to the top of greased poles, if you are lucky.

ing to the old Julian calendar – the fact that Russia changed to the Gregorian calendar back in 1918 is not seen as any reason to deny the nation one last party to brighten up the cold, dark winter).

FEBRUARY

Defenders of the Fatherland Day, informally known as 'Men's Day', is celebrated on the 23rd. Men of all ages, regardless of their experience (or lack) of defending the fatherland, are congratulated by their womenfolk, and nobody goes to work.

MARCH

On the 8th, it is the turn of women to bask in the limelight. Only former Soviet Union countries take **International Women's Day** this seriously. Weary men stand in line at the florist's, traffic police hand out carnations instead of fines to speeding female drivers, and all the restaurants

Left: parade on Nevsky Prospekt.

The phenomenon of the **White Nights**, when the sun barely sets for several weeks around the Summer Solstice in June, is due to St Petersburg's northerly latitude of 60 degrees. During these nights of surreal daylight, people roam the streets and embankments drinking champagne or take boat trips to watch the opening of the bridges. Some suffer from insomnia and long for proper darkness, others wish they would never end, and the city buzzes with a feeling of abandon and mild insanity.

are fully booked. Going to work does not feature anywhere in the festivities.

APRIL
Orthodox Easter
SEE ALSO CHURCHES, P.48

MAY
1 May is **Labour Day** – another day off, but not marked as solemnly as 9 May – **Victory Day**, when Russia celebrates the anniversary of the end of World War II. It is a particularly poignant holiday in St Petersburg, where siege survivors and veterans are paid tribute to by their relatives and the city. There is a parade down Nevsky and a moving remembrance ceremony at the Piskaryovskoe cemetery, where many of those who perished during the siege are buried.

On a more cheerful note, 27 May is **City Day** – the anniversary of the founding of the city. It's not a day off,

so the City Carnival that celebrates the occasion is usually held on the Saturday after the 27th.

JUNE
Stars of the White Nights Festival
An annual series of premieres and unique performances by leading opera and ballet stars at the Mariinsky and some of the city's other theatres. See www.mariinsky.ru for up-to-date information.

This month's obligatory day off work is on the 12th, for **Russia Day**.

NOVEMBER
Until 2005, Revolution Day

was celebrated on 7 November, but was then replaced with the less Communist **People's Unity Day**, celebrated on 4 November. Most Russians are vague on the 1612 uprising against the Poles that it commemorates, but are relieved that the overall number of public holidays has not decreased.

DECEMBER
Arts Square Winter Festival
Ten days of classical music, opera, jazz and much more held at the Shostakovich Philharmonic and directed by the celebrated maestro Yury Temirkanov.

Left: generals singing at parade. **Right:** sandcastle competitions at Peter and Paul Fortress.

Film

St Petersburg has served as the backdrop for numerous foreign films and TV series, as well as for hundreds of Russian productions – anything set before the 1917 revolution is usually filmed in St Petersburg, since it has retained its Tsarist appearance far more than Moscow, which has a highly distinctive Soviet look. The city's film studio, Lenfilm, is Russia's second-largest after Moscow's Mosfilm and has contributed greatly to Russia's rich film heritage. St Petersburg's many cinemas show all the latest Hollywood hits as well as the occasional arty film, though almost exclusively in Russian.

On Location

One of the city's most famous appearances was in the James Bond film *GoldenEye* (1995), which showed Pierce Brosnan driving a tank past St Isaac's Cathedral, through the arch of the Senate building down Galernaya Ulitsa and along the Moika embankment past Pushkin's apartment.

Alexander Sokurov's 2002 film *Russkii Kovchyog* (Russian Ark) was filmed in the Hermitage in a single take. The film features 33 of the rooms in the Winter Palace to explore 300 years of Russian history and culture. The Winter Palace also featured in Sergei Eisenstein's 1927 silent movie *Oktyabr: Desyat Dnei Kotorye Potryasli Mir* (October: 10 Days that Shook the World), in which the real events of the storming of the Winter Palace were reconstructed.

The city was also the setting for part of *Ironiya Sudby, ili S Lyogkim Parom* (The Irony of Fate, 1975) and its 2007 sequel.

The plot of Eldar Ryazanov's classic comedy *The Irony of Fate* revolves around the Soviet city-planning system, in which streets and squares in cities all over Russia had the same names and layouts – and even, sometimes, the same locks. The central male character, Zhenya, wakes up after a drinking bout on New Year's Eve thinking he is in his home city, Moscow – but in fact he is in Leningrad, as St Petersburg was then known. He gets a taxi to his Moscow address, which not only exists in Leningrad, but differs very little from his own apartment. Conflict and romance ensue when the apartment's real inhabitant, Nadya, comes home to find a strange, drunk man in her bed insisting that she is the intruder and not him. The film is a Soviet classic that is still immensely popular

Left: *The Russian Ark.*

smaller and quirkily Soviet, with its rows of wooden chairs and ornate ceiling. Like its neighbour, it shows a lot of foreign films and festivals, as well as older cult movies.

Avrora
Nevsky Prospekt 60; tel: 315 5254; www.avrora.spb.ru; M: Gostiny Dvor; map p.137 E2
Avrora, which opened in 1913, has been restored to its full Tsarist glory and is enjoyable to visit both for its opulent interior and the range of films it shows, which include rare and precious screenings of films in the original language.

For Hollywood blockbusters and other mainstream films, the following cinemas have good, modern sound systems and facilities:

Khudozhestvenny
Nevsky Prospekt 67; tel: 314 0045; www.poravkino.ru; M: Mayakovskaya; map p.138 A2

Mirage Cinema
Bolshoy Prospekt 35; tel: 498 0758; www.mirage.ru; M: Chkalovskaya

If you understand Russian, the films *Progulka* (A Walk), *Piter FM* and the classic *Neveroyantye Prikliucheniya Italiantsev v Rossii* (The Amazing Adventures of the Italians in Russia) are also set in St Petersburg, and all feature extensive views of the city.

today, and is traditionally shown every New Year's Eve in Russia.

Lenfilm Studios

Lenfilm on Kamennyostrovsky Prospekt on the Petrograd Side remains the city's main film studio, though a new state-of-the-art facility is under construction. The city's most famous directors include Sokurov and Alexei Balabanov, whose films have included *Brat* (Brother, 1996) and *Brat 2* (2000), which portrayed the gang wars taking place in the city in the '90s and were immensely popular.

Cinemas

Foreign films are almost always dubbed (often badly) into Russian, but are occa-sionally shown in the original language with subtitles at Avrora, or as part of regular film festivals. Check the Friday edition of *The St Petersburg Times* for weekly film listings. In June, the annual *Poslanie k Cheloveku* (Message to Man) film festival is held at Dom Kino and Rodina, showing a variety of animated, documentary and short films.

Dom Kino
Karavannaya Ulitsa 12; tel: 314 5614; www.domkino. spb.ru; M: Nevsky Prospekt; map p.137 E2
Dom Kino (House of Cinema) is the city's best art cinema, showing foreign films rarely seen elsewhere in St Petersburg. It regularly holds festivals of films from all over the world, and also shows alternative Russian films.

Rodina
Karavannaya Ulitsa 12; tel: 571 6131; www.rodinakino.ru; M: Nevsky Prospekt; map p.137 E2
Housed in the same building as Dom Kino, Rodina is

Left: Alexander Sukorov.
Right: memorial outside Lenfilm Studios.

59

Food and Drink

Russian cuisine and the hospitable culture that accompanies it are one of the highlights of any trip to St Petersburg: it is certainly a lot more than pickled beetroot and potatoes. In the city it is also well worth sampling the national cuisine of some of the former Soviet republics, especially Georgia, which bear little resemblance to Russian food but are just as delectable. Drinking is also a big part of Russian culture, regardless of the time and place. *See Restaurants, p.114–21*, for a broad selection of the best places to try all the local delicacies.

Business Lunches

The typical Russian meal consists of a salad, soup and main meal, usually involving meat and some source of starch, such as potatoes, rice or pasta. The business lunch deals on offer at many of the city's eateries usually include all three courses and are a good way to fill up on a range of dishes for a reasonable price.

Soups

Soups are an essential course of any Russian meal, which is perhaps not surprising, given the climate.

The most famous is of course *borshch*, most commonly translated as beetroot soup, though in fact beetroot is just one of many ingredients, including beef, onion, cabbage and other vegetables. Even if you can't stand beetroot, don't be put off – most visitors quickly acquire a taste for this tangy, warming pink soup.

Shchi, or cabbage soup, is also a bit of a misnomer, and bears no resemblance to the stuff of '80s diet plans.

Salads

Traditional Russian salads

differ somewhat to those of France, Italy and Greece, for example. You are unlikely to find anything resembling a lettuce leaf in a Russian salad, and the main ingredient is usually mayonnaise, so if you have ordered a salad as a healthy option, you may be in for a surprise. Once you know what to expect, you are less likely to be disappointed, so go ahead and take the plunge.

Olivier salad is a Russian favourite and is as essential on the New Year table as turkey at an English Christmas dinner. It contains ham, peas, boiled egg, onion, and naturally, plenty of mayonnaise.

Other Favourites

Pelmeni, or ravioli-like dumplings stuffed with meat, are popular as a quick bite served with the obligatory *smetana*.

Another Russian staple is *blini*, or pancakes. Eat them with caviar, *smetana*, ham and cheese, salmon, dill,

Left: *blini* and caviar.

Left: caviar, in volume.

Whatever you choose, make sure you order a *khachapuri* to go with it. *Khachapuri* is a very rich and filling dish consisting of bread stuffed with cheese and baked in the oven. There will usually be several variations on a menu – some come served with an egg on top (which is supposed to fry on the hot bread but in reality doesn't always, for the salmonella-conscious) and some are more like pastry than bread. Staff in Caucasian restaurants are often more friendly than their Russian counterparts and are usually more than happy to advise you on what to order. While the names of dishes may vary slightly from place to place, the standard dishes are usually the same regardless of the part of the Caucasus from which they originate.

Vodka Etiquette

Russia's national spirit should be downed straight, as a single or, more frequently, double shot. Russians like to chase it with *zakuski*, an assortment of picked vegetables, or black bread.

Essential accompaniments to any Russian meal are black rye bread and *smetana* or sour cream. The latter gets dolloped in soup, salads, on *pelmeni*, and indeed anywhere else you fancy. An essential garnish to all savoury dishes, Russian or otherwise, is dill *(ukrop)*, and in copious amounts. Sometimes you may be pushed to see your chips/pizza/salad/soup for the carpet of dill concealing it, but Russians maintain it is very good for you.

jam, condensed milk and virtually anything else you can think of. *See Cafés, p.40–41*, for some prime *blini* joints.

Caucasian Cuisine

There is a wealth of Georgian, Armenian and Azerbaijani restaurants all over the city. If you start to feel a bit jaded by the blandness of many Russian dishes and long for something spicier than a dill plant, then head

for one of them and try some of the following mouth-watering dishes.

Shashlyk (lumps of meat barbecued on a skewer) is the speciality at Caucasian restaurants. The juicy meat is usually served adorned with fresh onion, herbs and the odd pomegranate seed.

Popular starters include aubergine rolls *(baklazhany)* served with a garlic and nut paste; *adzhabsandali*, similar to a spicy ratatouille; and *lobio* – a kind of kidney bean stew with onion and herbs.

Right: buffet and its natural accompaniment.

Left: fine produce is available at markets that have changed little over the years.

pagne) is available in any food shop from as little as 1 euro. Look for the Brut – it's less sweet than the other kinds.

Wine is not widely consumed in Russia. Georgian and Moldovan wine is considered to be the most drinkable of those available, but the former was banned in Russia, along with Georgian mineral water, in 2006 following a dispute between the two countries. Though it has disappeared from the menu, in reality it is still freely available in the city, though it is not a good idea to ask for it loudly – try asking sweetly for *domashnoe vino* (house wine) instead.

Non-alcoholic drinks include *Mors*, a bittersweet drink made from cranberries, and *kvas*, a fermented drink made from rye bread. Russians swear it is the most thirst-quenching drink, and it is sold from barrels in the street during the summer in some places, such as the fountain in front of the Admiralty.

SEE ALSO CAFÉS, P.40

In recent years, beer has actually overtaken vodka in popularity. Popular local brands include Nevskoe and Baltika. Highly recommended is the *myod*, or honey beer available at **Teremok**, some other cafés and occasionally from barrels in the street. It is worth remembering that it is no less alcoholic than regular beer, though it may slip down as easily as a soft drink.

Champagne is a must at any celebration – weddings,

birthdays, and many far less formal occasions such as picnics and walks during the White Nights. *Sovietskaya Shampanskoe* (Soviet cham-

---

If you are offered a meat-and-jelly dish that bears an alarming resemblance to Pedigree or Whiskas, try to contain your surprise. *Kholodets* is a Russian delicacy and an essential part of every wedding feast and formal celebration.

Food Shopping

Until recently, buying food in Russia involved asking the shop assistant for individual products from the shelves behind the counter. Usually there were multiple counters – and multiple queues – for different sections, such as dairy, meat, fruit and vegetables and tinned goods. However, times are changing, and Western-style supermarkets have sprung up around the city and all along the road to the airport. Many of them are open 24 hours,

Russians are extremely hospitable, and if you are invited to someone's house, you may want to consider starving yourself for a day in advance, since you are likely to be plied with plate upon plate of food and a slab of rich cream cake with your tea to top it all off. Refusal may cause offence, especially among the older generations, so it's best to forget about your diet until you can escape.

as are some of the smaller shops in the centre, which may retain the Soviet system of service described above. There are also several fresh produce markets around the city that are far cheaper than the supermarkets.

Supermarkets

Land

Vladimirsky Passazh shopping centre, Vladimirsky Prospekt 19; tel: 331 3233; 24 hours; M: Vladimirskaya/Dostoevskaya; map p.138 A3

Land, located in the basement of Vladimirsky Passazh, is fairly pricey, but its range of items is good – you can even, on occasion, find hummus here.

Perekryostok

Pik shopping centre, Ulitsa Yefimova 2; tel: 336 4790; 24 hours; M: Sennaya Ploshchad/Sadovaya; map p.137 C4

Perekryostok resembles a smart Western supermarket in every way, apart from the occasional rat seen scuttling under the shelves. It is cheaper and more spacious than Land, but its range of food products is just as good.

Markets

Kuznechny Rynok

Kuznechny pereulok 3; tel: 312 4161; Mon–Sat 8am–8pm, Sun 8am–7pm; M: Vladimirskaya; map p.137 E3

Located just a stone's throw from the metro, this is one of the city's smartest, best-stocked and most expensive markets.

Sennoy Rynok

Moskovsky Prospekt 4a; tel: 310 1209; 8am–7pm; M: Sennaya Ploshchad/Sadovaya

One of the biggest and cheapest markets in the city. The produce sold outside is

Above and below: the upmarket Vladimirsky Passazh, home of Land.

considerably cheaper than that sold inside, but do watch to make sure you are not being given bruised or rotten fruit.

Sytny Rynok

Sytninskaya Ploshchad 3/5; tel: 233 2293; 8am–7pm; M: Gorkovskaya; map p.132 B1

The city's oldest market, and still one of the cheapest, Sytny Market is very well stocked and considered by many to be the best in the city.

History

1703

Peter the Great chooses a small island in the swampy Neva delta as the site for a new fortress to protect the territory from Sweden. The new city planned around the fortress is to be a "window on the West."

1712

St. Petersburg officially replaces Moscow as the capital of the Russian Empire and the court is forced to leave their Moscow palaces and move up north. Peter bans construction in all Russian cities with the exception of St. Petersburg in order to ensure its development.

1725

Peter dies, and in 1728 his son, Peter II, moves the capital back to Moscow. The half-finished buildings are left to decay.

1732

Peter the Great's niece, Empress Anna, restores St. Petersburg to its status as capital.

1736

Fire destroys the centre of the city.

1741

Peter's daughter Elizabeth ascends the throne. Her reign sees the building of many Baroque masterpieces.

1754

Francesco Bartolomeo Rastrelli begins building the Winter Palace.

1762

The future Catherine the Great deposes her unpopular husband and takes the throne. During her reign, St. Petersburg acquires a more restrained, Classical appearance.

1782

Bronze Horseman monument is unveiled.

1799

Paul I's brief and unpopular reign comes to an end when he is murdered in the newly-built Mikhailovsky Castle.

1811

Kazan Cathedral completed.

1812

The Russian army defeats Napoleon's France, unleashing an unprecedented wave of patriotism.

1825

Alexander I dies, and the Decembrist Uprising takes place on Senate Square on Dec.14. Its leaders call for a constitution and liberal reforms, but are unsuccessful and are executed a year later.

1837

Russia's leading poet, Alexander Pushkin is killed in a duel.

1850

The Annunciation Bridge, now Lt Schmidt Bridge, opens as the city's first permanent river crossing.

1858

St Isaac's Cathedral is finished.

1861

The liberal Alexander II abolishes serfdom and introduces government reforms. It is not enough for revolutionaries, who make persistent attempts on the life of the Tsar.

1881

On March 1, Alexander II is mortally wounded by a terrorist's bomb on the site where the Church on the Spilled Blood now stands, bringing to power the far more reactionary Alexander III.

1898

Russian Museum opens.

1905

On Jan. 9, a day now known as Bloody Sunday, a peaceful demonstration of workers and their families on their way to the Winter Palace is massacred on Palace Square by royal troops, sparking the first Russian Revolution.

1914
With the outbreak of WWI, the city's name is changed to the less German-sounding Petrograd.

1916
A Siberian peasant by the name of Grigory Rasputin is murdered at the Yusupov Palace after his influence over the imperial family becomes perceived as a threat to the country's stability.

1917
Following the 1917 February Revolution, Tsar Nicholas II was forced to abdicate. A Provisional Government was formed but faced opposition from the Socialist radicals. In October, the Bolsheviks seized control of the country's railways, power station and central bank, directed by Vladimir Ilyich Lenin from the Bolshevik headquarters in the Smolny Institute. On Oct. 25, a single blank shot fired by the Aurora at the Winter Palace signalled the beginning of the storming of the Winter Palace, where the Provisional Government was in conference.

1918
The capital of new, Communist Russia is moved back to Moscow.

1924
Lenin dies and Petrograd is renamed Leningrad.

1934
Sergei Kirov is assassinated in his office in Smolny, sparking the Great Terror, in which millions are arrested and shot or sent to the gulags, Russia's growing network of labour camps.

1941
In June, Nazi Germany attacks Russia. On Sept. 8, the 900-day Siege of Leningrad begins as Nazi troops encircle the city.

1944
The siege is lifted on Jan. 27. At least 670,000 citizens perished during the devastating Siege of Leningrad, mostly from cold and starvation.

1955
City's underground railway opens.

1964
Peterhof finally reopens to the public after a lengthy restoration to repair extensive war damage.

1989
UNESCO makes the city a World Heritage Site.

1998
Millions see their life savings wiped out as the ruble plummets after the government defaults on its debt.

2000
Vladimir Putin, a former KGB officer and native Petersburger, replaces Yeltsin as President of Russia.

2003
The city celebrates its 300th anniversary amid much restoration work.

2008
Dmitry Medvedev, another Petersburger and Putin's chosen candidate to succeed him as president, is elected by a landslide majority at the presidential elections.

Hotels

Having gone from a monopoly of grim, Intourist hotels that provided basic needs at best during the Soviet era to a boom of top-of-the-range luxury hotels that left the average tourist at the door during the '90s and first years of the 21st century, a category of mid-range hotels is finally beginning to develop in St Petersburg. It is worth bearing in mind that during the summer months, especially May and June, hotels are very busy, so booking well ahead is recommended, especially for the mini-hotels, which by definition only have a few rooms.

Nevsky Prospekt

Apricot Hostel
Nevsky Prospekt 106; tel: 272 7178; €; M: Mayakovskaya; map p.138 A2
Ideal for those travelling on a strict budget, Apricot Hostel has everything you would expect from a cheap and cheerful residence in the city centre. Luridly painted cupboards, self-conscious Soviet kitsch, shared showers – this place could easily be located in any up-and-coming European capital. A good choice for students.

Corinthia Nevskij Palace
Nevsky Prospekt 57; tel: 380 2001; www.corinthia.ru; €€€€; M: Mayakovskaya; map p.138 A2
Ultra-modern and boasting all mod cons (including a swimming pool, fitness centre and spa), this five-star hotel is not for those seeking the historical and architectural charm of classical St Petersburg. The hotel's restaurants are very good, and the view from the top-floor Landskrona restaurant is superb.

Hotel Moscow
Ploshchad Alexandra Nevskovo 2; tel: 274 2052; www.hotel-moscow.ru; €€; M: Ploshchad Alexandra Nevskovo; map p.139 D4
A Soviet-era hotel renovated to Western standards, Hotel Moscow is all about BIG. Big building, big corridors, big breakfast, this place is perfect for visitors to the city who want to stay central

without paying the mammoth prices of some of the more stylish hotels. Staff are friendly and rooms are satisfactorily clean.

Nevsky Forum
Nevsky Prospekt 69; tel: 333 0222; www.forumhotel.ru; €€€; M: Nevsky Prospekt; map p.138 A2
The bubbly, helpful staff are the real attraction at this centrally located but somewhat overpriced hotel. They are uncommonly eager to help, so expect to be met, greeted and seated by the receptionist and porter on your arrival, your bags whisked away and

Prices for a standard double room in high season:
€ under 3,000 rubles
€€ 3,000–6,000 rubles
€€€ 6,000–10,000 rubles
€€€€ over 10,000 rubles

Left: Moika 22.

have a great night's sleep whatever St Petersburg's nightbirds get up to outside your window. The location of this place is ideal – within walking distance of the Hermitage and most of the city's other attractions.

Palace Square to Liteiny Prospekt

Ermitage Hotel
Millionaya Ulitsa 11; tel: 571 5497; www.ermitage.spb.ru; €€; M: Nevsky Prospekt; map p.133 C4
The main attraction of this mini-hotel (just four rooms) is its central position within walking distance of Vasilievsky Island and the Petrograd Side, as well as Palace Square and the Field of Mars. The historic building itself is well preserved, but the rooms are a bit dated.

Grand Hotel Europe
Mikhailovskaya Ulitsa 1/7; tel: 329 6000; www.grandhotel europe.com; €€€€; M: Nevsky Prospekt; map p.137 D2
For this sort of money, you may expect to be served the moon on a stick, and the Grand Hotel Europe certainly does not disappoint. Combine massage therapists with French champagne breakfasts, a caviar bar and live show and you start to get some idea of what's in store here. If you like to indulge in obscene decadence this is the place for you.

Kempinski Moika 22
Nab. Moika 22; tel: 335 9111; www.kempinski-st-petersburg.com; €€€€; M: Nevsky Prospekt; map p.137 C1
Overlooking Palace Square and the Winter Palace, this hotel enables guests to flee

---

your every need attended to. Good internet connection is another bonus, although the rooms themselves might be much better equipped for the money.

Oktyabrsky Hotel
Ligovsky Prospekt 10; tel: 578 1515; www.oktober-hotel. spb.ru; €€; M: Ploshchad Vosstaniya; map p.138 B2
Boasting the somewhat puzzling epithet of 'oldest hotel of the mid-19th century', this place is sensibly priced for what it offers and conveniently located for those arriving at the city by train from Moscow. Having

undergone significant restoration in recent years, the hotel has managed to preserve some of the Soviet-era accoutrements. Expect to encounter kitschy upholstery and lots of atmospheric uplighting!

Radisson SAS Royal Hotel
Nevsky Prospekt 49/2; tel: 322 5000; www.stpetersburg. radissonsas.com; €€€€; M: Nevsky Prospekt; map p.138 A2
Located right on Nevsky, the five-star Radisson SAS Royal Hotel is remarkable for its tranquil atmosphere. Carefully soundproofed rooms ensure that you will

Far Left: Corinthia Nevskij Palace. **Left:** Radisson SAS.

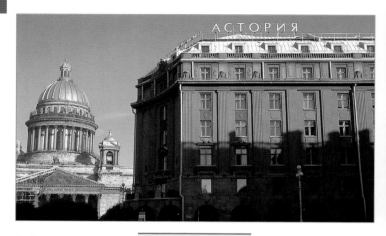

the Gazprom building sites and blinking Baltika adverts and step back in time to Tsarist Russia. The rooms of the hotel have been decorated with an opulence that strives to live up to the building's historic surroundings. Needless to say, all your technological and personal needs will be anticipated.

Nevsky Grand Hotel
Bolshaya Konyushennaya 10; tel: 312 1206; www.hon.ru; €€€; M: Nevsky Prospekt; map p.137 C1

A rare example of a reasonably priced, friendly and well-located hotel, the dis-

Many of the larger hotels such as the Kempinski Moika 22 and the Astoria offer special packages at certain times of the year, such as Valentine's Day, Easter and winter weekend breaks. These are usually far better value than the standard rates, so it's worth checking for such offers before you make your booking.

cerning tourist to St Petersburg could do a lot worse than Nevsky Grand Hotel. Staff are fluent in English and French, and while the rooms might be criticised for

being 'over-cosy', the fantastic location makes up for any domestic drawbacks. The Grand is part of the Nevsky Hotel Group, which has similar hotels dotted around the centre.

Pushka Inn
Nab. Reki. Moiki 14; tel: 312 0957; www.pushkainn.ru; €€€; M: Nevsky Prospekt; map p.137 C1

The staff here speak great English, which is definitely an advantage for those travelling to the city for the first time. Breakfast is free and copious and the rooms are quiet, clean and spacious. Perched on the river, this is a great

Left: Astoria.

place for wandering around the meandering backstreets, and is equally well located for sightseeing.

The Admiralty to St Nicholas's Cathedral

Ambassador
Prospekt Rimskovo-Korsakova 5–7; tel: 331 8844; www.ambassador-hotel.ru; €€€€; M: Sadovaya/Sennaya Ploshchad; map p.136 B4
Something about this luxurious four-star hotel makes regular visitors to the city want to stay here every time. Situated near the Yusupov Gardens, the Ambassador is about a 20-minute walk from Nevsky Prospekt, but is only a stone's throw away from Sadovaya and Sennaya Ploshchad metro stations, making it handy for the Mariinsky.

Angleterre
Malaya Morskaya Ulitsa 24; tel: 494 5666; www.angleterre hotel.com; €€€€; M: Sadovaya; map p.136 B2
The Astoria's sister hotel is not quite as opulent as its famed relative, and only fractionally less expensive. It still has the amazing views of the cathedral, but the rooms are smaller and less luxurious. Facilities include a mini-gym and even more diminutive pool.

Astoria
Bolshaya Morskaya Ulitsa 39; tel: 494 5757; www.roccoforte collection.com; €€€€; M: Sadovaya; map p.136 B2
Housed in a Style Moderne beauty built by Fyodor Lidval at the beginning of the 20th century, the Astoria is one of the city's top hotels. The elegant interiors of the ground-floor lobby are con-

tinued in the rooms upstairs, the best of which have views to kill for of St Isaac's Cathedral.

Casa Leto
Bolshaya Morskaya Ulitsa 34; tel: 600 1096; www.casa leto.com; €€€; M: Nevsky Prospekt; map p.136 B2
This small boutique hotel in an excellent location between St Isaac's and Nevsky Prospekt is a converted apartment, which has been beautifully decorated to retain the homely atmosphere of an apartment rather than a hotel. Rooms are spacious and airy with high ceilings. The hotel has a very luxurious feel to it, and the visa service here is excellent.

Comfort Hotel
Bolshaya Morskaya 25; tel: 570 6700; www.comfort-hotel.spb.ru; €€; M: Nevsky Prospekt; map p.136 B2
An excellent mini-hotel perfectly positioned midway between St Isaac's and

Prices for a standard double room in high season:
€ under 3,000 rubles
€€ 3,000–6,000 rubles
€€€ 6,000–10,000 rubles
€€€€ over 10,000 rubles

Nevsky. The rooms are not large, but they are adequate and manage to find the perfect balance between tasteful decor and a cosy atmosphere. Tea and coffee are served all day in the breakfast room.

Cuba Hostel
Kazanskaya Ulitsa 5; tel: 921 7115; www.cubahostel.ru; €; M: Nevksy Prospekt; map p.137 C2
Cuba Hostel is perfect for budget travellers, situated right in the centre next to Kazan Cathedral. As well as the dorms, there are 14 rooms, a communal kitchen and other communal areas.

Herzen House
Bolshaya Morskaya 25; tel: 315 5550; www.herzen-hotel.ru;

Left: Moika 22 *(see p.67)*.
Right: Casa Leto.

€€; M: Nevsky Prospekt; map p.136 B2

Housed in the same building as Comfort Hotel, Herzen House has more rooms, some of which are also more spacious than those of its neighbour. The hot breakfast here is just what is needed to set you up for a day of sightseeing.

Nevsky Inn
Kirpichny Pereulok 2, Apt 19; tel: 972 6873; www.nevsky inn.ru; €€; M: Nevsky Prospekt; map p.136 C2

This seven-room guesthouse tucked away just off Nevsky has bright, immaculate rooms and excellent service. It is a good budget option in a handy location with a light, spacious, well-equipped communal kitchen. The free internet is a bonus.

Northern Lights
Bolshaya Morskaya 50; tel: 571 9199; www.nlightsrussia.com; €€; M: Nevsky Prospekt; map p.136 B2

Northern Lights is a small, welcoming hotel with a per-

sonal feel. Rooms are sparkling and newly decorated, with either en suite or shared bathroom facilities. The staff are knowledgeable about the city and very keen to help.

Petro Palace Hotel
Malaya Morskaya Ulitsa 14; tel: 571 2880; www.petro palacehotel.com; €€€; M: Nevsky Prospekt; map p.136 B2

The Petro Palace is situated in the heart of the city between St Isaac's and the Hermitage and is surrounded by great places to eat. Standard rooms are a decent size, renovated to a modern design.

Renaissance St Petersburg Baltic Hotel
Pochtamtskaya Ulitsa 4; tel: 380 4000; www.renaissance hotels.com; €€€€; M: Nevsky Prospekt; map p.136 B2

Reminiscent of a boutique hotel with its intimate feel, the standard rooms are a decent size, with original decor and attention to detail. The hotel is situated in a quiet location with a lovely outdoor bar terrace overlooking St Isaac's Square.

Petrograd Side

Iskra
Malaya Posadkaya Ulitsa 24/1; tel: 230 6027; www.iskra

Prices for a standard double room in high season:
€ under 3,000 rubles
€€ 3,000–6,000 rubles
€€€ 6,000–10,000 rubles
€€€€ over 10,000 rubles

Left: Holiday Club.
Right: Grand Hotel Emerald.

hotel.spb.ru; €; M: Gorkovskaya; map p.133 C1

Iskra is a bargain mini-hotel a five-minute walk from Gorkovskaya metro. Rooms are basic but have a quaint charm to them, and for the slight difference in price, it may be worth paying for the smarter de luxe rooms.

Stony Island Hotel
Kasmennoostrovsky Prospekt 45; tel: 337 2434; www.stony island.ru; €€; M: Petrogradskaya

Situated in a fashionable, sought-after district, this boutique hotel is perfectly placed for shopping and exploring the calmer Petrograd Side, while still only two stops from Nevsky Prospekt. Rooms are fitted out in an individual, modern approach in keeping with its boutique image.

Vasilievsky Island

Holiday Club
Birzhevoi Pereulok 2–4; tel: 335 2200; www.holidayclubhotels.ru; €€€€; M: Vasileostrovskaya

Holiday Club is a five-star oasis of Nordic tranquillity. Its high-tech open-brick industrial interior is unusual for the city, and the quirky coffee bar, perched between raised walkways under a glass roof, is worth visiting even if you're not staying in the hotel. Rooms are luxurious, individual and functional. The hotel's pride and joy is its luxury spa.

Marco Polo
12th Liniya 27; tel: 449 8877; www.mpolo-spb.ru; €€; M: Vasileostrovskaya

The rooms at this smart hotel are spacious, elegant and fitted out in an old St Petersburg style. Staff are polite and helpful, and there is a whole heap of extra services available at an additional cost.

Park Inn Pribaltiyskaya
Ulitsa Korablestroitelei 14; tel: 329 2626; www.pribaltiyskaya.parkinn.com.ru; €€€; M: Primorskaya

Although claiming to be modern, this vast Soviet-era hotel has not quite lost its 1984 feel. The hotel provides a shuttle service to Nevsky Prospekt, since it is quite a walk from the metro. Rooms have been renovated, but the service could be better. Its location right on the Gulf of Finland and Waterville aqua park are its main selling points.

Vladimirskaya, Liteiny and Smolny

Grand Hotel Emerald
Suvorovsky Prospekt 18; tel: 740 5000; www.grandhotel emerald.com; €€€€; M: Ploshchad Vosstaniya; map p.138 C2

The rooms at least are tastefully designed, if not the hotel's exterior. Service can at times leave a little to be desired. Ploshchad Vosstaniya is a 10-minute walk away, but Suvorovsky Prospekt is well served by the Nos 5 and 7 trolleybuses.

Hotel Dostoevsky
Vladimirsky Prospekt 19; tel: 331 3200; www.dostoevsky-hotel.ru; €; M: Vladimirskaya; map p.137 E3

Rooms at the Dostoevsky, which is conveniently located right between two metro stations and a five-minute walk from Nevsky, are a reasonable size but can get quite hot in the summer. The service is very average. The best rooms have views of St Vladimir's Cathedral.

Ibis
Ligovsky Prospekt 54; tel: 622 0100; www.ibishotel.com; €€; M: Ploshchad Vosstaniya; map p.138 B4

Left: Ibis's lounge bar.

Ibis hotels may be the same the world over, but in a city with a disproportionately large number of super-expensive five-star giants, the arrival of Ibis 10 minutes from Ploshchad Vosstaniya is very welcome. Rooms are small but sparkling clean and func-tional, and the staff are smart and helpful.

International Youth Hostel

3rd Sovietskaya Ulitsa 28; tel: 329 8018; www.ryh.ru; €; M: Ploshchad Vosstaniya; map p.138 C2

The oldest hostel in the city is still one of the best options for students. Staff are extremely helpful and friendly, facilities are clean, and the double rooms are very reasonably priced.

Peter's Walking Tours

depart from outside the hostel.

SEE ALSO WALKS AND VIEWS, P.128

> Prices for a standard double room in high season:
> € under 3,000 rubles
> €€ 3,000–6,000 rubles
> €€€ 6,000–10,000 rubles
> €€€€ over 10,000 rubles

> Nearly all hotels will provide your visa invitation and take care of your registration for you when you arrive, for a reasonable fee. This service is definitely worth taking advantage of to save having to sort it all out yourself.

Kristoff Hotel

Zagorodny Prospekt 9; tel: 712 4787; www.kristoffhotel.com; €€; M: Dostoevskaya; map p.137 E3

Kristoff is an immaculate, comfortable and welcoming mini-hotel within easy walking distance of Nevsky Prospekt, as well as being well served by metro. Rooms are large and overall the hotel has a cosy feel to it, despite the dominance of beige in the rooms.

Novotel

Ulitsa Mayakovskogo 3A; tel: 335 1188; www.novotel.spb.ru; €€€€; M: Mayakovskaya; map p.138 A2

True to its name, Novotel is ultra-modern. Rooms have a light, airy feel to them and are a decent size. Staff are friendly and professional.

Left: Sokos Hotel Olympic.
Right: Park Inn Pulkovskaya.

Left: Novotel's simple, but accommodating interiors.

The hotel is in a good position for Nevsky Prospekt, but it is a long walk to the Hermitage and St Isaac's.

Smolninskaya Hotel
Tverskaya Ulitsa 22; tel: 576 7262; www.smolninskaya hotel.com; €€; M: Cherny-shevskovo/Ploshchad Vosstaniya; map p.135 D3

The four-star Soviet-era Smolninskaya was fully renovated in 2007, and rooms are now very well equipped, if not particularly inspired. For inspiration, just look out of the window at Smolny Cathedral. Its proximity to City Hall, housed in the Smolny Institute, means it attracts government guests, who have their own drivers and are therefore not inconvenienced by the lack of transport in this area.

Moskovsky Prospekt

Park Inn Pulkovskaya
Ploshchad Pobedy 1; tel: 740 3900; www.pulkovskaya.park inn.com.ru; €€;
M: Moskovskaya

Rooms are spacious and clean, but overall the hotel is dated. The standard of service is variable, and something about the hotel doesn't make you want to stay there for too long. It's a decent metro ride from St Petersburg's main sights, but is very conveniently located for both the domestic and international airports.

Sokos Hotel Olympic Garden
Bataisky Pereulok 3A; tel: 335 2270; www.shotels.ru; €€€€;
M: Tekhnologichesky Institut

One of the newest hotels in St Petersburg; rooms are individually decorated and have all the latest technical amenities. Staff are kind and

If you're staying for more than a few days, it's definitely worth considering renting an apartment. A spacious, very comfortable apartment in the centre will usually work out cheaper than a less luxurious hotel further from the centre, but you will not have the benefit of a concierge service and advice from staff, which is an asset when visiting Russia for the first time. The best agency is Pulford, Nab. Reki Moiki 6; tel: 320 7560; www.pulford.ru; M: Nevsky Prospekt; map p.133 C4.

attentive. The hotel's claim to fame is that its mattresses were designed using NASA technology. You will have to use the metro to get around, as it's a little way from the city's major sights and is not well served by overground transport.

Language

The Russian language is notoriously difficult, so do not be discouraged if you fail to pick up a basic knowledge of it during a trip to St Petersburg; mastering the alphabet alone can take students several weeks. Luckily the locals are very accommodating. Nearly all cafés and restaurants have an English-language menu, and most young people speak at least a little English. However, street and shop signs and signs in the metro are in Russian only, so life will be considerably easier if you can at least read the Cyrillic alphabet before your arrival.

Alphabet

А а a Pronounced like **ar**chaeology
Б б b Pronounced like **b**uddy
В в v Pronounced like **v**ow
Г г g Pronounced like **g**lad
Д д d Pronounced like **d**ot
Е е ye Pronounced like **ye**s
Ё ё yo Pronounced like **yo**ke
Ж ж zh Pronounced like compo**s**ure
З з z Pronounced like **z**est
И и i Pronounced like **see**
Й й i Pronounced like **see**
К к k Pronounced like **k**ind
Л л l Pronounced like **l**ittle
М м m Pronounced like **m**emory
Н н n Pronounced like **n**ut
О о o Pronounced like **o**n
П п p Pronounced like **p**arty
Р р r Pronounced rolled
С с s Pronounced like **s**ound
Т т t Pronounced like **t**itle
У у u Pronounced like **oo**
Ф ф f Pronounced like **f**lower
Х х kh Pronounced like ich in German
Ц ц ts Pronounced like ten**ts**
Ч ч ch Pronounced like **ch**ild
Ш ш sh Pronounced like **sh**y

Щ щ shch Pronounced like **sh**ocking
ъ Hard sign that follows other letters
Ы ы iy Pronounced with the tongue in the same position as for g or k
ь Soft sign that follows other letters
Э э e Pronounced like **e**ncourage
Ю ю yu Pronounced like **you**
Я я ya Pronounced like **ya**rd

Below are some basic words with a pronunciation guide (the capital letters show where the emphasis in the word is, which is crucial in making yourself understood).

Numbers

1 *adEEn* один
2 *dva* два
3 *tree (with rolled r)* три
4 *chutEEri* четыре
5 *pyat* пять
6 *shest* шесть
7 *syem* семь
8 *vOsem* восемь
9 *dYEvit* девять
10 *dYEsit* десять
11 *adEENatsat* одиннадцать
12 *dveNATsat* двенадцать

13 *treeNATsat* тринадцать
14 *chutEErnatsat* четырнадцать
15 *pitNATsat* пятнадцать
16 *shestNATsat* шестнадцать
17 *semNATsat* семнадцать
18 *vosemNATsat* восемнадцать
19 *devitNATsat* девятнадцать
20 *DVATsat* двадцать
21 *DVATsat adEEn* двадцать один
30 *TREEtsat* тридцать
40 *SOARok* сорок
50 *PitdesYAT* пятьдесят
60 *ShestdesYAT* шестьдесят
70 *SEMdesit* семьдесят
80 *VOSemdesit* восемьдесят
90 *DeviNOSTi* девяносто
100 *Stow* сто
200 *DVEsti* двести
300 *TREEsta* триста
400 *ChutEEriysta* четыреста
500 *PitSOT* пятьсот
600 *ShestSOT* шестьсот
700 *SemSOT* семьсот
800 *VosemSOT* восемьсот
900 *DevitSOT* девятьсот
1,000 *TIYsicha* тысяча

Useful Words and Phrases

Hello *ZdrAZdvutye*
Здравствуйте

Left: Cyrillic street sign.

Places

Avenue *PrasPEKT* Проспект
Bridge *Most (short 'o')* Мост
Cathedral *SabOR* Собор
Embankment *NABerezh-naya* Набережная
Garden/Park *Sad* Сад
Island *OSTrov* Остров
Lane *PereOOlok* Переулок
Market *RInok* Рынок
Palace *DvORets* Дворец
Restaurant *RestaurAN* Ресторан
Street *OOlitsa* Улица
Square *PlOshchad* Площадь

Transport

Bus *avTOWbus* автобус
Trolleybus *trollAYbus* троллейбус
Train *POezd* поезд

Days of the Week

Monday *PoneDELnik* понедельник
Tuesday *FtORnik* вторник
Wednesday *SREDa* среда
Thursday *ChetvAIRg* четверг
Friday *PYATnitsa* пятница
Saturday *SubORta* суббота
Sunday *VoskresENye* воскресенье

Goodbye *DusvidANya* До свиданья
OK/Good *KharashO* Хорошо
Yes *Da* Да
No *Nyet* Нет
Thank you *SpasEEba* Спасибо
Big *BalshOY* Большой
Small *MALinky* Маленький
Where is the toilet? *GdYE tooalYEt?* Где туалет?
Metro *MetrO* Метро
Pharmacy *AptYEka* Аптека
How much? *SkOLko stOeet?* Сколько стоит?
Can I try this on, please? *MOzhno paMYErit?* Можно померить?
Ticket *BeelYET* Билет

Eating Out

Tea *Chai* Чай
Coffee *COffee* Кофе
Beer *PEEva* Пиво
Wine *VinO* Вино
Red *KrASnoye* Красное
White *BEloye* Белое
Juice *Sock* Сок
Water *VaDA* Вода
Sparkling *S GAZom* С газом
Still *Bez GAZa* Без газа
Chicken *KOOritsa* Курица

Pork *SvinEEna* Свинина
Beef *GavYAdina* Говядина
Lamb *BarANina* Баранина
Fish *RIYba* Рыба
Soup *Soop* Суп
Salad *SalAT* Салат
Caviar *IkRA* Икра
Ashtray *PEpelnitsa* Пепельница
Lighter *ZazhigALka* Зажигалка
The bill, please *ShchOT, pazhalsta* Счёт, пожалуйста

Right: bilingual signs to help tourists navigate the centre.

Literature

St Petersburg has inspired generations of great Russian poets and novelists, from the country's most celebrated poet, Alexander Pushkin, to the late 19th-century novelists Nikolai Gogol and Fyodor Dostoevsky and the Silver Age poets of the early 20th century such as Anna Akhmatova, Alexander Blok and Osip Mandelshtam. The city not only inspired them; in their stories and verse it was often a complex character in itself, both beautiful and dangerous, majestic and sordid. Many of the city's greatest writers have museums dedicated to their lives and work.

Akhmatova

The Silver Age poet Anna Akhmatova (1889–1966) moved from Odessa to Tsarskoe Selo (now Pushkin) with her family when she was one year old. Growing up in the place that had proved so formative for Pushkin was no less inspirational for Akhmatova, who began writing verse at the age of 11. In 1910 she married her fellow poet, Nikolai Gumilyov, and two years later gave birth to a son.

She did not support the 1917 revolution, but did not leave Russia and did not agree with those who fled. In 1921, her husband was shot for counter-revolutionary activity and her son was imprisoned in Leningrad's infamous Kresty Prison. During his imprisonment, Akhmatova spent 17 months waiting outside the prison trying desperately to obtain news of her son, and her most famous cycle of poems, *Requiem* (1935–40) was inspired by the fates of those imprisoned and executed during the Terror of the

Akhmatova *(left)* is also commemorated in a statue of the poetess and the Shemiakin sphinxes, whose bases are inscribed with quotes by her and other Silver Age poets. Both of the monuments are situated on the bank of the Neva opposite Kresty prison, where Akhmatova spent so long queuing with hundreds of other women, all waiting for news of their imprisoned relatives.

1930s. During the siege she was evacuated to Tashkent, but continued to write poems dedicated to those who remained in Leningrad, which was never far from her thoughts. In her 'Poem without a Hero', written between 1940 and 1962, the city is treated as a living entity, left to die during the siege.

Akhmatova died in 1966, and is buried in Komarovo outside the city. The Fontanny Dom on the Fontanka where she lived for many years now houses the **Anna Akhmatova Museum**. SEE ALSO MUSEUMS AND GALLERIES, P.86

Further Reading
Selected Poems (Penguin Classics)
Anna of All the Russias: A Life of Anna Akhmatova – Elaine Feinstein (Phoenix)

Blok

The Symbolist poet Alexander Blok (1880–1921) was born in St Petersburg and witnessed the workers' strikes and demonstrations of 1905. Blok's collection of poems

Left: Pushkin Memorial outside the Mikhailovsky Palace.

appearance of St Petersburg. The theme is explored in 'White Nights', the story of a couple who meet during the magical White Nights in May, and discover that hopes and dreams can turn into disillusionment just as quickly as the romantic and ephemeral White Nights turn into the cold light of day.

Dostoevsky often housed his heroes in the same districts and areas in which he himself lived, describing their surroundings and lives with incredible detail. Once, when walking with his wife, he showed her the courtyard on Voznesensky Prospekt where the protagonist of *Crime and Punishment*, the student Raskolnikov, hides the valuables that he steals from the money-lender after killing her and her sister. The action of his most famous novel mainly takes place in the area around Sennaya Ploshchad.

entitled *The City* (1904–8) were inspired by St Petersburg itself, and his most famous poem, 'The Twelve', depicts the march of 12 Red Army soldiers through Petrograd amidst a blizzard.

The apartment in which he lived and died at 57 Ulitsa Dekabristov now houses the **Alexander Blok Apartment Museum**.
SEE ALSO MUSEUMS AND GALLERIES, P.92

Further Reading
Selected Poems (Carcanet Press)

Dostoevsky

The writer Fyodor Dostoevsky (1821–81) was born in Moscow and moved to St Petersburg at the age of 16 to study at the Military Engineering Academy, housed in the gloomy Mikhailovsky Castle *(see p.88)*. Like Gogol, Dostoevsky had a complex attitude to the city that featured in so many of his works. His first novel, *Poor People*, written in 1845, por-

trays the Gogol-esque theme of love being destroyed by harsh reality. The everyday lives and surroundings of the working class of St Petersburg are described in detail in the book, from the courtyards to the dingy stairwells.

Dostoevsky also shared Gogol's idea of the deceptive

Right: Dostoevsky.

77

In 1847, Dostoevsky began to attend the meetings of the Petrashevsky circle, whose members sought economic reform and the abolition of serfdom. Made nervous by the revolutions that swept Europe that year, in 1848 Nicholas I ordered the arrest of the Petrashevsky circle. Dostoevsky was imprisoned for eight months in the infamous **Alexeevsky Ravelin** of the Peter and Paul Fortress before being sentenced to death.

On a cold morning in December 1849, on the square behind which now stands the Theatre of the Young Spectator near Pushkinskaya metro station, Dostoevsky and his friends were lined up before the firing squad. Instead of being shot, however, they were informed that the Tsar had commuted their sentences to hard labour.

During his four years at a Siberian penal colony, Dostoevsky lived with murderers and other criminals who were later the inspiration for some of the heroes in his works.

A wall plaque at Grazhdanskaya Ulitsa 19 marks the building in which Raskolnikov 'lived', while the moneylender and Sonya Marmeladova lived on the Canal Griboedova at Nos 104 and 73 respectively.

The last apartment in which Dostoevsky lived and died (while writing *The Brothers Karamazov*) at Kuznechny Pereulok 5, now houses the **Dostoevsky Museum**. The writer is buried in the Tikhvin cemetery of the **Alexander Nevsky Monastery**.

SEE ALSO CHURCHES, P.44; MUSEUMS AND GALLERIES, P.97

Further Reading
Crime and Punishment
(Vintage Classics)

The Brothers Karamazov
(Vintage)

Gogol

The satirical writer Nikolai Gogol (1809–52) moved to St Petersburg from his native Ukraine at the age of 19, and was bitterly disappointed by the famed northern capital, which seemed cold and damp after his childhood in

the sunny south. In 1830 he got a job as a bureaucrat, which provided him with much inspiration for his later stories about petty officials. Gogol wrote many short stories set in the city, including 'Nevsky Prospekt', in which the city itself is portrayed as a beguiling destructive force that crushes and corrupts ordinary people.

Gogol never did get accustomed to St Petersburg and its climate, and spent much of his time abroad after writing the play *The Government Inspector* in 1836. After he completed the full-length novel *Dead Souls* in 1842, his physical and mental health deteriorated, and after burning the manuscript of the second volume of *Dead Souls* and

Left: Gogol. **Right:** The Mandelshtam family with special guest Anna Akhmatova.

Left: performance of Gogol's *The Government Inspector*. **Right:** Nabokov.

Further Reading
Plays and Petersburg Tales (Oxford World's Classics)
Dead Souls (Penguin Classics)

Mandelshtam

The poet Osip Mandelshtam (1891–1938) was born in Warsaw but moved to St Petersburg when he was six years old. Many of his early poems, such as the 'St Petersburg Stanzas' (1913) were inspired by the architecture and various places in the city. The later part of his life was spent in Moscow, Voronezh and finally in a labour camp near Vladivostok, where he died from dystrophy in 1938.

Further Reading
Selected Poems (Penguin 20th-Century Classics)

Nabokov

The writer Vladimir Nabokov, best-known as the author of the novel *Lolita*, is commemorated at the **Vladimir Nabokov Museum**, located in the house where he spent

the first 18 years of his life before his family fled Russia after the Bolshevik Revolution in 1917.

SEE ALSO MUSEUMS AND GALLERIES, P.92

Further Reading
Speak, Memory: An

refusing to eat anything, he died in Moscow on 21 February 1852.

Gogol is remembered in the monument to him on Malaya Konushennaya Ulitsa and in the unique monument to the eponymous nose of his story at Prospekt Rimskovo-Korsakova 11.

At the start of 'Nevsky Prospekt', the beauty, grandeur and social aspect of the city's main street are extolled enthusiastically by the narrator, but later on it becomes apparent that the glitter and beauty of Nevsky are merely a sham concealing squalor and cold indifference. 'Everything is a lie, a daydream, nothing is what it seems!' laments the narrator. In the story 'The Nose', which is also set in St Petersburg, a major wakes up one morning to find that his nose is missing. The nose goes on to become a high-ranking state official and parades around the city, where its owner is forced to bow to it due to its senior rank. The story is a reflection of the importance of rank and hierarchy and the absurd proportions it could reach in pre-revolutionary St Petersburg.

Autobiography Revisited (Penguin Modern Classics)

Pushkin

Russia's greatest poet and national hero, Alexander Pushkin (1799–1837) was born in Moscow, but his life and work are inextricably linked to St Petersburg. In 1811, he was a member of the very first class of students to start studying at the newly established **Lyceum at Tsarskoe Selo** – now a museum, many of whose exhibits are related to the school's most famous graduate.

Many of St Petersburg's favourite meeting places featured in his poems, such as the Summer Gardens, the Admiralteisky Boulevard, and most famously, the monument to Peter I, which only became known as the **Bronze Horseman** after

Pushkin wrote the eponymous poem.

In 1837, Pushkin was shot in a duel with Dantes, the adopted French son of the Dutch ambassador to Russia.

Dantes had for some time been in love with Pushkin's wife, Natasha, and had even married her sister. Nevertheless, Dantes continued to pursue Natasha, and on 27 January 1837, the two men met at Chernaya Rechka, which was at that time located outside the city boundary. Dantes shot first, and Pushkin fell to the snowy ground, wounded. He was taken back to his home on the River Moika, where he died two days later from his injuries. Thousands of people crowded the streets on the day of his funeral, and no other figure, even today, holds the same special place in Russian hearts.

Right: Russian National Library.

Pushkin is paid tribute to at the **Pushkin Apartment Museum** in his former apartment on the Moika, the **Lyceum** at Pushkin, as Tsarskoe Selo is now named, and numerous monuments to the poet around the city.

SEE ALSO OTHER EXCURSIONS, P.24; MONUMENTS, P.82; MUSEUMS AND GALLERIES, P.89

Further Reading

Eugene Onegin (Penguin Classics)
The Queen of Spades (Penguin Classics)
Pushkin (Everyman Poetry)
Pushkin's Button – Serena Vitale and Ann Goldstein (Fourth Estate)

Further Reading

Petersburg – Andrei Bely (Indiana University Press)
Bely's Symbolist masterpiece, written in 1913, depicts a young revolutionary ordered

Below: Russia's literary maestro, Alexander Pushkin.

The story of 'The Bronze Horseman', written in 1833, takes place during the great flood of 1824. An impoverished clerk, Yevgeny, wanders the city crazed with grief after his fiancée drowns during the flood. Yevgeny rages at the statue of Peter the Great, whom he blames for the tragedy for choosing to build a city in an area prone to flooding. Suddenly, the face of the statue turns to look at the clerk, who runs away, only to be pursued by the sound of bronze hoofs on the street behind him. Yevgeny's body is later found washed up on an island in the Neva. The poem is partly a reflection on the rights of individuals versus the will of an autocrat.

to assassinate his own father – a Tsarist official – in 1905. It was described by Nabokov as one of the four great novels of the 20th century.

To the Hermitage – Malcolm Bradbury
(Overlook TP)

A clever and witty novel combining the dual stories of the 18th-century French encyclopedist Diderot visiting the court of Catherine the Great and a British academic attending an international Diderot conference in 1993.

Bookshops

Anglia
Nab. Reki Fontanki 38; tel: 579 8284; www.anglophile.ru; 10am–9pm; M: Mayakovskaya/ Nevsky Prospekt; map p.137 E2

Anglia specialises in English-language books, with a selection of translated Russian classics and the latest English-language books on Russian history and politics.

Dom Knigi
Nevsky Prospekt 28; tel: 448 2355; www.spbdk.ru; 9am– midnight; M: Nevsky Prospekt; map p.137 C2

The city's favourite bookshop has a reasonable selection of English-language novels and a wealth of tourist books about the city.

John Parsons Bookshop
Nab. Reki Fontanki 38; tel: 331 8828; www.bookshop. center.com.ru; 10am–8pm; M: Mayakovskaya/Nevsky Prospekt; map p.137 E2

Situated in the same building as its fellow English-language bookshop Anglia, it has a wider range and is cheaper.

Below: Russians are proud of their literary past, and well-preserved vintage editions are easy to find.

Monuments

Unsurprisingly, given the dramatic events and influential people the city has spawned, there are hundreds of monuments in St Petersburg, ranging from tiny birds to vast victory arches. Unlike Moscow, most of the city's monuments commemorate people and events from the pre-Soviet period. Some have superstitions and traditions associated with them, and many feature in the photos of almost every newlywed couple, who according to tradition drive around various monuments with their wedding party and champagne in tow to observe the rituals associated with each one.

Alexander Column

Dvortsovaya Ploshchad; M: Nevsky Prospekt; map p.136 C1
The Alexander Column, designed by Auguste de Montferrand, was erected in 1834 to commemorate Russia's victory under Tsar Alexander I over Napoleon in 1812. The column is not fixed to the ground, but is anchored by its own immense weight.

The face of the angel at the top of the Alexander Column is said to resemble that of Alexander I.

Alexander III

Marble Palace, Millionaya Ulitsa; M: Nevsky Prospekt; map p.133 D4
The equestrian monument to the unpopular penultimate Tsar, Alexander III, was unveiled in 1909 at the centre of Ploshchad Vosstaniya (then known as Znamenskaya Ploshchad). It was mocked by the public for its cumbersome appearance and moved in 1937 to the courtyard of the Russian Museum, which the Tsar founded, and then to its current location in the courtyard of the Marble Palace after perestroika.

Bronze Horseman (Medny Vsadnik)

Ploshchad Dekabristov; M: Sadovaya; map p.136 B2
The city's most famous monument, the Bronze Horseman

has become a symbol of the city itself. The statue was modelled by the French sculptor Etienne Falconet for Catherine the Great and completed in 1782. The serpent being trampled by the horse represents evil. The horse stands on an enormous granite boulder found in a forest 10km (6 miles) outside the city and painstakingly dragged to the site. The inscription reads 'To Peter I from Catherine II' in Russian on one side and Latin on the other.

Catherine the Great

Ploshchad Ostrovskovo; M: Gostiny Dvor; map p.137 D2
Catherine in turn is immortalised in the majestic monument unveiled in 1873 at the centre of the Catherine Garden. The figures around the base of the statue include the

Chyzhik Pyzhik was the nickname of a cadet and the subject of the Soviet rhyme, *'Chyzhik Pyzhik, gde ty byl? Na Fontanke, vodku pil?'* ('Chyzhik Pyzhik, where have you been? On the the Fontanka, drinking vodka?').

Left: Alexander Column on Palace Square.

82

Left: the Bronze Horseman.

A local joke about the poses of the statues has de Tolly complaining to Kutuzov that his stomach aches, to which the latter is replying, 'There's a pharmacy over there.'

Lenin

Moskovskaya Ploshchad; M: Moskovskaya

Of the many statues of the Bolshevik leader around the city, the background of the immense House of the Soviets makes this one, sculpted in 1970, particularly impressive. If you look at the monument from the corner of Leninsky Prospekt and Moskovsky Prospekt, it looks uncannily like Lenin is look-ing directly at you.

Monument to the Heroic Defenders of Leningrad

Ploshchad Pobedy; M: Park Pobedy

This gigantic Soviet monu-ment honours those who fought and died to defend the city during the devastating 900-day siege it suffered dur-ing WWII. Beneath the monu-ment is a small museum.
SEE ALSO MUSEUMS AND GALLERIES, P.99

18th-century *philosophes* Voltaire and Diderot, with whom the great empress corresponded.

Chyzhik Pyzhik

Inzhenerny Bridge; M: Nevsky Prospekt; map p.133 E4

The small bird statue located on the side of the granite embankment of the Fontanka near the water level is one of the best-loved – and most frequently stolen – monu-ments in the city, despite having only appeared in 1994. There is usually a crowd on the embankment above throwing coins at the statue – it is said to bring good luck if the coin lands on the plinth without bouncing off into the water, and to ensure that you will return to St Petersburg.

Krylov

The Summer Garden; M: Nevsky Prospekt; map p.133 D3

Amid the classical statues that adorn the Summer Gar-den is a monument to the writer Krylov, best-known for his fables. The base of the

monument is decorated with various animals from his tales, which are still read by Russian children today.

Kutuzov and de Tolly

Kazan Cathedral, Kazanskaya Ploshchad 2; M: Gostiny Dvor; map p.137 C2

The two statues at each end of the colonnade of Kazan Cathedral are Field Marshal Kutuzov, who is buried inside the cathedral, and Mikhail Barclay de Tolly, heroes of the 1812 war with Napoleon.

Right: Catherine the Great.

Left: Krylov Monument, *see p.83*. **Right:** Nicholas I.

and were buried here the following month.

Moscow Triumphal Arch (Moskovskiye Vorota)

Moskovsky Prospekt;
M: Moskovskaya

The Moscow Triumphal Arch was completed in 1838 by Vasily Stasov to commemorate the Russian victory in the Russo-Turkish war of 1828–9.

Narva Triumphal Arch (Narvskaya Triumfalnaya Vorota)

Ploshchad Stachek;
M: Narvskaya

The Narva Triumphal Arch commemorates Russia's victory over Napoleon in 1812. The current structure was erected by Stasov in 1834 to replace an earlier wooden arch built by Quarenghi to greet the victorious Russian soldiers.

Monument to Victims of Political Repression

Nab. Robespiera; M: Chernyshevskaya; map p.134 B3

The pair of Sphinxes opposite Kresty Prison on the embankment is another creation of Mikhail Shemiakin and was unveiled in 1996. While the side of their faces furthest from the water is that of a woman, the side nearest the prison is a chilling skull, signifying the horror experienced by so many during the aftermath of the 1917 revolution and Stalin's purges. Engraved on the plinths are verses by poets including Anna Akhmatova, whose son was incarcerated in Kresty. A small replica of a cell window in the embankment wall frames the view across the river of the dreaded prison.

Monument to Victims of the Revolution on the Field of Mars

M: Nevsky Prospekt;
map p.133 D4

The eternal flame and surrounding monuments commemorate those who died during street fighting in the February Revolution of 1917

Nicholas I

Isaakievskaya Ploshchad;
M: Sadovaya; map p.136 B2

The equestrian monument to Nicholas I unveiled in 1859 was designed by Auguste de Montferrand – the architect of

the cathedral that soars above it. The reliefs around the base of the monument represent episodes from the Tsar's reign, while the allegorical figures of Faith, Wisdom, Justice and Power around the pedestal were made to resemble Nicholas's wife and daughters.

Peter the Great at the Mikhailovsky Castle

Sadovaya Ulitsa; M: Nevsky Prospekt; map p.137 E1
The second, less famous equestrian monument to the city's founder stands in front of the Engineers' Castle. Commissioned by Peter himself, it was only completed after his death, and only erected at last under Paul I, who chose the location in front of his new castle. The inscription has echoes of Catherine's dedication on the Bronze Horseman: 'To great-grandfather from great-grandson.'

Peter the Great at the Peter and Paul Fortress

M: Gorkovskaya; map p.132 C3
Mikhail Shemiakin's controversial statue of 'Peahead Peter' was unveiled in 1991. Despite

Left: Monument to Victims of the Revolution.

its seeming lack of proportion, its head is modelled on a mask taken by the sculptor Bartolomeo Carlo Rastrelli during the Tsar's lifetime.

Pushkin

Ploshchad Iskusstv; M: Nevsky Prospekt; map p.137 D1
This monument to Russia's favourite poet, Alexander Pushkin, was sculpted by Mikhail Anikushin in 1957.

Rostral Columns (Rostralnye kolonny)

The Spit of Vasilievsky Island; M: Vasileostrovskaya/Sportivnaya; map p.132 B4

To the south of the Mikhailovsky Zamok stands a monument to Peter I, which despite being considerably less famous than its counterpart, The Bronze Horseman, has its own tradition. The plaque on the side of the base nearest to Sadovaya Ulitsa features a battle at sea. The heel of one of the sailors being rescued has been worn a much brighter colour than the rest of the mural, due to the fact that dozens of people come here every day to rub the heel. It is said to being good luck with important events, such as job interviews or exams.

The soaring red Rostral Columns, built from 1805–10 by Jean-François Thomas de Thomon, continue a tradition from ancient Rome of building columns decorated with the prows of defeated enemy ships to celebrate naval victories. The four figures at the base of the columns represent the four great rivers of Russia: the Volga, Dnieper, Neva and Volkov.

Sphinxes in front of the Academy of Fine Arts

Universitetskaya Naberezhnaya; M: Vasileostrovskaya
The awe-inspiring pair of Sphinxes are genuine Egyptian artefacts discovered in ancient Thebes dating from 1455–1419 BC, making them 1,000 years older than the river on which they now stand. They were brought to St Petersburg in 1832 and have become a favourite symbol of the city.

Suvorov

Suvorovskaya Ploshchad; M: Nevsky Prospekt; map p.133 D3
Overlooking the Field of Mars from his pedestal in the square, General Suvorov is depicted in the guise of Mars, the Roman god of war.

85

Museums and Galleries

The cultural capital of Russia is best-known for its unimaginable Hermitage Museum, a collection of millions of priceless works of art from all over the world begun by Catherine the Great and housed in the stunning Winter Palace and adjacent buildings. However, there is far more to St Petersburg than this, and while a visit to the biggest museum in the world is essential, there are many smaller, but no less fascinating museums, from preserved writers' apartments to unusual collections begun by Peter the Great.

Right: Museum of Decorative and Applied Arts.

Nevsky Prospekt

Stroganov Palace

Nevsky Prospekt 17; tel: 571 8238; www.rusmuseum.ru; Wed–Mon 10am–6pm; admission charge; M: Nevsky Prospekt; map p.137 C2

The ornate Stroganov Palace on the corner of the Moika and Nevsky was built for Count Sergei Stroganov by Rastrelli in 1753. The Stroganov family lived in the palace until the 1917 revolution, when the palace was turned into a museum. The rooms are being restored

It was in the Stroganov Palace that the eponymous dish was invented by the Stroganov family chef. Allegedly the chef devised the dish of small strips of beef for Count Pavel, who could no longer eat steak because he had lost his teeth.

gradually, and those that are ready contain temporary exhibitions of work from the State Russian Museum *(see p.91)*, of which the palace is a branch. It also contains a rather tacky waxworks exhibition. When restoration is complete, the museum will house Russian decorative and applied art from the 19th and 20th centuries.

Palace Square to Liteiny Prospekt

Anna Akhmatova Museum

Nab. Reki Fontanki 34; tel: 272 2211; www.akhmatova.spb.ru; Tue–Sun 10.30am–6.30pm, Wed 1–9pm; admission charge; M: Mayakovskaya; map p.137 E2

The apartment in which Russia's greatest poetess lived

Left: Akhmatova Museum.

for nearly 30 years is located in the Fontanny Dom (Fountain House) wing of the splendid Sheremetev Palace. The tranquil, evocative museum includes a recording of Akhmatova reading some of her poems, as well as some personal possessions and drafts of poems, and the interiors are interesting even for those with no experience of the poet's work. One room is dedicated to the poet Josef Brodsky, whom Akhmatova encouraged and inspired in his work. Downstairs is a collection of documentaries in English and Russian about the poet that can be watched in the cosy video room.

Decorative and Applied Arts Museum

Solyanoi Pereulok 13; tel: 273 3258; Sept–July Tue–Sat 11am–4pm; admission charge; M: Chernyshevskaya; map p.133 E4

The museum was founded in 1878 by the entrepreneur and banker Baron Shtieglitz, who had the stunning eclectic

Left: Rembrandt at the Hermitage, *see p.89.*

Museum Picks

Art-lovers will not be disappointed by St Petersburg. In addition to the celebrated Hermitage Museum *(see p.89)*, Russian art throughout the ages is chronicled and presented in the several branches of the State Russian Museum *(see p.91)*. Both collections are housed in historic palaces and buildings worthy of the masterpieces they contain, comprising a work of art themselves.

The city of three revolutions is steeped in world-changing **history**, and this is reflected in the city's museums. The era and personality of Peter the Great, the city's founder, and the creation of the city are documented in the Cabin of Peter the Great *(see p.95)*, the Summer Palace and the museums of the Peter and Paul Fortress *(see p.93)* – the foundation of Peter's new city. Those interested in the turbulent history of the 20th century will find new perspectives and rare collections in the Kirov Museum, the Museum of Political History *(see p.95)* and the writers' apartment museums, which along with their literary value also offer a fascinating look at how people lived and worked. **Science buffs** should head to the Popov Museum of Communications *(see p.93)*, where they can interact with the hi-tech exhibitions and trace the development of radio, telephony, internet and just about every other means of communication imaginable.

building housing the collection constructed from 1885–96 next door to the Academy of Applied Arts. Each room is designed in a different style that corresponds to the contents of that room – most impressive is the Terem room, designed in the style of the medieval Terem Palace in the Kremlin. Though much of the museum's pre-revolutionary collection is now in the Hermitage, it contains an impressive collection of 18th-century Russian stoves, medieval furniture and contemporary work by the academy's students.

From time to time the museum hosts exhibitions of jewellery and precious stones

– these are an excellent opportunity to pick up inexpensive, original trinkets.

Defence of Leningrad Museum

Solyanoi Pereulok 9; tel: 275 7208; Thur–Sat 10am–5pm, closed last Thur of month; M: Chernyshevskaya

Devoted to the 900-day siege of Leningrad, the museum is a very moving experience. It contains images of the city during the siege, including the small garden in front of St Isaac's transformed into a potato field, and of people dragging their dead on sledges through snowy streets. A visit to the museum is highly recommended as a way to

understand more about one of the darkest periods in the history of St Petersburg.

Ethnography Museum

Inzhenarnaya Ulitsa 4/1; tel: 570 5421; www.ethnomusem.ru;

Left: Ethnography Museum.

Mikhailovsky Castle
Sadovaya Ulitsa 2; tel: 570 5112; www.rusmuseum.ru; Mon 10am–5pm, Wed–Sun 10am–6pm; admission charge; M: Nevsky Prospekt; map p.137 D1

The Mikhailovsky, or Engineers' Castle as it is also known, was built for Paul I, the son of Catherine the Great. Paul lived in fear of an attempt being made on his life, and the castle was designed to be as secure as possible – surrounded by water with a drawbridge and secret escape passage. The castle was completed in 1801, and Paul moved in – only to be murdered just 40 days later in his bedroom by his own guards, who wanted to see his son Alexander accede the throne. After Paul's death, the castle became a Military Engineering Academy, whose students later included Dostoevsky. Now part of the

Tue–Sun 10am–6pm, closed last Fri of month; M: Nevsky Prospekt; map p.137 D1

The Ethnography Museum details the culture and lives of 158 peoples of the Russian Empire, the Soviet Union and modern-day Russia, including ethnic groups from the Caucasus, Eastern Europe and Central Asia. The impressive building was purpose-built to house the collection. Objects on display include clothes made from nettles and fish-skin, jewellery, weapons and possessions of the shamans of Siberia and the Far East.

Marble Palace
Millionaya Ulitsa 5/1; tel: 312 9196; www.rusmuseum.ru; Mon 10am–5pm, Wed–Sun 10am–6pm; admission charge; M: Nevsky Prospekt/Gorkovskaya; map p.133 D3

The magnificent Marble Palace, decorated inside and out with over 30 kinds of marble, was built by Rinaldi from 1768–85 as a gift from

Catherine the Great to her lover Grigory Orlov. Orlov did not live to see its completion, however, and the palace became the residence of the Grand Dukes until 1917. After the revolution, the palace was turned into the city's principal Lenin Museum. Now part of the Russian Museum, it houses exhibitions devoted to foreign artists in Russia in the 18th and 19th centuries, and a popular section of 20th-century art that includes work by Warhol, Lichtenstein and Koons.

> Pushkin is a revered figure to this day, and this museum is just one part of the National Pushkin Museum – it also includes the Lyceum Museum at Pushkin.

Right: Mikhailovsky Palace; Loggia Hall and a masterpiece by Raphael in the Hermitage.

Left: Pushkin's study.

drawn by the poet himself, as well as manuscripts of his poetry and his personal belongings. His study, which includes an extensive library of books in several languages, has been preserved, with the clock stopped at the time of his death. Some poignant original notes on the door of the apartment inform concerned callers about Pushkin's condition – the first says that the poet is making a recovery; the last reports his death.

Russian Museum, the exhibitions include the reign of the ill-fated Paul I and a portrait gallery of Russian royals and aristocrats, as well as temporary exhibitions.

Pushkin Apartment Museum

Nab. Reki Moiki 12; tel: 571 3531; www.museumpushkin.ru; Wed–Mon10.30am–6pm, closed last Fri of month; admission charge; M: Nevsky Prospekt; map p.137 C1

This elegant apartment on the River Moika was where Russia's greatest poet lived and died after being fatally wounded in a duel. The collection includes witty caricatures and sketches of Pushkin's contemporaries

State Hermitage Museum

Dvortsovaya Nab. 38; tel: 571 3420; www.hermitagemuseum. org; Tue–Sat 10.30am–6pm, Sun until 5pm; admission charge; M: Nevsky Prospekt; map p.136 B1

The city's most famous museum began life as the Winter Palace of Peter the Great, though the existing tour de force is the work of Rastrelli, who began rebuilding the palace for Elizabeth in 1754 and completed it under Catherine in 1762. The interiors are spectacular, making a fitting background for the world art treasures located in its depths. Countless top architects contributed to the

The Winter Palace is 200m (655ft) long, 10m (32ft) wide and 30m (100ft) tall. It has 1,057 rooms, 117 staircases, 1,786 doors and 1,945 windows. It is said that to visit all 400 rooms and halls of the Hermitage, you would have to walk 22.5km (14 miles), and if you spent eight hours in the museum every day, it would take you almost 15 years to see every item on display. Bearing all this in mind, you might want to plan your trip in advance to decide what you want to see. One of the most popular attractions in the vast Hermitage is the Peacock Clock in the stunning Pavilion Hall. The ornate gold construction built by James Cox in the 18th century includes a life-sized peacock, which spreads its enormous tail feathers and turns around 360 degrees as it chimes to mark the hour. To preserve the mechanism, it only does so once a week, at 5pm on Wednesdays.

decor, including de la Mothe, Rinaldi, Starov and Quarenghi, but a fire in 1837 destroyed most of the interior, and it was reconstructed by Stasov and Briullov.

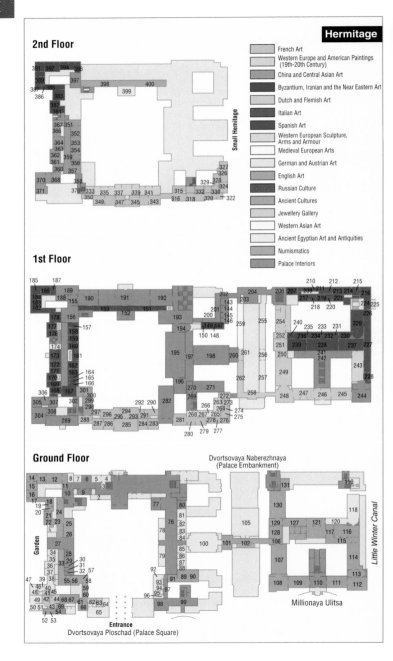

2nd Floor

Small Hermitage

Hermitage

French Art

Western Europe and American Paintings (19th-20th Century)

China and Central Asian Art

Byzantium, Iranian and the Near Eastern Art

Dutch and Flemish Art

Italian Art

Spanish Art

Western European Sculpture, Arms and Armour

Medieval European Arts

German and Austrian Art

English Art

Russian Culture

Ancient Cultures

Jewellery Gallery

Western Asian Art

Ancient Egyptian Art and Antiquities

Numismatics

Palace Interiors

1st Floor

Ground Floor

Dvortsovaya Naberezhnaya (Palace Embankment)

Garden

Little Winter Canal

Millionaya Ulitsa

Entrance
Dvortsovaya Ploschad (Palace Square)

Clockwise from top: the Winter Palace; icon and bust at the Russian Museum; Hermitage portrait.

Besides the Winter Palace, the art collection is housed in the adjacent Small Hermitage, which was built from 1764–8 to house the art collection of Catherine the Great, which became the foundation of the largest museum in the world. As the Empress's collection grew and grew, the Large Hermitage was built next door from 1771–87, followed by the New Hermitage. Along with the spectacular state rooms, the 3 million works of art contained in the extravagant interiors include masterpieces by da Vinci, Rembrandt, El Greco, Renoir, van Gogh, Picasso, as well as large sections devoted to classical art, Egyptian and Scythian artefacts, and much, much more. The General Staff building on the other side of Palace Square houses more of the never-ending collection, including 20th-century French art.

The State Russian Museum

Mikhailovsky Palace, Inzhenarnaya Ulitsa 4; tel: 595 4248; www.rusmuseum.ru; Mon 10am–5pm, Wed–Sun 10am–6pm; admission charge; M: Nevsky Prospekt; map p.137 D1

The city's second colossal museum is dedicated to Russian art. The museum was opened by Tsar Nicholas II in 1898 in the Mikhailovsky Palace, built by Rossi from 1819–25. The collection

comprises over 40,000 works, from medieval icons to contemporary art. The Benois wing (entrance from the Canal Griboedov) is one of the most interesting sections, covering the avant-garde, Symbolism and other 20th-century movements. The collection is arranged chronologically and represents a history of Russian art, from icon-painting to the Wanderers to Constructivism. More much manageable than the Hermitage, it is no less impressive, with its masterpieces by Rublev, Briullov, Repin, Vrubel, Kandinsky, Malevich and many more masters.

The Admiralty to St Nicholas's Cathedral

Blok Museum
Ulitsa Dekabristov 57; tel: 713 8631; www.spbmuseum.ru; Thur–Mon 11am–6pm, Tue 11am–5pm; admission charge; M: Sadovaya

The life and work of the Symbolist poet is celebrated in two apartments where Alexander Blok lived with his wife. It was here that Blok wrote his controversial masterpiece 'The Twelve'. One flat has been preserved almost as it was during his lifetime, and the other contains some personal belongings of Blok, including photos and manuscripts. A sketch of the poet on his deathbed and his death mask are displayed in the room in which he died in 1921.

Nabokov Museum
Bolshaya Morskaya Ulitsa 47; tel: 315 4713; www.nabokov museum.org; Tue–Fri 11am–6pm, Sat–Sun noon–5pm; admission charge, free

Left: statue of Blok; portrait of Nabokov as a young man.

Left: Briullov's *Last Day of Pompeii* at the Russian Museum.

Thur; M: Sadovaya; map p.136 B2
Vladimir Nabokov, author of *Lolita* and many other classics of Russian and world literature, was born in this house on Bolshaya Morskaya Ulitsa in 1899, and spent the first 18 years of his life here before his wealthy family fled the Bolshevik Revolution in 1917. The museum only occupies the ground floor of the family mansion – the other two floors are now occupied by the offices of a local newspaper. The small museum contains family photographs, some butterflies from the collection of the keen lepidopterist, the wood-panelled library that the great writer recalled so longingly in *Speak, Memory*, and a small selection of souvenirs, including some elegant postcards with quotations from Nabokov's work.

Popov Museum of Communications
Pochtamtsky Pereulok 4; tel: 323 9718; www.rustelecom-museum.ru; Tue–Sat 10.30am–6pm, closed last Thur of month; admission charge; M: Sadovaya; map p.136 B2
The Popov Museum is one of the oldest science museums in the world, founded in 1872 and named after Alexander Popov, whom the Russians credit with the invention of the radio. It is also one of the most modern museums in Russia, featuring dozens of screens and interactive displays – a far cry from the worn, dusty spaces of many of the city's other museums. The museum documents items relating to post, teleph-

Right: Peter and Paul Cathedral and Fortress.

> Ticket offices at museums usually close one hour before the official closing time, so make sure you get there before then.

ony, radio, television, space communication and the latest developments in communication technology.

Peter and Paul Fortress
Tel: 230 6431; www.spbmuseum.ru; M: Gorkovskaya; map p.132 C2
One ticket provides entrance to all the museums in the Peter and Paul Fortress, with the exception of the belfry and the walk along the ramparts. There are tours around the belfry (tel: 498 0505; admission charge) at 12, 1.30, 3.30 and 4pm May–Sept. Visitors can see how the bell-ringing mechanism

works, and climb to the top of the tower for a superb view of the city.
The rest of the complex's museums are open 11am–6pm (5pm Tue), Thur–Tue.
The **Museum of the History of St Petersburg and Petrograd 1703–1918** contains some fascinating depictions of the city at various stages in its history, including when the Strelka was still a working port and before the embankments were covered in granite.
The Museum of Old St Petersburg contains lithographs, photographs, blueprints and other documents illustrating how the city has grown and changed over the years, along with some quirky vintage typewriters and sewing machines. One of the most poignant items is a 1917 calendar illustrated with

portraits of Nicholas II, Alexandra and their son and heir, Alexei.

The Museum of Space Exploration and Rocket Technology is located in the Ioannovsky Ravelin, where from 1932–3 the first Soviet liquid-fuelled rocket was developed. It documents the Soviet space programme and the Space Race, and includes a re-entry capsule in which Soviet cosmonauts returned to Earth.

Petrograd Side

Artillery Museum
Alexandrovsky Park 7; tel: 232 0296; www.artillery-museum.spb.ru; Wed–Sun 11am–6pm, closed last Thur of month; admission charge; M: Gorkovskaya; map p.133 C2
Military enthusiasts will be enthralled by the collection at this museum, which includes ammunition, decorative pistols, jewel-encrusted sabres, objects relating to military engineer-ing, uniforms and battle standards, as well as paintings and sculptures of battlegrounds, victorious generals and officers. Its pièce de résistance is the armoured car in which Lenin triumphantly returned from his rapturous reception at the Finland Station in 1917.

Avrora
Petrogradskaya Nab. 2; tel: 230 8440; www.aurora.org.ru; Tue–Thur, Sat–Sun 10.30am–4pm; free; M: Gorkovskaya; map p.133 D2
The cruiser *Avrora* fired a blank shot at the Winter Palace on the night of 25 October 1917, signalling the storming of the palace where the provisional government was in conference and the start of the October Revolu-tion. As part of the Central Naval Museum, the crew's quarters are open to visitors, along with exhibitions on the ship's turbulent history (the cruiser was deliberately scut-tled in shallow water off Oranienbaum to protect it from German artillery during World War II) and tokens of

Left: *Avrora*. **Right:** Cabin of Peter the Great.

Left: Artillery Museum.
Right: State Museum of the
Political History of Russia.

friendship and support from
Socialist organisations across
the world.

**Cabin of Peter the Great
(Muzey Domik Petra I)**
Petrovskaya Nab. 6; tel: 232
4576; www.rusmuseum.ru;
Mon 10am–5pm, Wed–Sun
10am–6pm; admission charge;
M: Gorkovskaya; map p.133 D2
Peter the Great's cabin, a
simple log cabin hastily
erected by army carpenters
in 1703 to accommodate the
energetic Tsar while he
supervised the building of the
Peter and Paul Fortress, is
the oldest structure in the
city. The modest hut contains
just three rooms, but was
perfectly adequate for Peter's
simple tastes while the Summer Palace across the Neva
was being built. In 1844 the
wooden building was in danger of collapsing and was
encased in the brick structure
that surrounds it. The exhibits
include some of Peter's personal belongings, such as his
pipe and some of his clothes,
as well as his death mask,
bronze casts of the Tsar's
large hands and a rowing
boat built by Peter himself.
The cabin is a branch of the
State Russian Museum.

**Kirov Museum
(Muzey S.M. Kirova)**
Kamennoostrovsky Prospekt 26;
tel: 346 0217; www.spb
museum.ru; Thur–Mon 11am–
6pm, Tue 11am–5pm;
M: Gorkovskaya/Petrograd-
skaya; map p.132 C1
The apartment in which
Leningrad party boss Sergei
Kirov lived for 10 years
before he was murdered has
been preserved for visitors to
stare at the portraits of Stalin
(a regular visitor) and a
somewhat bourgeois
bearskin rug. The personal
items on display include a
delightful portrait of Kirov
made out of feathers – a gift
from local factory workers –
and the clothes he was
wearing when he was shot
dead in the Smolny Insitute –
blood stains and all. The
museum also contains an
interesting exhibition on
Leningrad in the 1920s and
30s, and another entitled 'To
Our Happy Childhood',
which covers the creation of
the Pioneers movement in
Petrograd and has on display
toys and books from the
1920s and 30s.

**Museum of Political
History**
Ulitsa Kubysheva 2–4; tel: 233
7052; www.polithistory.ru;
Fri–Wed 10am–5pm; admis-
sion charge; M: Gorkovskaya;
map p.133 C2
The former mansion of the
famed ballerina Matilda

95

Kshessinskaya was taken over by the Bolsheviks for their headquarters when she fled Russia in 1917. Lenin made frequent speeches from the balcony of the building, and his office comprises one of the exhibitions. The collection is not limited to Communism, however – political figures from Catherine the Great to the local liberal politician Galina Starovoitova, shot dead in the city in 1998, are represented in documents and photographs. Another exhibition focuses on the life of Kshessinskaya herself.

Vasilievsky Island

Central Naval Museum

Birzhevaya Ploshchad 4; tel: 328 2501; www.museum.navy.ru; Wed–Sun 11am–6pm; admission charge; M: Gorkovskaya; map p.132 B4

Housed in the stately former Stock Exchange building, the Naval Museum was another of Peter the Great's ideas. There are about 2,000 vessels for maritime enthusiasts to ogle, as well as paintings and photographs. The pride of the museum is a 3,000-year-old oak canoe and the legendary boat of Peter the Great – 'Botik' – or, as the sailing-mad Tsar himself said, 'the grandfather of the Russian Navy.'

Kunstkamera (Museum of Anthropology and Ethnography)

Universitetskaya Nab. 3; tel: 328 9744; www.kunstkamera.ru; Tue–Sun 11am–7pm, closed last Tue of month; admission charge; M: Vasileostrovskaya; map p.132 B4

Definitely one of the most macabre and unusual muse-

ums in St Petersburg, the Kunstkamera (Chamber of Curiosities) is Russia's oldest purpose-built museum, founded on the orders of Peter the Great in 1714 to display natural curiosities. The museum has interesting, if dated, sections on peoples from Russia and around the world, but the most memorable part is undoubtedly Peter's collection of malformed foetuses, displayed pickled in jars.

Right: Central Naval Museum.

Left: Kunstkamera.

The collection also includes the surgical instruments of Peter, who was a keen amateur dentist, much to the misfortune of his hapless courtiers.

Zoology Museum (Zoologichesky Muzey)
Universitetskaya Nab.1; tel: 328 0112; www.zin.ru; Wed–Mon 11am–6pm; admission charge; M: Vasiliestrovskaya; map p.132 B4
Children in particular will enjoy the Zoology Museum, which contains over 40,000 mounted animals, most notably a 44,000-year-old woolly mammoth found in 1902 preserved in the Siberian permafrost, and a live insect zoo. As well as regular displays, part of the collection is exhibited in ecological dioramas.

Vladimirskaya, Liteiny and Smolny

Arctic and Antarctic Museum
Ulitsa Marata 24a; tel: 571 2549: www.polarmuseum.ru; Wed–Sat 10am–6pm, Sun 10am–5pm, closed last Thur of month; admission charge; M: Vladimirskaya/Mayakovskaya; map p.138 A3
The largest museum of its kind in the world, the Arctic and Antarctic Museum occupies the unlikely setting of the Old Believers' Church of St Nicholas – yet another illustration of the uses churches were put to during the Soviet era. The exhibitions focus on Soviet polar expeditions and include a stuffed polar bear, which, along with the family of penguins surrounded by the ornate columns of the church, makes for fairly surreal viewing.

Bread Museum
Ligovsky Prospekt 73; tel: 764 1110; Tue–Sat 10am–5pm, closed last Thur of month; admission charge; M: Ploshchad Vosstaniya/Ligovsky Prospekt; map p.138 B4
The Bread Museum is a lot more interesting than it might sound. The museum aims to record the development of mankind via the prism of bread-baking, and the items on display include special kinds of bread baked for weddings and other occasions. There is also a sombre note in the photos of the 1920s famine and the exhibition dedicated to the siege, which includes an example of the bread ration.

Dostoevsky Museum
Kuznechny Pereulok 5/2; tel: 571 4031; www.md.spb.ru; Tue–Sun 11am–6pm; admission charge; M: Dostoevskaya; map p.138 A3
The collection of the Fyodor Dostoevsky Museum is divided into two well-organised sections, one focusing on the great writer's life, housed in the recreated interiors of his rooms, and the other focusing on his work. *Crime and Punishment* aficionados will love the large map showing the addresses around the city where the writer and his fictional heroes lived.

Nekrasov Apartment Museum
Liteiny Prospekt 36; tel: 272 0165; www.museumpushkin.ru; Wed–Sun 11am–6pm, closed

When visiting Russian museums, you will often have to wear a pair of *tapochki*, or slippers, over your own shoes to protect the floors. These can range from a pair of small elasticated plastic bags to large, bizarre and cumbersome felt creations that can make navigating staircases tricky and rather dangerous. There is usually a large box full of *tapochki* at the entrance to the exhibitions – don't worry about getting a matching pair, but try and get ones that are only a few sizes larger than your feet, rather than twice their size, as it will make walking in them slightly less difficult. Watch out for the hilarious spectacle of Russian girls in stiletto boots moonwalking around in their oversize felt *tapochki*.

Left: Dostoevsky
Museum, *p. 97.*

Rimsky-Korsakov Museum

Zagorodny Prospekt 28; tel: 575 6587; www.theatremuseum.ru; Wed–Sun 11am–6pm; M: Vladimirskaya; map p.137 E4

Strangely enough for a city with such a rich musical history, the Rimsky-Korsakov Museum is the only museum devoted to a composer in St Petersburg. It was in this apartment that the composer wrote the opera *Sadko*, among other masterpieces. The tradition of 'Korsakov Wednesdays', at which Glazunov, Repin and Chaliapin were regular guests during the composer's lifetime, has been resumed by the museum's curators, featuring concerts by young musicians.

Suvorov Museum

Kirochnaya Ulitsa 43; tel: 579 3914; Thur–Mon 10am–6pm, closed first Mon of month; M: Chernyshevskaya; map p.135 C4

You can't miss this museum devoted to the Russian general and military strategist Alexander Suvorov (1730–1800), housed as it is in a purpose-built whimsical building designed to resemble an ancient Russian castle. If the idea of the general himself doesn't grab everyone, then the country's largest collection of tin soldiers (over 60,000) will appeal to attic fanatics at least.

World of Water

Shpalernaya Ulitsa 56; tel: 275 4325; Tue–Sun 10am–6pm; admission charge; M: Chernyshevskaya; map p.135 C3

World of Water is a recent addition to the city's museum scene, having been opened in an old red-brick water

Despite large numbers of foreign tourists in the city, signs in museums are often only in Russian. If there is an audioguide available, it is usually worth renting it, as it allows you to appreciate the collection fully while letting you wander around in your own time. In some museums, such as the Yusupov Palace, this is included in the ticket price. You may have to leave a deposit. In the out-of-town imperial palaces, it is definitely worth joining a group excursion, as there is very little information available without one.

last Fri of month; M: Chernyshevskaya; map p.138 A1

From this apartment, Nikolai Nekrasov – whom Dostoevsky described as the greatest Russian poet since Pushkin and Lermontov – edited the literary journals *Sovreminnik* (The Contemporary), founded by Pushkin, and *Otechestvennie Zapiski* (Notes from the Fatherland). Turgenev, Tolstoy, Dostoevsky and many other great writers were regular guests here. The collection includes personal belongings of the poet, first editions and illustrations of his work and paintings.

Right: Repin's Penaty studio.

pressure tower dating from the 1860s by the water company Vodokanal. The interactive exhibitions include the history of water supply in antiquity, and in St Petersburg. One building is devoted to temporary exhibitions. The tower itself now contains a large transparent pipe through which the water can be seen on its journey – a unique and impressive sight.

Moskovsky Prospekt

Monument to the Heroic Defenders of Leningrad
Ploshchad Pobedy 1; tel: 373 6563; www.spbmuseum.ru; Thur–Tue 10am–6pm, Tue and Fri until 5pm; free; M: Moskovskaya

Beneath the monument unveiled in 1975 to commemorate the 30th anniversary of Victory Day in World

During the White Nights, the museum stays open later some evenings, when films based on Dostoevsky's work are shown. If you're visiting during this period, check the museum's site for more details.

War II is a dim memorial hall, whose reverent atmosphere is enhanced by sombre, haunting music, and the steady sound of a metronome (during the war, this was the only sound that besieged Leningraders heard on the radio other than emergency announcements, to symbolise the city's heartbeat. Nine hundred plaques document the siege of Leningrad – one for each day that the siege lasted.

Other Excursions

Penaty
Primorskoye Shosse 411, Repino; tel: 432 0834; Wed–Sun 10.30am–4pm, June–Aug until 5pm; admission charge

Penaty was the country estate of the outstanding painter Ilya Repin, who was one of the leading figures of the *peredvizhniki* or Wanders' art movement – a group of students who left the Academy of Arts because they felt stifled by its constraints and formalism. Most of Repin's most celebrated works hang in the Russian Museum, but there are another hundred on display at Penaty, where the painter spent the last 30 years of his prolific life.

FOR DETAILS OF HOW TO GET TO REPINO, SEE OTHER EXCURSIONS, P.25

Music

A s in so many other respects, the cultural capital leads the way in music and concerts. The city has been home to Tchaikovsky, Stravinsky, Shostakovich and many other musical giants, and was the scene of Russia's underground rock movement in the '70s and '80s, spawning the country's two biggest bands, Akvarium and Kino. Musical traditions remain strong, and there is always something going on to interest music-lovers of all kinds, including regular festivals of classical and contemporary music. For other performing arts venues, *see Ballet, Opera and Theatre, p.32–3.*

Classical

St Petersburg Philharmonic

Grand Hall
Mikhailovskaya Ulitsa 2; tel: 312 9871; www.philharmonia. spb.ru; M: Nevsky Prospekt; map p.137 D2

Small Hall
Nevsky Prospekt 30; tel: 312 4585 www.philharmonia. spb.ru; M: Nevsky Prospekt; map p.137 D2

The city's resident orchestra is the St Petersburg Philharmonic, which performs an extensive repertoire of Baroque, classical and Romantic music under the baton of its acclaimed artistic director, Yuri Temirkanov, and other conductors including Maxim Shostakovich, son of the great composer. The Philharmonic is closed in July and August.

St Petersburg Rimsky-Korsakov Conservatory
Teatralnaya Ploshchad 3; tel: 312 2519; www.conservatory.ru; M: Sadovaya or buses 3, 22 and 27; map p.136 A4

The alma mater of Tchaikovksy, Shostakovich, Prokofiev and countless other

Shostakovich's 7th symphony, dedicated to Leningrad, is often known as the 'Siege Symphony'. It was completed in December 1941 and was performed in the besieged city on 9 August 1942. The performance was broadcast on the radio and from loudspeakers throughout the city, as well as to the German troops surrounding the city. It was hailed by the Soviet Union and their allies as a stirring expression of determination to defeat Nazi Germany. Though the inspiration and themes depicted in the symphony have since come under question, it remains a poignant part of local repertoires, and in 2005 was conducted by the composer's son to a backdrop of footage of the siege of Leningrad and World War II.

greats, the Conservatory has its own theatre with a repertoire of opera and symphonic classics performed by new generations of maestros.

Seasonal Events

The **Stars of the White Nights** festival held from May to July and directed by Termikanov attracts classical performers from around the world and is hugely popular, while the **Palaces of St Petersburg** festival held June–July presents a programme of classical music performed in some of the city's most opulent and sumptuous palaces, including the Marble, Menshikov, Yusupov and Catherine palaces. During the summer months, the superb Male Choir of St Petersburg performs at 7pm on Mondays and Fridays at the atrium of the Peter and Paul Fortress (tel: 933 3094), and September sees the holding of the annual **Early Music Festival**, which showcases Baroque and medieval music at venues around the city.

SEE ALSO FESTIVALS, P.57

Jazz

St Petersburg is home to several decent jazz clubs, while the summer brings the traditional White Nights Swing jazz festival.

Jazz Philharmonic Hall
Zagorodny Prospekt 27; tel: 764 8565; www.jazz-hall.spb.ru;

Left: concert at Palace Square.

influenced Billy's Band, the legendary punk-ska band Leningrad, fronted by Sergei Shnurov and notorious for its obscene lyrics, and the more lyrical rock group Splean.

The annual **Sergei Kuryokhin International Festival** (www.kuryokhin.ru) in April brings together alternative music artists from around the world in memory of the late Kuryokhin – a leading figure of the Leningrad underground music scene.
SEE ALSO NIGHTLIFE, P.102–3

Music Stores

Just a few years ago, bootleg CDs in Russia cost as little as one pound ($2) and were sold on every street corner and in every underpass. Since the G8 summit held in the city in 2005 and in line with WTO negotiations, the city has tightened up the laws. Music is still a bargain compared to Western prices – expect to pay no more than 300 rubles (£6, $12) for an album – but the selection available is usually limited to recent best-sellers. The following local chains are worth a visit:

Iceberg
Liteiny Prospekt 63; tel: 579 0148; 10am–10pm;
M: Mayakovskaya; map p.137 E2

Playland
Ulitsa Marata 3; tel: 314 3364; www.play-land.ru; 10am–10pm;
M: Mayakovskaya; map p.138 A3

Boris Grebenshchikov and his seminal band Akvarium rode the crest of the underground rock wave in the 70s, earning Grebenshchikov the nickname of 'the grandfather of Russian rock'. The group and its leader are still going strong and regularly perform their folk-influenced, poetic music in venues around the city. The next generation of Russian rock was led by the group Kino, headed by the iconic Viktor Tsoy. Tsoy's untimely death in a car crash in 1990 cemented his status as a cult figure, and Kino songs can still be heard on the radio, in bars and clubs, and performed by young buskers on the street.

JFC Jazz Club
Shpalernaya Ulitsa 33; tel: 272 9850; www.jfc-club.spb.ru; 7pm–11pm; admission charge; M: Chernyshevskaya; map p.134 A3
The city's most respected, innovative and popular jazz club. It is small, so booking a table in advance is recommended. Concerts of all kinds of jazz, from blues to acid jazz, are held every evening.

Popular
St Petersburg has a wealth of popular home-grown bands which perform regularly around the city in clubs such as **Griboedov**, **Mod**, **Achtung Baby**, **Zoccolo**, **Sochi** and **Fish Fabrique**. They include the ever-popular alt-rock band Tequilajazzz, the Tiger Lilies-

admission charge;
M: Vladimirskaya/Dostoevskaya;
map p.137 D4
The state jazz venue has two halls. Concerts start at 7pm in the large hall and 8pm in the smaller hall. Try to get seats in one of the balconies of the big hall when buying tickets.

Right: Rimsky-Korsakov.

Nightlife

Russians know how to party, and this is reflected in the city's nightlife. The scene has diversified from the days of strip clubs for goggle-eyed foreigners, though there are still plenty of such places. Going out in Russia tends to be an all-night affair. While the city's bars fill up after 9pm, the clubs stay empty until around midnight, and it's quite normal to be getting the last metro into town rather than out, and to arrive at a club or bar at 3, 4 or even 5am. Most stay open until 6am, by which time transport is already running again. For places to have a quieter drink *see Bars and Pubs, p.36–7.*

Alternative/Rock

Achtung Baby
Konyushennaya Ploshchad 2; www.achtungbaby.ru; 5pm–6am; admission charge Fri–Sat; M: Nevsky Prospekt; map p.137 C1
A good time is practically guaranteed at this inexpensive indie club decorated

with furry pink lampshades and sumptuous red velvet curtains. The first room is more Spartan in design and hosts live bands from time to time, while the second room is where it's really happening, with a young crowd dancing 'til dawn to 80s pop, 90s rock and modern anthems.

Fish Fabrique
Pushkinskaya Ulitsa 10 (entrance through the arch at Ligovsky Prospekt 53); tel: 764 4857; www.fishfabrique.spb.ru; 3pm–6am; admission charge; M: Ploshchad Vasstaniya; map p.138 A3
Located in the Artists' Colony Pushkinskaya 10, quirky metal fish are about the only decoration in this small underground grungy bar. The long wooden benches lend themselves to a friendly, communal atmosphere. There are concerts most days at 11pm, when it can get a bit too loud for conversation.

Griboedov
Voronezhskaya Ulitsa 2a; tel: 764 4355; www.griboedov club.ru; midnight–6am; admission charge; M: Ligovsky Prospekt
Located in an old bomb shelter, Griboedov is one of the best clubs in the city. Underground in all senses of the word, it has low ceilings, a small dance-floor and stage

Left: bling counts at many nightclub doors.

Left: expats have a less than spotless reputation when it comes to behaving.

charge Fri–Sat; M: Nevsky Prospekt; map p.137 C2

Plans by Sochi's directors to host a gay and lesbian film festival at the bar finally achieved what a barmaid attacking a customer and a bouncer killing another customer could not – the authorities immediately closed the bar citing fire hazards (a common pretext used to close down establishments that have fallen foul of City Hall). Neither of the above incidents dented the popularity of the bar, and at the time of research it looked set to open again soon.

Zoccolo (Tsokol)

3rd Sovietskaya Ulitsa 2/3; tel: 274 9467; www.zoccolo.ru; Thur–Sun 6pm–midnight; admission charge; M: Ploshchad Vosstaniya; map p.138 B2

A small underground club with dangerously cheap beer. It hosts regular concerts by local rock, punk and ska bands.

Pop and Dance

Buddha Bar

Bolshaya Morskaya 46; tel: 314 7007; free; M: Sadovaya; map p.138 B2

where local rock bands regularly perform, and a small chill-out room. Its modest size has recently been increased by the addition of Griboedov Hill, a glass structure above ground. The outside area between the underground and overground parts is a great place to sit and while away the White Nights.

Mod Club

Konnyushennaya Ploshchad 2g; tel: +7 921 881 8371; 6pm–6am; admission charge Fri–Sat; M: Nevsky Prospekt; map p.137 C1

Popular with students, this cavernous bar has live bands and a cosy upper gallery.

Money Honey

Sadovaya Ulitsa 28–30; tel: 310 0549; www.money-honey.ru; 10am–5am; admission charge; M: Nevsky Prospekt; map p.137 D2

If you like rockabilly, then Money Honey is the place for you. This sprawling club has live bands and hundreds of cowboy enthusiasts.

Sochi

Kazanskaya Ulitsa 7; tel: 312 0140; 11am–6am; admission

Bridge opening times

Missing the bridges, which are raised during summer to let large ships along the Neva *(see left)*, is always a good excuse to stay out all night. The combination of bridges and White Nights seems to prove fatal, and during this time the sheer number of people walking the streets and drinking in simple impromptu café-bars set up on the street can create the impression that very few of the city's residents have to get up to go to work the next day.

Classic New Russian-spotting territory. You will see more sunglasses among the hookah pipes and cushions here than on a crowded beach.

Decadance
Scherbakov Pereulok 17; tel: 947 7070; Wed–Thur 6pm–1am,

Fri–Sat 6pm–late; free; M: Vladimirskaya; map p.137 E3
This pretentious club just off Ulitsa Rubinshteina is the favourite hangout of the city's glamorous crowd. The atmosphere is akin to being backstage at the final of a beauty competition. Drinks

If you have the munchies after a hard night's partying, the city's late-night junk food speciality is the *shaverma*, or kebab. There are plenty of *shaverma* joints around the city, but the hygiene standards of the kiosks from which they are usually served cannot be guaranteed – the ones located near metro stations in particular are best avoided.

are expensive, and there is no beer.

Magrib
Nevsky Prospekt 84; tel: 275 1255; 11pm–6am; admission charge; M: Mayakovskaya; map p.138 A2
Magrib lures tourists in with its prime location on Nevsky and smart, Moroccan-style interiors, but tends to be full of mercenary Russian women on the hunt for hapless foreign men, of whom there are also plenty.

Metro
Ligovsky Prospekt 174; tel: 766 0204; www.metroclub.ru; 10pm–6am; admission charge; M: Ligovsky Prospekt
Metro is a huge dance club on three floors, popular with teenagers from the outskirts. The entertainment includes men dancing in thongs on podiums.

Purga
Nab. Reki Fontanki 11; tel: 570 5123; www.purga-club.ru; 4pm–6am; Purga 2: tel: 571 2310, 8pm–last person leaves; admission charge; M: Nevsky Prospekt/Mayakovskaya; map p.137 E2
There are actually two Purgas next door to each other on the Fontanka, a five-minute walk from Nevsky. The first hosts a surreal New Year's party every night,

Left: Purga adopts a war theme for the night.

Above and right: cocktails, especially white Russians, are popular.

including a countdown with sparklers. In Purga 2, psychadelic stuffed rabbits decorate the ceilings and walls and the staff are dressed as brides. Both venues are small, so it can be difficult to get in late at night without booking a table in advance. The music varies, but is usually good for a dance.

Rossi's
Ulitsa Rossi 1–3; tel: 710 4016; www.rossis.ru; 11am–6am; admission charge; M: Gostiny Dvor; map p.137 D3

Rossi's has all the traditional elements of a Russian club: discounts for girls, karaoke and strippers. It also has live music and a good atmosphere – it lacks the posey element of many mainstream clubs – and the end result of all of these things is generally a good time.

Sphinx
Nevsky Prospekt 118; tel: 717 6868; restaurant 11am–2am, club Fri–Sat 10pm–6am (admission charge); M: Ploshchad Vosstaniya; map p.138 B3

This large, modern joint right on Ploshchad Vosstaniya is a café by day, a restaurant and bar at night and a club at weekends, playing RnB and hip hop. It is free of the snooty, glamorous crowd and is good for a dance.

Getting Home

There are no nightbuses in St Petersburg. The last buses are at around 11.45pm, the last metro runs at 12.30am, and after that, the only options are taking a taxi or staying out until the metro opens again at 5.45am.

If you want to get a taxi, it is of course safer to use a proper cab rather than hail down the first Lada that comes along like the locals do. Proper taxis can be found at regular intervals along Nevsky but do not have meters, so you should agree on the price before you get in. Alternatively, there are always official taxis waiting outside the biggest hotels, though their prices are prohibitively expensive. If you order a taxi by telephone, they usually arrive promptly and will tell you a rough price when you phone up. The following companies are tried and tested:

Petersburg Taxi
Tel: 068; www.taxi068.spb.ru
Just dial 068.

Six Million
Tel: 600 0000; no web
Very popular with girls due to its trustworthy reputation.

Taxi Blues
Tel: 321 8888; www.taxiblues.ru
Not the cheapest, but reliable.

Dumskaya Ulitsa behind Gostiny Dvor is home to a whole host of tiny alternative bars that are insanely popular with students and foreigners. Datscha (6pm–6am), Fidel (www.barfidel.ru; 8pm–6am) and Belgrad (http://belgrad-club.livejournal.com; 8pm–6am) are all located at Dumskaya Ulitsa 9; no phones; M: Gostiny Dvor; map p.137 D2. Datscha and Fidel play soul, funk, ska and disco, while Belgrad hosts concerts by punk bands. Entrance to the bars is free, and beer is cheap. Several times the bars have announced they are closing because the building in which they are located is due to be restored, but they seem to keep going indefinitely, and the crowds keep coming.

Palaces and
Houses

S t Petersburg's rivers and streets are lined
with magnificent palaces. Along with the
royal palaces, the aristocracy and royal
favourites built themselves luxurious residences
no less opulent than those of the royal family.
After the revolution, some of the palaces were
turned into institutes or galleries and some are
now hotels, but many have been painstakingly
restored to their former glory, and represent a
fascinating insight into the houses, lives and
interests of their former occupants.

Around the City

Menshikovsky Palace
Universitetskaya Nab. 15;
tel: 323 1112; www.hermitage
museum.org; Tue–Sun
10.30am–5.30pm; admission
charge; M: Vasileostrovskaya
Peter gave the whole of
Vasilievsky Island to his best
friend and assistant Alexander Menshikov when he
made him Governor of St
Petersburg in 1703 at the
very founding of the city.
The palace was begun in
1710 by Marion Giovanni
Fontana, and later extended
by Johann Gottfried

Schädel. Peter allowed his
friend to build a palace that
far surpassed his own, the
relatively humble Summer
Palace across the Neva, on
condition that Peter would
host formal receptions for
ambassadors and other
important guests in the
grander Menshikov Palace.
The combination of Russian
traditions and foreign inno-
vations in the decor offers a
valuable insight into the
thinking of the Petrine era,
and the views over the river
and city from the famed
Walnut Drawing Room and
other first-floor rooms are
superb. The palace is a
branch of the State Her-
mitage Museum.

**Summer Palace of Peter I
(Letny Dvorets)**
Letny Sad; tel: 314 0374;
www.rusmuseum.ru; Wed–Mon
10am–6pm; admission charge;
M: Nevsky Prospekt; map
p.133 D3
This simple two-storey brick
building in the corner of the
Summer Gardens was
designed by Trezzini from

Left: Menshikov Palace.

1710–14, who was also
involved in drawing up the
plans for the gardens.
It is an excellent example
of early 18th-century Russian
interior design, with its cloth-
lined walls and tiled stoves.
Peter had his rooms on the
ground floor, which along
with a bedroom and study
included a turnery, where as
well as making things, he
liked to receive his guests,
while his second wife
Catherine had her apart-
ments on the first floor. The
exhibits include clothes and
other personal belongings of
Peter and Catherine, as well
as paintings, furniture, glass
and porcelain from the
Petrine era, and a complex
German device for measur-
ing the wind that was Peter's
pride and joy.

Yusupov Palace
Nab. Reki Moiki 94; tel: 332 1991;
www.yusupov-palace.ru; daily
11am–5pm; admission charge;
M: Sadovaya; map p.136 A3
The austere classical facade
of the Yusupov Palace,
home to five generations of
one of Russia's wealthiest
aristocratic families, con-

P

106

Left: theatre at the Yusupov Palace.

After the exile and execution of the entire royal family, the left wing of the Alexander Palace was turned into a sanatorium for members of the NKVD, or secret police. When the town of Pushkin was occupied during WWII, the palace was used to house the headquarters of the German Gestapo, and its basement was turned into a prison. The area in front of the palace is the final resting place of SS soldiers buried there during the occupation.

Concerts of classical music are sometimes held in the small but magnificent theatre of the Yusupov Palace. See the board outside the palace, or ask inside or at any of the city's box offices for details.

ceals interiors that are no less impressive than those of the royal palaces. If you haven't got time to go to one of the out-of-town estates – or even if you do – the fascinating Yusupov Palace in the centre is highly recommended. The palace was drastically remodelled from 1830–38 by Andrei Mikhailov to give it its current appearance, while the exquisite theatre and main staircase were created by Hyppolito Monighetti from 1858–9. Look out for the decadent Moorish Drawing Room.

On 17 December 1916, the basement of the palace was the scene of the murder of the controversial royal favourite, Grigory Rasputin, by Prince Felix Yusupov, Grand Duke Dmitry Pavlovich and three other conspirators – now the subject of a gruesome and fascinating separate tour *(see box, p.11)*. The tour is once a day at 1.45pm in Russian, but tours in English can be booked in advance by calling the museum.

Outside the City

For details on how to get to the suburban imperial residences, *see Other Excursions, p.25*.

Alexander Palace
Pushkin; tel: 465 2024; www.tzar.ru; Wed–Mon 10am–6pm; admission charge
Catherine had a second palace built at Tsarskoe Selo (now Pushkin) for her beloved grandson, the future Alexander I. Built by Cameron, the palace is an example of austere Classicism, though the facade is in need of restoration. It was here that Nicholas I and his family were kept under house arrest following the

Right: Moorish Room at the Yusupov Palace; Amber Room at the Catherine Palace, *see p.108*.

revolution, and from here that they were taken to the Urals. Some of the rooms in the right wing, where Nicholas and Alexandra had their private apartments, have been restored to create a very moving exhibition on Russia's last royal family, including a sailor suit belonging to Alexei, family photos and other personal possessions.

Catherine Palace

Sadovaya Ulitsa 7, Pushkin; tel: 465 2024; www.tzar.ru; Wed–Mon 10am–6pm; admission charge

The estate at Tsarskoe Selo dates back to 1708, when Peter the Great gave the land to his wife Catherine. The palace's 300m (985ft) long gilded facade is the work of Rastrelli, who worked on the palace for Empress Elizabeth. The interior is no less extravagant, with its legendary Amber Room and its Golden Enfilade of dozens of consecutive gilded door frames, through which Elizabeth liked

to approach, framed in gold. The abrupt change in interior design halfway through the rooms marks the influence of Catherine the Great. The gilt and mirrors give way to soothing pastel colours and Classicism – the work of her favourite architect, Cameron, who also built the elegant gallery that bears his name, and the Agate Rooms decorated with precious stones from around the empire. The end of the exhibition is devoted to the restoration of the palace, to which people have dedicated their life's work, and includes many

photographs showing the devastation caused by the war – the roof was destroyed, and the long corridors lie in thick snow.

There is not much information in English inside the Catherine Palace, so it's worth joining a guided tour group, or alternatively, buying one of the booklets about the palace in the gift shop near the ticket desk.

FOR MORE ABOUT THE HISTORY OF THE AMBER ROOM, SEE OTHER EXCURSIONS, P.24

Gatchina

Krasnoarmeisky Prospekt 1, Gatchina; tel: 81371 21509;

Right and above: Catherine Palace at Pushkin.

Right: Peterhof's Grand Cascade. **Below:** Pavlosk.

Tue–Sun 10am–6pm, closed first Tue of month; admission charge

One of the least visited of all the imperial estates, the village of Gatchina was given by Catherine the Great to her lover, Grigory Orlov, in 1776 as a token of gratitude for his help in despatching her husband. The palace was built in 1781 by Rinaldi in the style of early Russian Classicism. Its interiors were destroyed in a fire in 1944, but the state rooms on the first floor have been recreated using archival documents. The rooms on display include the lovely Raspberry Sitting Room, Paul I's throne room and the White Hall. The exhibition also covers the history of the palace.

Pavlovsk

Tel: 452 1536; www.pavlovsk museum.ru; Sat–Thur 10am–5pm; admission charge

The palace was originally designed by Cameron from 1782–6, but was badly damaged in a fire in 1803, after which Voronikhin supervised reconstruction. Though less spectacular than some of the other palaces, it has its points of interest, such as the luxurious bedroom of Maria Fyodorovna, which is decorated

with idyllic pastoral scenes on silk, representing the Tsar's wife's yearning for a simple life. The Egyptian vestibule with its winding staircase is particularly impressive.

Peterhof

Razvodnaya Ulitsa 2; tel: 450 6223; www.peterhof museum.ru; Tue–Sun 10.30am–6pm, closed last Tue of month; admission charge

The Great Palace at Peterhof, which stands proudly on the Upper Terrace, was founded in 1705 by Peter. Today's palace is the result of efforts during different periods by Jean-Baptiste Le Blond

(1714–24), Rastrelli (1745–55) and Vallin de la Mothe, who designed the pair of richly ornamented Chinese drawing rooms. The rooms include Peter the Great's throne room and his Oak Study, whose navigation equipment illustrates the Tsar's passion for sailing. Like most of the suburban residences, Peterhof was ruined during the war while under occupation, and has been painstakingly and lovingly reconstructed. Like the Catherine Palace, there is little information available in the rooms, so it is best to tag on to a tour group.

Peter's favourite residence at Peterhof was not the magnificent Great Palace, but the more modest Monplaisir (10.30am–6pm daily from May–Sept), designed by Johann Friedrich Braunstein from 1714–23. Peter loved to be near water, and from the terrace of Monplaisir he could look out across the Gulf of Finland towards his new capital, St Petersburg.

Parks and Gardens

You will find that you are never far away from a park or garden in St Petersburg, even in the very heart of the city. Since no one living in the centre has their own garden, the parks are particularly dear to locals, who walk with their children and dogs here, congregate to squash onto the benches, drink beer and set the world to rights, and sunbathe en masse in the summer. As well as being nice places to enjoy an ice cream and some tranquillity, many of the parks are also objects of historic interest.

Imperial Estates

For details of how to get to Gatchina, Pavlovsk and Pushkin, *see Other Excursions, p.25*.

Gatchina
Tel: 81371 21509

The unkempt, rambling park at Gatchina is one of the most beautiful in and around the city, especially in the autumn. It is also one of the most romantic, with its Temple of Venus, Island of Love and White and Silver lakes. Look out for the Birch House (May–Sept Tue–Sun 10am–6pm; admission charge) – its simple log cabin exterior

conceals a lavish mirrored interior. The park has a wistful aura of wild tranquillity, and is well worth visiting.

Pavlovsk
Tel: 452 2155; www.pavlovsk museum.ru; main gate: 8am–8pm; admission charge before 6pm

Pavlovsk has the reputation of being the most beautiful and wild of the suburban parks, though Gatchina is in fact no less enchanting. The park, which is divided by a river, contains a myriad of bridges and pavilions, some of which have been restored and can be visited, including the Tem-

ple of Friendship designed by Charles Cameron, and the Rose Pavilion. Only the part of the park near the palace is enclosed; the rest is open 24 hours and free.

Peterhof
Grounds: daily 9am–7pm, fountains operate: 11am–5pm, Sat–Sun until 6pm, May–Sept
SEE ALSO PETERHOF, P.22–3

Pushkin
Alexandrovsky Park
Free

The park surrounding the more humble Alexandrovsky Palace is very different to the Catherine Park. Its vast, sprawling wilderness is mostly empty, giving it a slightly desolate feel, though it is no less enjoyable to stroll around than its neighbour. Since the palace was the favourite residence of the last Tsar and his family, their favourite Grigory Rasputin was originally buried here after his murder in 1916, but his body was later moved by Red Army soldiers.

Left: Peterhof's grounds. **Right:** Catherine Garden, Botanical and Tauride gardens.

Left: the wooded estate of Catherine Park.

ing, you might encounter young cadets from the Naval Academy training – whatever the weather. It is also a popular meeting place for the same cadets and their girlfriends. The busts around the majestic fountain depict great Russians including Gogol, Lermontov and Glinka.

Alexandrovsky Park
M: Gorkovskaya; map p.132 C2
The bustling park behind Gorkovskaya metro is more of a busy thoroughfare than a place to relax, but it is dotted with interesting features such as sculptures of children and a monument to the crew of the *Steregushchy*, who scuttled their torpedo boat to avoid being captured by the Japanese in 1904.

Botanical Gardens (Botanichesky Sad)
Ulitsa Professora Popova 2; tel: 346 3639; Sat–Thur 11am–4pm; grounds: free, greenhouse: admission charge; M: Petrogradskaya
Aptekarsky (Apothecary) Island takes its name from the herb garden founded here in 1714 on the orders of Peter the Great. By the beginning of the 20th century, the original kitchen garden had grown into an impressive botanical garden,

Many of the parks listed here are unenclosed open spaces. Unless stated otherwise, the parks are free and open to the public 24 hours.

Catherine Park
Tel: 465 2124; www.tzar.ru; Wed–Mon 9am–6pm; admission charge May–Sept
There are two parks at Pushkin. The Catherine Park is laid out in front of the palace of the same name, beginning with some formal French gardens laid out in the 1740s, which then give way to a hilly expanse punctuated by the Great Lake, pavilions and

bridges. The expansive park also contains a small pyramid marking the spot where Catherine the Great used to bury her beloved Italian greyhounds, and some sculptures, including the 'Girl with a Pitcher' statue that inspired Pushkin to write the poem 'Fountain at Tsarskoe Selo'.

Around the City
Alexandrovsky Garden (also known as Admiralteysky Sad)
M: Nevsky Prospekt; map p.136 B2
If you walk through the long, narrow garden in front of the Admiralty early in the morn-

Left from top: Victory Park; Tauride Gardens; Tauride Palace.

Central Park of Culture and Leisure (TsPKO)
Yelagin Island; tel: 430 0911; www.elaginparkspb.ru; 6am–midnight; Mon–Fri free, Sat–Sun admission charge; M: Krestovsky Ostrov

The whole of Yelagin Island, landscaped by Rossi in the 19th century, is given over to this popular weekend destination. To explore the island, you can rent skates, bikes and even rowing boats. If you find yourself in the park towards sunset, go to the western tip of the island to get an unparalleled view of the sun setting over the Gulf of Finland.

Field of Mars (Marsovo Pole)
M: Nevsky Prospekt; map p.133 D4

Originally the site of imperial military parades in the 19th century, the flat, open expanse of the Field of Mars is the burial ground of those who died during the February Revolution in 1917, marked by an eternal flame in the centre. This sombre fact does not deter sunbathers or newlyweds on their post-ceremony photo opportunities tour around the city.

Mikhailovsky Gardens
9am–10pm; M: Nevsky Prospekt; map p.137 D1

At one time the Mikhailovsky Gardens behind the main

second only to London's Kew Gardens. Sadly, many of the plants died during World War II, and now the gardens are somewhat overgrown, but this only adds to the charm of the place as a secluded place to stroll. The beautiful 19th-century greenhouses cover an entire hectare (2½ acres) and house plants from all over the world.

Catherine Garden (Yekaterinsky Sad)
Ploshchad Ostrovskovo; M: Gostiny Dvor; 8am–11pm; map p.137 D2

The small garden in front of the Alexandriinsky Theatre is dominated by the impressive monument to Catherine the Great. Its location halfway along Nevsky makes it the perfect place to have a rest and an ice cream if you are feeling weary. By evening, however, it becomes a cruising spot for gay men and young army recruits who are forced into prostitution by their officers, who then appropriate the money earned.

The beaches at Solnechnoye, Repino and Komarova are packed with sunbathers on hot days. The fact that the water is polluted and officially unsafe to swim in does not seem to stop anyone from doing so. *See Other Excursions, p.25, for details on how to get to the resorts.*

> There are plans to close the Summer Gardens for a whole five years for reconstruction, though rumour has it the apparently excessive timeframe is all part of a money-laundering scheme by corrupt bureaucrats.

building of the Russian Museum used to be a favourite place for picnics, but the grass is now out of bounds and its rectangular pond is lifeless and uninspiring. If you are in this area, both the Field of Mars *(see left)* and the Summer Gardens *(see right)* make more interesting options.

Peter and Paul Fortress Beach
9am–8pm; M: Gorkovskaya; map p.132 C3

If the sun is out, head to the Peter and Paul Fortress to work on your tan. Some locals also come here in the depths of winter to go swimming in the Neva in a hole made in the ice by such enthusiasts, known as *morzhi* or walruses. These hardy creatures, many of whom are elderly, swear this extreme sport is the secret of their longevity. A blue walrus painted on the wall of the fortress marks the spot at which they congregate.

Seaside Victory Park (Primorsky Park Pobedy)
M: Krestovsky Ostrov

The city's other Victory Park was laid out in the 1930s, but only planted in 1945, when city residents turned out en masse one Sunday in October in response to an appeal to plant 45,000 trees in honour of those who died during the siege. Bikes and skates are available to rent. The main avenue is flanked with stalls selling corn on the cob and candy floss to the

crowds of locals who come here at weekends, and leads to a statue of the murdered party boss Kirov, who gave the demolished football stadium behind him its name.

Smolny Institute
M: Chernyshevskaya or No. 5 trolleybus; map p.135 E3

The small symmetrical gardens in front of the Smolny Institute are a quiet, peaceful place to relax, surrounded by fragrant lilac bushes and elegant fountains. They are also a popular place for newly-weds to come and be photographed.

Summer Gardens (Letny Sad)
May–Sept 10am–10pm, Oct–Mar 10am–6pm, closed Apr; free; M: Nevsky Prospekt; map p.133 D4

The Summer Gardens are the oldest park in the city, laid out from 1704–12 as a private garden for Peter the Great. Originally the site was laid out with numerous ponds, fountains, aviaries and exotic trees, but the gardens were destroyed by a flood in 1777, and all that remains of the original park are the Baroque statues, which are boxed up during the winter to protect them from the elements. Along with the monument to Krylov, of particular note is the beautiful wrought-iron fence flank-

ing the side of the gardens on the embankment, dating from 1771.

Tauride Gardens (Tavrichesky Sad)
8am–10pm; M: Chernyshevskaya; map p.133 C3/C4

The rambling Tauride Gardens, with their lake, basketball court and hilly mounds are another of the city's favourite outdoor spots. Despite the large sign prohibiting swimming in the lake, it is not unusual in warm weather to see the locals splashing around with their children. In the winter, a trip to the adjacent floral exhibition hall (Potyomkinskaya Ulitsa 2; tel: 272 5448; Tue–Sun 11am–7pm; admission charge; M: Chernyshevskaya) is a good way to warm up and forget you are in a cold northern land.

Victory Park (Park Pobedy)
8am–10pm; M: Park Pobedy

Park Pobedy, or Victory Park, is one of the most popular parks in the city. Laid out in remembrance of those who died during WWII and the siege of Leningrad, its perfectly straight avenues are lined with statues of war heroes. It also contains a rickety antique funfair.

> Nearly all of the city's parks and gardens (at least those that are fenced off) are closed during April for the annual *prosushka*, or drying out of the ground after a winter under snow and sludge. Locked gates are no deterrents to the locals, however, who cheerfully pass their sleeping children in their prams over the railings to accomplices on the other side and then climb over to continue their stroll.

Restaurants

St Petersburg's wealth of restaurants offers a diverse range of cuisine from around the world to please all tastes and budgets. If you are looking to try some authentic Russian food during your visit, you will find many possibilities on the list below, along with the national cuisine of Georgia, Ukraine, France, Italy, Japan and many more. Whatever district you might find yourself in, and whatever cravings you might have, St Petersburg is almost guaranteed to be able to satisfy them. For background on Russia's culinary traditions *see Food and Drink, p.60–63*.

Nevsky Prospekt

Bagrationi
Ploshchad Alexandra Nevskovo 2; tel: 333 2260; noon–midnight; €€€; M: Ploshchad Alexandra Nevskovo; map p.139 D4
A smart, modern take on Georgian cuisine, Bagrationi serves generously portioned classics in comfortable, well-heeled surroundings. With *shashlyks* (kebabs) prepared before your very eyes and traditional music playing, Bagrationi tries hard to let its hair down, but its cool, chic atmosphere and robotic service make a meal here more formal than bacchanalian.

Bistro Garcon
Nevsky Prospekt 95; tel: 717 2467; www.garcon.ru; 9am–1am; €€; M: Ploshchad Vosstaniya; map p.138 B3
An authentic French café where you can still puff on Gauloises over your morning croissant, Bistro Garcon has been offering a good-quality breakfast, lunch and dinner menu, sophisticated wine list and solid service for more than a decade. A real hit among St Petersburg intelligentsia with Parisian pretentions.

Dom Aktora
Nevsky Prospekt 86; tel: 272 9482; 11am–11pm; €; M: Mayakovsakya; map p.138 A2
Visiting Dom Aktora is like taking a trip back to the Soviet Union. The restaurant is in a large, draughty hall with ornate ceilings and curtains, on the top floor of the building. It's very atmospheric and dirt cheap, but you may find that much of what is on the menu is not really available – in true Soviet style.

Palkin
Nevsky Prospekt 47; tel: 703 5371; www.palkin.ru; 24 hours; €€€; M: Mayakovskaya; map p.138 A2
One of St Petersburg's most famous and exclusive restaurants is a recreation of a pre-revolutionary establishment of the same name and now associated with the upscale Premier Casino. Pricey Palkin is elegant and formal, with good views of Nevsky Prospekt, while the classic Russian/French menu and superb wine list are nothing short of exemplary.

Sakartvelo
Nevsky Prospekt 22; tel: 314 3858; 11am–midnight; €€; M: Gostiny Dvor; map p.137 C2
A brightly lit basement restaurant styled as a traditional eatery from old Tiflis, as Tblisi, the capital of Georgia, was once known. The classics of Georgian cuisine – lobio bean salad, egg-filled cheese breads, chargrilled meat and fish kebabs – are served in mountainous quantities.

Palace Square to Liteiny Prospekt

Bellevue Brasserie
Kempinski Hotel Moika 22; tel: 335 9111; www.kempinski-

> The tip is not usually included on the bill in Russia. If the service was decent, 10 percent is the norm.

> Prices for an average two-course meal with a glass of wine:
> € under 700 rubles
> €€ 700–1,500 rubles
> €€€ over 1,500 rubles

Left: chef Didier Reibel from the Bellevue Brasserie. **Below:** his creations.

Unusual Ukrainian specialities such as green *borshch* and apple vodka are available at this full-on theme restaurant opened in 2006. Waitresses dressed as buxom maidens, minstrels serenading diners and even a huge fake tree at its centre giving the place the feel of a gigantic rustic treehouse make for an unforgettable experience.

Le Borshch
Nab. Reki Fontanki 11; tel: 314 0056; www.le-borshch.ru; noon–1am; €€; M: Gostiny Dvor; map p.137 E2

With a quirky collection of white pots lining Welsh dressers and blinding white tablecloths and walls, this trendy new eatery wants to break the rules and presents a modern take on French/Russian cooking that turns this tired formula on its head by playing up the Russian ingredients but applying a French lightness of touch.

NEP
Nab. Reki Moiki 37; tel: 571 7591; www.neprestoran.ru; noon–last customer; €€€; M: Nevsky Prospekt; map p.136 C1

st-petersburg.com; 10am–2pm; €€€; M: Nevsky Prospekt; map p.137 C1

With a breathtaking all-round panorama of the city skyline, Bellevue's location on the roof of the Kempinski Hotel Moika 22 makes it one of St Petersburg's most distinctive dining spots. But its brasserie-style menu is also top-notch, featuring French/Asian dishes with an accent on seafood worth every penny of the five-star prices you'd expect from a high-class hotel.

Dve Palochki
Italianskaya Ulitsa 6; tel: 570 6262; http://dvepalochki.ru; 24 hours; €€; M: Gostiny Dvor; map p.137 D2

A central branch of the black-and-red themed sushi chain offering fast, friendly service and a reliable selection of Japanese cuisine, Dve Palochki (Two Chopsticks) is never empty and rarely disappoints.

Khutor Vodograi
Karavannaya Ulitsa 2; tel: 570 5737; 11am–last customer; €€; M: Gostiny Dvor; map p.137 E1

The recently opened NEP evokes the decadence of early 20th-century Russia with a lively, professional cabaret programme (extra charge), Art Deco styling and diverse menu featuring Soviet, European and even Thai dishes. Despite the glitz, NEP delivers on food and service standards and has become popular with well-heeled local denizens.

Park Giuseppi

Nab. Kanala Griboedova 2b; tel: 571 7309; www.park-restaurant.ru; 11am–3am; €€; M: Nevsky Prospekt; map p.137 D1

A pleasant eatery in a stunning park location near to the Church on the Spilled Blood, Park Giuseppi features pasta and pizza from the Italian regions and an extensive wine list. Wheat and cream tones dominate its terrazzo-style interior, while large win-

dows make the most of its views on three sides.

The Admiralty to St Nicholas's

Dvorianskoe Gnezdo (Noble Nest)

Ulitsa Dekabristov 21; tel: 312 3205; www.dvgnezdo.ru; noon–midnight; €€€; M: Sennaya Ploshchad; map p.136 A3

When princes, presidents and prime ministers dine out in St Petersburg, they go to the Noble Nest, once described by The New York Times as 'the most romantic restaurant in Russia'. An interior that stands as a monument to Empire-style luxury

with an haute-cuisine menu to match, the length of the waiting list for reservations at this exclusive venue is matched only by the size of the wallets of its patrons.

The Idiot

Nab. Reki Moiki 82; tel: 315 1675; 11am–1am; €€; M: Sennaya Ploshchad; map p.136 B3

A legendary basement salon with mismatched antique furniture and laid-back waitresses that pulls in foreigners and Russians alike. They drink up its bookish, cosy atmosphere – and free vodka shots – as well as savour the hearty, vegetarian cuisine that has made The Idiot quite simply a St Petersburg institution.

Krokodil

Galernaya Ulitsa 18; tel: 314 9437; 12.30pm–midnight; €; M: Nevsky Prospekt; map p.136 A2

Krokodil is a real find tucked down Galernaya Ulitsa, a stone's throw from the Bronze Horseman. It's small, highly original and serves

Left and above: NEP's intimate dining room and colourful entertainment. **Right:** Noble Nest.

Prices for an average two-course meal with a glass of wine:
€ under 700 rubles
€€ 700–1,500 rubles
€€€ over 1,500 rubles

Right: relaxing at The Idiot.

true gourmet food at ridiculously cheap prices.

Sadko
Ulitsa Glinki 1; tel: 920 8228; www.probka.ru; noon–midnight; €€; M: Sadovaya/Sennaya Ploshchad; map p.136 A3

This large vaulted Russian restaurant named after the folk hero about whom Rimsky-Korsakov wrote an opera is covered with traditional designs *(Gzhel)* and located just steps away from the Mariinsky Theatre. A crowd-pleasing menu features all the Russian classics, and draws both artists and audiences from the nearby theatre.

Stroganoff Steak House
Konnogvardeisky Boulevard 4; tel: 314 5514; noon–midnight; €€€; M: Sennaya Ploshchad; map p.136 A2

Seating up to 300 guests, the Stroganoff Steak House may be right in its claim to be the biggest steak house in Russia. But more important is its range of dry matured cuts from Argentina, grilled to order and served with rich sauces, fresh salads and well-made side orders. It also features possibly the best burgers in town.

Tandoor
Voznesensky Prospekt 4; tel: 312 8772; www.tandoor. restaurant.ru; noon–11pm; €€; M: Nevsky Prospekt; map p.136 B2

Tandoor is a well-established beacon of authentic Indian cuisine in the northern capital with a plush interior, outstandingly friendly service and varied curry menu that doesn't hold back on the spices – as many places do to suit mild Russian palates.

Teplo
Bolshaya Morskaya Ulitsa 45; tel: 310 8270; 9am–midnight; €€; M: Sennaya Ploshchad; map p.136 B2

A very comfortable basement restaurant arranged like a smart but lived-in house with stuffed toys, a large fireside sofa and bookshelves with art books, Teplo offers welcoming service and a mouth-watering menu based on Italian classics. The restaurant also features a breakfast menu with home-made cakes and pastries.

Testo
Grivtsova Pereulok 5/29; tel: 310 8270; 11am–11pm; €; M: Sennaya Ploshchad; map p.136 C3

A cute little Italian eatery serving home-made pastas cooked al dente and tempting pizzas with fresh ingredients, Testo (Dough) is a popular lunch spot as well as being perfect for a cosy candlelit dinner.

Peter and Paul Fortress

Austeria
Ioannovsky Ravelin (Bastion), Peter and Paul Fortress; tel: 230 0369; noon–midnight; €€; M: Gorkovskaya; map p.133 C2
The restaurant, located in one of the bastions of the Peter and Paul Fortress, is full of 18th-century curios and torture devices, and serves authentic old Russian cuisine such as 'serf' broth dating from before the time potatoes were introduced, made of beef and beans.

> Prices for an average two-course meal with a glass of wine:
> € under 700 rubles
> €€ 700–1,500 rubles
> €€€ over 1,500 rubles

Petrograd Side

Chekhov
Petropavlovskaya Ulitsa 4; tel: 347 6045; noon–midnight; €€; M: Petrogradskaya
Chekhov evokes a genteel dacha from the end of the 19th century with meticulous and tasteful ease, even down to the live songbirds that chirp happily as diners devour home-made dishes made from Russian recipes of yesteryear using ingredients such as forest mushrooms, berries, game and fowl, washed down with home-brew beer and flavoured vodka.

Right: traditional tipples: tea from a samovar; flavoured vodka from a demijohn.

Left: Leningrad.

Demyanova Ukha
Kronverksky Prospekt 53; tel: 232 8090; http://demyanova-ukha.spb.ru; noon–midnight; €€; M: Gorkovskaya; map p.132 B2
Despite taking its name from a humourous fable about being forced to eat when you don't want to – the dark side of Russian hospitality – Demyanova Ukha ('Demyan's Fish Soup') is a long-established favourite dining spot, specialising in delicious traditional soups and fish dishes.

Leningrad
Kamennoostrovsky Prospekt 11a; tel: 644 4446; noon–1am; €€€; M: Gorkovskaya; map p.132 C1
This large new hotspot aches with trendy retro chic that both satirises and celebrates the restaurant culture of the Soviet Union. But for diners on whom this point is lost, there is still much to enjoy with its concise menu of such classics as Egg Mayonnaise, home-made meat, cabbage and mushroom pies and Herring in a Fur Coat, and its well-appointed modern interior.

Tbiliso
Sytninskaya Ulitsa 10; tel: 232 9391; www.tbiliso.ru; noon–

It is not easy to be a vegetarian in Russia. Most main meals are meat-based, and requests for vegetarian options are likely to be met with surprise, followed by the offer of chicken or fish.

Apart from the occasional vegetarian restaurant like The Idiot, the best approach is to try ordering a non-vegetarian dish but asking for it to be made without the meat. (This is also a good way to find out whether dishes are freshly prepared or not.) If you utter the magic phrase, 'For the same amount of money…' you will find chefs remarkably flexible. If that fails, a combination of side dishes is probably the best option, followed by a decadent dessert.

Above: shish kebabs are a Georgian trademark.

2am; €€; M: Gorkovskaya; map p.132 B1

One of St Petersburg's top Georgian restaurants, Tbiliso has a sumptuous if somewhat kitschy interior, staff in traditional costumes, a full live music and entertainment programme, and one of the most comprehensive selections of authentic Caucasian dishes in town, including specialities unique to Ossetia.

U Gorchakova
Bolshaya Monetnaya Ulitsa 17/19; tel: 233 9272;

www.gorchakov.restoran.ru; noon–last customer; €€; M: Gorkovskaya

'At Gorchakov's' you will find a charming slice of Slavic culinary culture delivered in stylish surroundings: open brickwork, beams, crimson tablecloths and hundreds of quirky objets d'art. With such rich pickings as goose and boar prepared to traditional recipes on the menu, U Gorchakova attracts a crowd and making a reservation is recommended.

Vasilievsky Island

Café Ketino
8th Liniya 23; tel: 326 0196; www.katino.allcafe.info;

noon–midnight; €€; M: Vasileostrovskaya

A comfortable Georgian café not to be confused with a fish restaurant of the same name on the next street, Ketino offers a comprehensible range of Georgian treats in pleasant surroundings with warm, friendly service.

New Island Restaurant Boat
Moored at Rumyantsevsky dock; tel: 963 6765; www.concorde-catering.ru; during navigation season, sets sail at 2pm, 6pm, 8pm and 10.30pm; €€€; M: Nevsky Prospekt

St Petersburg's only luxury restaurant boat makes 90-minute trips along the River Neva. New Island's reputation as one of the most exclusive fine dining experiences the city has to offer was burnished by the occasional patronage of Vladimir Putin in recent years.

Restoran
Tamozhenny Pereulok 2; tel: 327 8979; www.elbagroup.ru; noon–midnight; €€€; M: Nevsky Prospekt

Large windows and a minimalist touch give Restoran a stylish, modern edge over its more fussy rivals, and care has been lavished on its white, airy interior. The

119

Clockwise from top left: red caviar; *borshch*; *pelmini*; fresh fish.

same can be said for its excellent menu, which adds contemporary flair to traditional Russian recipes, making Restoran one of St Petersburg's world-class dining spots.

Russky Kitsch

Universitetskaya Nab. 25; tel: 325 1122; 11am–midnight; €€€; M: Nevsky Prospekt

As its name suggests, Russky Kitsch is a one-joke theme restaurant where parties and pranks take a back seat to the creative Russian cuisine on offer. With its riverside location and Hermitage views, Russky Kitsch features an unforgettable,

over-the-top interior that includes a mural of Brezhnev and Castro amorously entwined.

Vladimirskaya, Liteiny and Smolny

Congo

Ulitsa Zhukovskogo 57; tel: 275 9954; noon–midnight; €€; M: Ploshchad Vosstaniya; map p.138 B2

Congo, an African-themed restaurant that has been around for years but remains popular for its relaxed atmosphere and unusual menu, offers dishes inspired by African cuisines as well as exotic drinks and cocktails.

Ket Cafe

Stremyannaya 22; tel: 571 3377; noon–midnight; €€; M: Mayakovskaya; map p.138 A3

Ket (Cat) is a small but perfectly formed Georgian restaurant a few steps from

Nevsky Prospekt that fills up quickly with diners relishing its amazing, authentic Georgian food, its dark and atmospheric (but non-smoking) interior and friendly, efficient service.

Mops

Ulitsa Rubinshteina 12; tel: 572 3834; 1pm–1am; €€€; M: Mayakovskaya; map p.137 E3

Ignore the unusual name – it means 'pug dog' in English – Mops is a delightful and classy Thai restaurant and cocktail bar with an attractive Art Deco interior, superior service and an irresistible selection of authentic Thai and Southeast Asian specialities.

Schastye

Ulitsa Rubinshteina 15/17; tel: 572 2675; Mon–Thur 9am–midnight, Fri 9am–7am, Sat 10am–7am, Sun 10am–midnight; €€; M: Vladimirskaya/Dostoevskaya; map p.137 E3

With a fresh, airy interior and inventive European menu, Schastye – 'Happiness' – is among the newest of the string of appealing restaurants on Ulitsa Rubinshteina that have made this street a dining hub. Schastye is also that rare thing in Russia, a restaurant with a breakfast menu.

Tres Amigos

Ulitsa Rubinshteina 25; tel: 572 2685; www.tres-amigos.spb.ru; noon–midnight; €€; M: Vladimirskaya; map p.137 E3

Manager Víctor Fernández Corres keeps the party atmosphere aloft at Tres Amigos, a lively Mexican joint on Ulitsa Rubinshteina, with a mix of spicy food, live music and a vast array of imported tequilas.

Prices for an average two-course meal with a glass of wine:
€ under 700 rubles
€€ 700–1,500 rubles
€€€ over 1,500 rubles

Right: a coffee and a view on Nevsky Prospekt.

Some of the city's restaurants list Vladimir Putin – a Petersburger himself – among those who have dined in their establishments. In a country where portraits of the glorious leader are a big business, this is some claim to fame. Tandoor, New Island, Podvorye and Russkaya Rybalka can all boast of having fed Russia's president-turned-prime minister. Strangely, none have yet hung framed photographs on the walls of Dmitry Medvedev, another Petersburger, dining in their restaurant.

Moskovsky Prospekt

Art Deco
Sadovaya Ulitsa 47; tel: 310 6454; 10am–2am; €; M: Sadovaya/Sennaya Ploshchad; map p.136 B4
Art Deco, a busy café with a dark green-and-red interior, fills up with office workers and students who come for its simple, hearty Russian and European menu and its laid-back Jazz Age atmosphere.

Mozzarella Bar
Moskovsky Prospekt 153; tel: 388 1482; www.probka.org; 10am–midnight; €€; M: Park Pobedy

Dining spots of this quality are difficult to find away from the city's central districts, but Mozzarella Bar, part of the Probka group of big-name restaurants, offers a pleasant, well-lit interior, a feast of Italian dishes made with fresh ingredients, and a solid selection of wine targeted at the discerning diner.

Peterhof

Shtandart
Lower Park of the Peterhof Museum and National Park; tel: 450 6281; www.peterhof.ru; 11am–9pm; €€; M: Avtovo/ Leninsky Prospekt
Located in a green-roofed one-storey building in the centre of the park and surrounded by its unique, fascinating fountains, Shtandart, named after Peter the Great's frigate, serves from its galley a satisfying range of Russian and European dishes.

Other Excursions

Podvorye
Filtrovskoe Shosse 16, Pavlosk; tel: 466 8544; www.podvorye.ru; 11am–midnight; €€€; train from Vitebsky Station or Kupchino metro station to Pavlovsk, turn left from the station and walk 300m/yds until

you see the restaurant
Recognised as a landmark in its own right, the extraordinary Podvorye represents Russian culture on steroids: a menu dedicated to Vladimir Putin (who dined here on his birthday once), a stuffed bear, folk costumes, a riot of black, red and gold and mountains of traditional feast foods like suckling pig designed for large groups, all set in a huge purpose-built log cabin with its own traditional tower.

Russkaya Rybalka in Komarovo
452a Primorskoye Shosse; tel: +7 901 310 9998; www.russian-fishing.ru; noon–midnight; €€; train from Finlandsky Station to Komarovo, cross over the railway line, turn left then right onto Morskaya Ulitsa, go straight until you reach the sea, turn left and keep walking until you see the sign
A well-known gimmick restaurant where you can catch your own dinner from its overpopulated fishponds, the real charm of Russkaya Rybalka is its location on the dramatic beach of the Gulf of Finland. Another branch is located on Krestovsky Ostrov within the city limits.

Shopping

If you're looking for gifts, a unique reminder of your trip to St Petersburg or just a haul of Soviet kitsch, there are plenty of variants to choose from. The souvenir stores lining Nevsky are often not the best option, as they tend to be overpriced and the range of goods unoriginal and not necessarily of the best quality. Along with traditional Russian dolls, a vast range of all kinds of other popular gift ideas can be found at the bustling tourist market. If you're after clothes or cosmetics to take home, see *Fashion, p.54–5*, and *Banya, p.34–5*; bookstores are listed in *Literature, p.81*.

Souvenirs

The classic Russian souvenir is a *matrioshka*, or set of nesting dolls. As well as the standard brightly vanished five-piece dolls, there is a whole range of *matrioshki* available to suit any kind of taste – elaborate, 10-piece sets; characters from Winnie-the-Pooh and Harry Potter, or Russian leaders from Lenin to Putin and Medvedev.

Another traditional Russian craft is the small papier-mâché boxes painted with flowers or scenes from Russian fairy tales, called *shkatulki*. These fall into two categories: outrageously expensive, exquisitely crafted boxes from the celebrated Palekh and Fedoskino schools, and cheaper imitations that make good souvenirs and presents.

Russian shawls are also widely available, decorated with the same kind of traditional patterns that have adorned this popular Russian accessory for centuries. If none of these options take

your fancy, there is always Soviet kitsch. You can snap up a Red Army hat – but don't wear it around the city, unless you want to declare yourself as a tourist to everyone around. Lighters and hip flasks decorated with hammers and sickles and Lenin make good presents.

Souvenir Market

Nab. Kanala Griboedova 1; tel: 962 2613; 11am–7pm; M: Nevsky Prospekt; map p.137 D1
The open-air souvenir market across the road that runs behind the Church on the Spilled Blood has by far the biggest range of traditional souvenirs, including all the classics described here. It's

also the cheapest place, though you must be prepared to haggle – the vendors, most of whom speak perfect English, will usually start the bidding at twice as much as what they really expect to get. Don't just buy at the first stall you come to, as prices can vary greatly around the market.

Bukvoyed

Nevsky Prospekt 13; tel: 312 6734; www.bookvoed.ru; 24 hours; M: Nevsky Prospekt; map p.136 C2
This store is handily located at the beginning of Nevsky and has the best range of posters, along with other reasonably priced gifts and souvenirs.

Dom Knigi

Nevsky Prospekt 28; tel: 448 2355; www.spbdk.ru; 9am–midnight; M: Nevsky Prospekt; map p.137 C2
Along with tourist books and postcards, Dom Knigi has a

Right: art market near the Church of the Spilled Blood.

Avoid buying souvenirs in hotels, as they are generally obscenely expensive. You can get items of the same quality at the tourist market or bookshops at a fraction of the price.

Left: fine shopping on Nevsky Prospekt.

Do keep in mind when you are shopping for Russian goods that no art, icons or printed material over 100 years old can be taken out of the country. For anything over 50 years old, you may need official permission to get it over the border.

Malevich-inspired designs, ensuring there is something for all tastes.

Varshavsky Express
Nab. Obvodnovo Kanala 118; tel: 333 1020; www.vokzala.net; 24 hours; M: Baltiiskaya
The old Warsaw Train Station has been converted into an upmarket shopping and entertainment center featuring an ice rink, bowling alley and three floors of shops. It's a refreshingly uncrowded alternative to the city center's shops and streets.

If you can't face haggling, many of the central bookshops have a good and reasonably priced range of souvenirs, including beautiful hardback books devoted to Russian art and St Petersburg, and quirky Soviet propaganda posters.

Cups and saucers made at the Imperial Porcelain Factory, founded in 1744, make elegant and original souvenirs. The collection ranges from traditional blue, white and gold patterns to edgy

range of traditional Lomonosov porcelain and small inexpensive animal figurines made at the same factory.

Gostiny Dvor
Nevsky Prospekt 35; tel: 710 5408; www.bgd.ru; 10am–10pm; M Gostiny Dvor; map p.xxx XX.
St. Petersburg's oldest department store contains just about everything you could possible need, from luxury food to souvenirs to electronics to fur and haute couture — though it's not the cheapest option.

Imperial Porcelain
Nevsky Prospekt 160; tel: 717 4838; www.ipm.ru; 10am–8pm; M: Ploshchad Vosstaniya/ Ploshchad Alexandra Nevskovo; map p.139 C3

Right: souvenirs for all budgets.

123

Sports

While visiting St Petersburg, don't pass up the opportunity to witness some local sports such as *gorodki* or even try your hand at them yourself. If you visit during the winter months, there are several open-air ice rinks to warm up (and get bruised) on, and there are always plenty of spectator sports going on; Russian football, in particular, is enjoying a renaissance. Cycling is becoming increasingly popular as a way to see less well-trodden parts of the city, which fortunately happens to be flat, and keep fit at the same time. See *Walks and Views, p.128–9*, for more information on cycling.

Participant Sports

ICE FISHING
The concept is simple – just take your rod, some bait and a stool, walk across the frozen ice to the middle of the Neva or the Gulf of Finland, cut a hole in the ice and wait for the fish to start biting. Don't let the fact that the ice may be melting put you off – Russians certainly don't.

ICE SWIMMING
It's similar to ice fishing, except that you need to cut a much bigger hole in the ice, then launch yourself into it for

some brisk breaststroke. If the idea of trying it on your own fills you with trepidation, join the friendly club of hardy *morzhki* on the beach of the Peter and Paul Fortress.

SKATING AND SKIING
Palace Square
Map p.136 C1
At the end of 2007, an open-air ice rink was erected for the winter on Palace Square despite opposition from Mikhail Piotrovsky, the director of the Hermitage, who argued it could cause damage to the Winter Palace. Towards

the end of winter, the rink was declared illegal, but it had been popular with skaters, and it seems likely to become a regular feature (the city government is not renowned for letting legislation get in the way of a money-making scheme). Prices are not the cheapest in town, but the surroundings are spectacular.

TsPKO
Yelagin Island 4; tel: 430 0911; www.yelaginpark.spb.ru; 11am–9pm; M: Krestovsky Ostrov
Since the whole of Yelagin Island is traffic-free, it is the perfect place for cross-

Left: kick about in the shadow of St Isaac's.

Most Russians have their own ice-skates, and you may find that those available to hire at rinks are old and uncomfortable. Don't be afraid to ask for several different pairs until you find some that won't shred your feet to bits.

venue and ice rink. The rink operates from 1.40–11pm most days, though the timetable is erratic, so it is worth checking the website (Russian only) or calling before you head out there.

TENNIS

The St Petersburg Open (http://spbopen.ru) is held annually at the end of October, attracting players from around the world. The men's tennis tournament is held at

SKK

Prospekt Gagarina 8; tel: 648 958; M: Park Pobedy

country skiing and ice-skating in winter. Equipment can be rented on the spot, including roller-skates and rowing boats in the summer months.

Yubileiny Sports Palace
Ulitsa Dobroliubova 18; tel: 323 9305; M: Sportivnaya; map p.132 A3

The all-night ice-skating sessions are Yubileiny are very popular, especially with students, as tickets are a bargain.

Spectator Sports

Tickets for matches can be bought at ticket offices around the city and at the venues themselves.

FOOTBALL
Petrovsky Stadium
Petrovsky Ostrov 2; tel: 328 8901; www.petrovsky.spb.ru; M: Sportivnaya

Petrovsky Stadium is where St Petersburg's beloved football club Zenit (www.fc-zenit.ru) plays its home games. Petersburgers are fiercely devoted to their club, which sparked large-scale street

parties when it won the UEFA Championship in June 2008, and football fans are sure to appreciate the electric atmosphere of a local match.

ICE HOCKEY
**Ice Palace
(Ledovy Dvorets)**
Prospekt Pyatiletok 1; tel: 718 6620; www.newarena.spb.ru; M: Prospekt Bolshevikov

The modern Ice Palace is home to the city's ice hockey club, SKA (www.ska.spb.ru), which plays here from September to June. The stadium also functions as a concert

Gorodki
Gorodki (left) is an ancient Russian folk game whose adherents have included Peter the Great, Lenin, Stalin and Tolstoy. The game consists of arranging small cylindrical blocks of wood into small formations and constructions, and then trying to knock as many blocks over in one go by throwing another block of wood from a designated distance. During the Soviet era, there was even a USSR Gorodki Championship, in which the team 'Hammer and Sickle' was a regular victor. After the fall of the Soviet Union, the game diminished in popularity, but can still be seen being played at the back of the Peter and Paul Fortress, and in other parks and squares around the city.

Left: enjoying the beach at Peter and Paul Fortress.

125

Transport

S t Petersburg is easy to get to. It is served by a ferry connection from Finland, is a regular on cruise-ship itineraries, served several times a day by trains from Eastern Europe and a key destination for most international airlines. If you are arriving from the UK, US, Australia or Asia, however, arriving by plane is probably the most realistic option – if not the greenest. Once in the city, most of its awe-inspiring attractions can easily be seen on foot, or reached by a quick trolleybus ride or a memorable journey on St Petersburg's ornate and efficient metro system.

Getting There

Arriving by Train

There are four train stations in St Petersburg at which international trains arrive; all are located next to metro stations. If you are not in a rush (it takes four days to get to St Petersburg from London), check out the highly informative rail travel website The Man in Seat 61 (www.seat61.com).

Arriving by Boat

If you arrive by ferry, you will arrive either at the old Morskoy Vokzal (Sea Port) on the southwestern side of Vasilievsky Island, or to the new Marine Facade on the western tip of the island. Both are served by regular buses, but it is a good idea to arrange transfer with your hotel if at all possible.

To minimise your energy impact, you can measure your travel usage and gain carbon emission credits. More information is available at www.carbonresponsible.com and www.climatecare.org.

If you arrive on a cruise ship, it will probably moor beside the Blagoveshchen-sky bridge in the centre, from where it is a 10-minute walk to the Hermitage.

Arriving by Plane

If you are travelling from abroad by plane, you will arrive at Pulkovo II, the city's international airport, about 17km (10 miles) from the city centre. British Airways flies direct from London Heathrow daily, but if you arrive from America, Australia or Asia, you will most probably have to change in Moscow or another European hub. From the airport, the No.13 or K13 buses or minibus (also K13) go to the

Left: the efficient metro.

nearest metro station, Moskovskaya, from where you can continue your journey. The Airport Express (tel: 388 0055; www.airportexpress.ru) goes to Pushkinskaya metro station via Moskovskaya.

Although officially since 2008 taxis outside the airport are not allowed to ask for more than 600 rubles to go to the centre, there is no guarantee that they will keep to this new law and may ask for up to 2,000 rubles.

Most hotels offer a transfer service, which is well worth taking advantage of, as long as it is reasonably priced (no more than 1,000 rubles one way). When you are leaving, it will be cheaper to order a taxi (no more than 700 rubles) to get to the airport.

Getting Around

Most of the major sights in St Petersburg can easily be accessed on foot, grouped as they are along Nevsky Prospekt, the Peter and Paul fortress across the river and St Isaac's Square.

Left: trolleybus passes the Kunstkamera.

Many of the metro stations are works of Soviet art, with ornate pillars and murals depicting Soviet workers, hammers and sickles and the like. Some of the most impressive stations are on the red line, including Ploshchad Vosstania, Pushkinskaya, Kirovsky Zavod and Avtova. But don't be tempted to photograph the grandeur – photography in the metro is strictly forbidden.

If on a bus or trolleybus you see a chair with a cushion or reading material on it, don't sit there! This is the conductor's seat, and occupying it could incur the wrath of the conductor, who is more often than not a ferocious *babushka*.

Buses

Buses have their destination and route clearly written (in Cyrillic) on the side of the bus. If in doubt, show the conductor where you want to go on a map and they will usually tell you when to get off. The flat fare is 16 rubles, payable to the conductor.

The major bus routes that a tourist is likely to need are 3, 22 and 27, which go from Ploshchad Vossstaniya, along Nevsky, and through St Isaac's Square to the Mariin-sky Theatre.

Trolleybuses

The antique trolleybuses may not be the quickest way to get around, but they are certainly atmospheric, and the routes are very convenient – the No. 5 runs all the way from

Smolny to Ploshchad Truda, via Nevsky Prospekt and St Isaac's Square, while the No. 10 is better than any sightsee-ing bus, running all the way from the Alexander Nevsky Monastery, along Nevsky Prospekt and over Dvortsovy bridge to Primorskaya metro station. These are a far cheaper alternative (16 rubles) to the extortionate ticket prices for the red double-decker tour buses, which at 550 rubles per ticket (including an audioguide) are mostly seen driving around empty.

Metro

St Petersburg's metro system is excellent – it is very rare to wait for more than three min-utes for a train. There are four colour-coded lines, covering most parts of the city. Tickets are sold at the windows in the stations in the form of a *zheton*, a metal token that you put in the slot of the turnstile. While on the escalator, it's not unusual to see people reading intently – this is because the metro is so deep underground

that it takes a good three or four minutes just to get down there. The underground was built in the 1950s, and is the deepest metro system in the world. This is partly due to the fact that it was built to double as a bomb shelter – to with-stand even a nuclear attack – and partly due to the swampy ground on which St Peters-burg is built and the necessity of building beneath the city's many waterways.

Water Taxis

In the summer, you can get around by water taxi – a good way to avoid jams and enjoy the views at the same time. The routes connect major sights and leave from the pier opposite the Admiralty and from outide Nevksy Prospekt metro station on the Canal Griboedov, but are not yet reg-ular. Check for more informa-tion at the departure points listed here, or in the Informa-tion Centre on Palace Square.

Right: sign for a metro stop.

Walks and Views

While the majestic facades of the palaces and glittering spires and cupolas of St Petersburg are undeniably beautiful, there is another side to the city – the side behind the facades, away from Nevsky and the great squares. This side of the city is just as fascinating to explore. The best ways to see all the different sides of the city for yourself are on foot or bike, or on a boat trip along the city's many rivers and canals. Exploring with a guide ensures you will get the most out of an excursion around the city and its awe-inspiring views, but in a city this beautiful, even aimless wandering guarantees reward.

Left: St Petersburg's bridges offer spectacular views.

On Foot

Peter's Walking Tours

Tel: 943 1229; www.peters walk.com; tours leave from outside the International Hostel on 3rd Sovietskaya Ulitsa (see p.72) or from Quo Vadis internet café, see web for timetables and details

If you want to take a more structured stroll around the city and see what lies behind the stately facades, by far the best English-language guided walking tours around the city are Peter's Walking Tours.

There is a whole range of walks, including WWII and the Siege of Leningrad Tour, Peter's Communist Legacy Tour, the Rasputin Walk, Dostoevsky Walk and a variety of pub-crawl options.

By Transport

One of the best ways to see the less well-trodden parts of St Petersburg is by bike. Since Russian driving is, to put it mildly, scary, going on an organised group bike tour is both a safer and more rewarding option, since an expert guide will add their insight and explanations to what you see.

Skat-Prokat

Goncharnaya Ulitsa 7; tel: 717 6838; www.skatprokat.ru; 10am–10pm; M: Ploshchad Vosstaniya; map p.138 B3

If 10.30 on a Sunday morning doesn't quite fit in with your plans for Saturday night, you can always rent a bike from Skat-Prokat for the day and follow your own route at your own speed.

Sunday Morning Bike Tour

The Sunday Morning Bike Tour (www.biketour.spb.ru) leaves at 10.30am from outside Skat-Prokat on Goncharnaya Ulitsa. It is led by the seemingly tireless Peter of Walking Tours fame. You can rent a bike there – just make sure you have your passport to leave as a deposit.

Right: Sunday Morning Bike Tour and sunset on the Neva.

Left: Church on the Spilled Blood from the Griboedov Canal.

A sociable and daring way to see the city at night – a truly beautiful sight – is by joining the unofficial group of young cyclists and rollerbladers who congregate at 11pm on Palace Square on Fridays during the summer months, and ride around the city until dawn.

boredom on their face reels off the dates of every building visible into an ancient megaphone, non-stop, for over an hour, there is now the welcome alternative of Anglotourismo – boat tours along the same routes, only in English.

The best way to watch the bridges open at night is also from the water. Boats leave at 1am from the intersections of the Moika, Griboedov and Fontanka with Nevsky, to get out onto the Neva in time to watch Dvortsovy go up. Instead of the non-stop commentary, nocturnal boats have prime Russian pop blaring out to get everyone in the party spirit.

Velocity
Nevsky Prospekt 3 (in the yard); tel: 922 6383; www.velocity-spb.ru; 10am–10pm; M: Nevsky Prospekt; map p.136 B2
As well as bike hire, Velocity also offers an Mp3 player and route map, so you still get the guided tour as you go along but can follow the route at your own speed. In summer, bikes can be rented for the night as well as for the day.

Boat Tours
An even more enjoyable way to see the city is by boat – none of the effort or danger of cycling, and a whole new perspective of St Petersburg, all while sitting down.

Anglotourismo
Nab. Reki Fontanki 21; tel: +7 921 989 4722; M: Nevsky Prospekt; map p.137 E2
Instead of the Russian-language tours, in which a person with a look of deathly

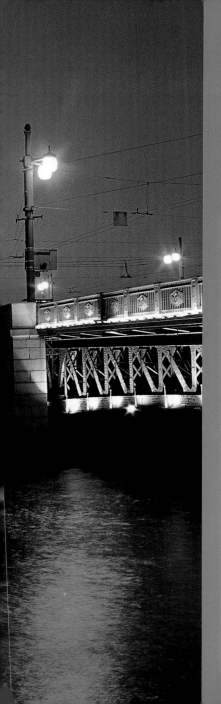

Atlas

The following streetplan of St Petersburg makes it easy to find the attractions listed in our A–Z section. A selective index to streets and sights will help you find other locations throughout the city.

Map Legend

Motorway		Railway	
Dual carriageway		Metro	
Main road		Library	
Minor road		Bus station	
Footpath		Airport	
Pedestrian area		Tourist information	
Notable building		Sight of interest	
Park		Cathedral/church	
Hotel		Theatre/concert hall	
Urban area		Synagogue	
Non urban area		Statue/monument	
Cemetery		Hospital	

p132	p133	p134	p135
p136	p137	p138	p139

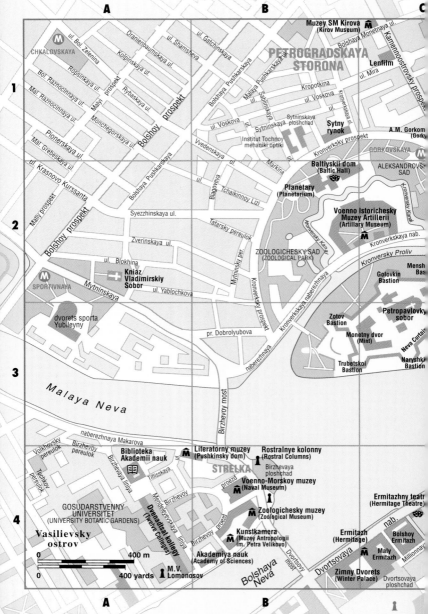

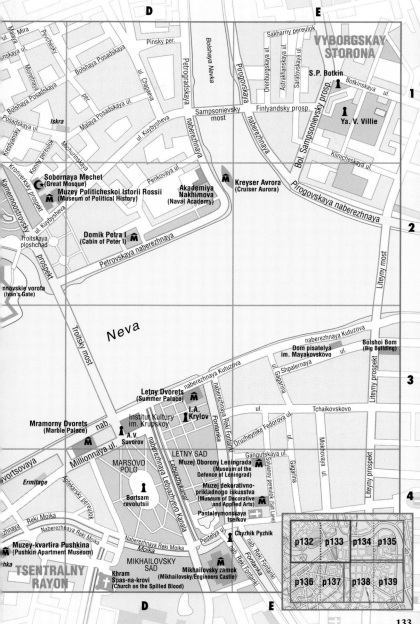

D

ul. Mira

Peychesky

Bolshaya Posadskaya

Pinsky per.

ul. Chapaeva

Petrogradskaya

Bolshaya Nevka

E

Sakharny pereulok

Orenburgskaya ul.

Astrakhanskaya ul.

Saratovskaya ul.

VYBORGSKAY STORONA

S.P. Botkin

Botkinskaya ul.

1

Malaya ul.

Monetnaya

Bolshaya Posadskaya per.

Malaya Posadskaya ul.

ul. Kuybysheva

naberezhnaya

Sampsonievsky most

Pirogovskaya

naberezhnaya

Finlyandsky prosp.

Bol. Sampsonievsky prosp.

Ya. V. Villie

Klinicheskaya ul.

Iskra

Kronverksky prospekt

Kamennoostrovskiy

Posadskaya ul.

Kronverksky per.

Krestyanskiy

Michurinskaya

Sobornaya Mechet (Great Mosque)

Muzey Politicheskoi Istorii Rossii (Museum of Political History)

ul. Kuybysheva

Penkovaya ul.

Akademiya Nakhimova (Naval Academy)

Kreyser Avrora (Cruiser Aurora)

Progovskaya naberezhnaya

2

Troitskaya ploshchad

Kamennoostrovskiy prospekt

Domik Petra I (Cabin of Peter I)

Petrovskaya naberezhnaya

Liteyny most

nnovskie vorota (Ivan's Gate)

Troitsky most

Neva

naberezhnaya Kutuzova

Dom pisatelya im. Mayakovskovo

ul. Shpalernaya

ul. Gagarina

Bolshoi Bom (Big Building)

Liteyny prospekt

3

naberezhnaya Kutuzova

Letny Dvorets (Summer Palace)

I.A. Krylov

naberezhnaya Reki Fontanka

Oruzheynike Fedorova ul.

ul. Tchaikovskovo

Mokhovaya ul.

Gagarina

Mramorny Dvorets (Marble Palace)

Millionnaya ul.

nab.

Institut Kultury im. Krupskoy

A.V. Suvorov

naberezhnaya Lebyazhkevo

LETNY SAD

Muzej Oborony Leningrada (Museum of the Defence of Leningrad)

Gangutskaya ul.

Solyanoy pereulok (Salt Lane)

Liteyny prospekt

4

vortsovaya

Ermitage

Aptekarsky pereulok

MARSOVO POLO

naberezhnaya Lebyazhkevo Kanala

Bortsam revolutsii

Muzej dekorativno-prikladnopo iskusstva (Museum of Decorative and Applied Arts)

Panteleymonskaya tserkov

Pestelya ul.

Chyzhik Pyzhik

naberezhnaya Reki Moyka

Muzey-kvartira Pushkina (Pushkin Apartment Museum)

naberezhnaya Reki Moyka

nab. Reki Fontanki

p132	p133	p134	p135
p136	p137	p138	p139

hka

TSENTRALNY RAYON

MIKHAILOVSKY SAD

Moika

Khram Spas-na-krovi (Church on the Spilled Blood)

Mikhailovsky zamok (Mikhailovsky/Engineers Castle)

nab. Reki Fontanki

D

E

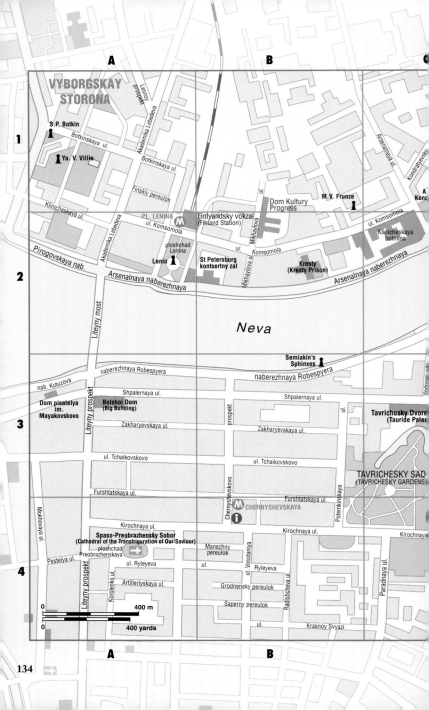

Pistkarevsky prospekt

Sverdlovskaya naberezhnaya

ul. Vatutina

Feodosiyskaya ul.

Neva

Smolnaya naberezhnaya

Smolnaya naberezhnaya

Smolnaya naberezhnaya

Orlovskaya ul.

2

Robespyera

Orlovskaya ul.

Orlovskaya ul.

Stavropolskaya

Smolnovo ul.

Smolnovo ul.

Tavricheskaya ul.

Tavricheskiy pereulok

Chesmenskaya ul.

Diktatury ul.

Smolny monastyr

Smolny sobor (Smolny Cathedral)

♟ Felix Dzerzinsky

Shpalernaya ul.

ploshchad Rastrelli

Kontsertno-Vystavochny kompleks

3

Tavricheskaya ul.

Kavalergardskaya

Stavropolskaya

C⌐ **Smolinskeya Hotel**

Kvarenghi

pereulok

Kvarenghi

SAD SMOLNOVO

Smolnaya naberezhnaya

Tverskaya ul.

Tverskaya ul.

ploshchad Proletarskoy Diktatury

Smolnovo alleya

♟ **F. Èngels**

Smolny

Smolny proyezd

♟ **V.I. Lenin**

Kaluzhskiy pereulok

Odesskaya ul.

Ochakovskaya ul.

Karl Marks ♟

Smolny Insitut (Smolny Institute)

Yunym geroyam oborony

proezd

Muzey-kvartira Kozlova ♟

Ⓜ

Smolny proyezd

Martinsky

Kavalergardskaya ul.

Suvorovsky prospekt

Tulskaya ul.

Pralietarskaya

Bonch-Bruev ul.

Smolny prospekt

Ⓜ **Memorialny muzey A.V. Suvorova (Suvorov Musuem)**

Yarostavskaya ul.

Tulskaya ul.

most Bolsheokhtinsky

Sverdlovskaya nab

4

Tavricheskaya ul.

Suvorovsky prospekt

Krochmaya ul.

Bolnitsa ✚

Novogorodskaya ul.

Krasnevo-Tekstilschig

Sinopskaya naberezhnaya

Malookhtinsky prospekt

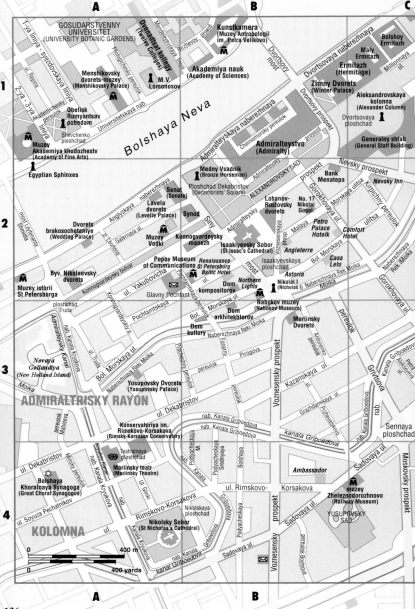

A

GOSUDARSTVENNY UNIVERSITET
(UNIVERSITY BOTANIC GARDENS)

1-ya liniya, sverdlovskaya liniya

ul. Repina

2-ya · 3-ya liniya

Menshikovsky dvorets-muzey
(Menshikovsky Palace)

Akademichesky pereulok

Obelisk Rumyantsav pobedam

Shevchenko ploshchad

M **Muzey Akademiya khudozhestv**
(Academy of Fine Arts)

Universitetskaya nab.

Egyptian Sphinxes

most Leytenanta Shmidta

Dvorets brakosochetaniye
(Wedding Palace)

Anglyskaya naberezhnaya

ul. Lborkta

Galernaya ul.

Byv. Nikolaevsky dvorets

M **Muzey istorii St Petersburga**

Dvenadtsat kollegy
(Twelve Colleges)

Mendeleyevskaya liniya

Filologichesky pereulok

Birzhevoy proyezd

M.V. Lomonosov

B

Kunstkamera
(Muzey Antropologii im. Petra Velikovo)

M

Akademiya nauk
(Academy of Sciences)

Dvortsovy most

Bolshaya Neva

C

Dvortsovaya naberezhnaya

Bolshoy Ermitazh

Maly Ermitazh

Millionnaya ul.

Ermitazh
(Hermitage)

Zimny Dvorets
(Winter Palace)

Dvortsovy proyezd

Dvortsovy prospekt

Aleksandrovskaya kolonna
(Alexander Column)

Dvortsovaya ploshchad

Generalny shtab
(General Staff Building)

Admiralteyskaya naberezhnaya

Chernomorsky pereulok

Admiralteystvo
(Admiralty)

Nevsky prospekt

2

Medny Vsadnik
(Bronze Horseman)

Ploshchad Dekabristov
(Decembrists' Square)

Senat
(Senate)

Lavela dvorets
(Levelle Palace)

Muzey Vodki

Synod

Konnogvardeysky manezh

Popov Museum of Communications

Konnogvardeysky bulvar

ul. Yakubovicha

ul. Yakubovicha

Admiralteysky prospekt

ALEXANDROVSKY SAD

Siny most

Isaakiyevsky Sobor
(St Issac's Cathedral)

Lobanov-Rostovsky dvorets

Voznesensky prosp

Malaya Morskaya ulitsa

Bol. Morskaya

Bank Menatepa

Gorokhovaya ulitsa

Nevsky Inn

No. 17 **Nikolai Gogol**

Petro Palace Hotelk

Angleterre

Morskaya ulitsa

Kirpichny pereulok

ulitsa

Comfort Hotel

Casa Leto

Naberezhnaya Rek Moika

Isaakiyevskaya ploshchad

Renaissance St Petersburg Baltic Hotel

Astoria

Pochtamtsky pereulok

Dom kompozitorov

Glavny Pochtamt

Bol. Morskaya

Northern Lights

M

Nikolai I (Nicholas I)

Moika

Nabokov muzey
(Nabokov Museum)

Gorokhovaya ul.

Dom arkhitektorov

Dom kultury

Pochtamtskaya ul.

Bol. Morskaya ul.

Pratechny pereulok

Naberezhnaya Reki Moika

Fonarny pereulok

Pirogova pereulok

Mariinsky Dvorets

Antonenko pereulok

Voznesensky prospekt

Kazanskaya ul.

Grazhdanskaya ul.

Pratechny pereulok

Grivtsova pereulok

Kanala Griboedova

Petra Alekseyeva nab.

3

Novaya Gollandiya
(New Holland Island)

Moika

ADMIRALTRISKY RAYON

Yusupovsky Dvorets
(Yusupovsky Palace)

ul. Dekabristov

Naberezhnaya Reki Moika

nab. Kanala Kryukova

Admiralteysky Kanal

pereulok Matveeva

ul. Truda

pereulok

Konservatoriya im. Rimskovo-Korsakova
(Rimsky-Korsakov Conservatory)

nab. Kanala Griboedova

nab. Kanala Griboedova

kanala Griboedova

Podyacheskaya M.

Podyacheskaya Srednaya

Bolshaya Podyacheskaya

Sennaya ploshchad

Sadovaya ul.

4

ul. Dekabristov

Teatralnaya ploshchad

Mariinsky teatr
(Mariinsky Theatre)

Bolshaya Khoralnaya Synagoga
(Great Choral Synagogue)

ul. Soyuza Pechatnikov

Minsky pereulok

Krukov kanal

nab. Kanala Kryukova

ul. Glinki

KOLOMNA

ul. Rimskovo-Korsakova

Rimskovo-Korsakova

Nikolsky Sobor
(St Nicholas's Cathedral)

Nikolskaya ploshchad

nab. Kanala Griboedova

kanal Griboedova

Podyacheskaya

ul. Rimskovo-Korsakova

Ambassador

Moskovsky prospekt

Sadovaya ul.

M **muzey Zheleznodorozhnogo**
(Railway Museum)

YUSUPOVSKY SAD

Voznesensky prospekt

pereulok Boyshoy

Sadovaya ul.

0 ————— 400 m

0 ————— 400 yards

A

B

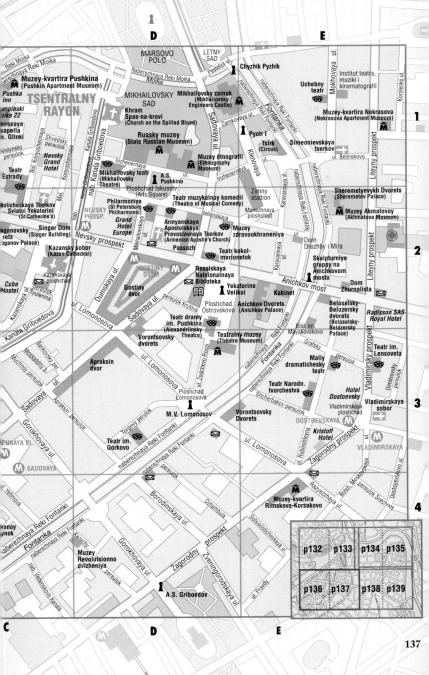

D   **E**

MARSOVO POLO

LETNY SAD

Naberezhnaya Reki Moika

verezhnaya Reki Moika

Muzey-kvartira Pushkina
(Pushkin Apartment Museum)

Pushka Inn

mpinski aika 22

orovaya apella . Glinki

TSENTRALNY RAYON

Shvedsky pereulok

Volynsky pereulok

Nevsky Grand Hotel

Teatr Éstrady

Kholicheskaya Tserkov Sviatoi Yekaterini (St Catherine's)

aganovsky rets oganov Palace)

Singer Dom (Singer Building)

Kazansky sobor (Kazan Cathedral)

Kazanskaya ploshchad

Cuba Hostel

pereulok Tyulenina

nab. Kanala Griboedova

Bol. Konyushennaya

Mal. Konyushennaya

Inzhenernaya

MIKHAILOVSKY SAD

Khram Spas-na-krovi
(Church on the Spilled Blood)

Russky muzey
(State Russian Museum)

Mikhailovsky teatr (Mikhailovsky Theatre)

A.S. Pushkina

Ploshchad Iskusstv
(Arts Square)

Philarmoniya (St Petersburg Philharmonic)

NEVSKY PROSP.

Grand Hotel Europe

Mikhailovsky

Nevsky prospekt

GOSTINY DVOR

Dumskaya ul.

Gostiny dvor

Sadovaya ul.

pereulok Krylova

Kazanskaya ul.

Kanala Griboedova

Bankovsky per.

Muchnoy pereulok

Moskatelny per.

Sadovaya

Apraksin dvor

ul. Lomonosova

Teatr im. Górkovo

SADOVAYA

MIKHAILOVSKY ZAMOK (Mikhailovsky / Engineers Castle)

Muzey étnografii (Ethnography Museum)

Inzhenernaya

Teatr muzykalnoy komedii (Theatre of Musical Comedy)

Italianskaya

Armyanskaya Apostolskaya Pravoslavnaya Tserkov (Armenian Apostle's Church)

Passazh

Teatr kokol-marionetok

Rossiskaya Natsionalnaya Biblioteka

Yekaterine Velikoi

Ploshchad Ostrovskovo

Anichkov Dvorets (Anichkov Palace)

Kabinet

Teatr dramy im. Pushkina (Alexandriinsky Theatre)

Teatralny muzey (Theatre Museum)

ul. Zodchevo Rossi

Ploshchad Lomonosova

M.V. Lomonosov

Vorontsovsky Dvorets

Borodinskaya ul.

Gorokhovaya ul.

Zagorodny

Dzhambula

Zvenigorodskaya ul.

prospekt

Muzey Revolutsionno dvizheniya

A.S. Griboedov

Sotsialisticheskaya ul.

C   **D**   **E**

Pestelya ul.

Chyzhik Pyzhik

Uchebny teatr

Mokhovaya ul.

Institut teatra, muziki i kinematografii

Korolenko ul.

Muzey-kvartira Nekrasova (Nekrasova Apartment Museum)

Pyotr I

Tsirk (Circus)

Simeonievskaya tserkov

ul. Belinskovo

Liteyny prospekt

Zamkovaya ul.

Klenovaya

Karavannaya

Manezhnaya ploshchad

Zimny stadion

naberezhnaya Reki Fontanki

ul. Belinskogo

Sheremetyevykh Dvorets (Sheremetev Palace)

Muzey Akmatovoy (Akhmatova Museum)

Muzey zdravookhraneniya

Dom Druzhby i Mira

Anichkov most

Skulpturniye gruppy na Anichkovom mostu

Dom Zhurnalista

Beloselsky-Belozersky dvorets (Beloselsky-Belozersky Palace)

Radisson SAS Royal Hotel

Bibl. im Mayakovskovo

Grafsky

Fontanka

Maliy dramatichesky teatr

Teatr im. Lensoveta

Dimitrovsky pereulok

Vladimirsky prospekt

pereulok

Teatr Narodn. tvorchestva

Shcherbakov pereulok

Vorontsovsky Dvorets

DOSTOEVSKAYA

Hotel Dostoevsky

Vladimirskaya ploshchad

Kristoff Hotel

Vladimirskaya sobor

VLADIMIRSKAYA

Zagorodny prospekt

ul. Rubinshteyna

Razyezzhaya ul.

Bolsh. Moskovskaya

Dostoevskovo ul.

pereulok Svechnoy

Muzey-kvartira Rimskovo-Korsakovo

naberezhnaya Reki Fontanki

naberezhnaya Reki Fontanki

ul. Lomonosova

4

1

2

3

| p132 | p133 | p134 | p135 |
| p136 | p137 | p138 | p139 |

137

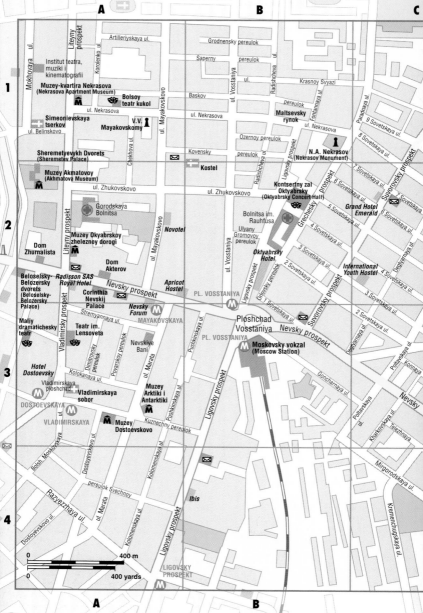

A

Mokhovaya ul.

Liteyny prospekt

Korolenko ul.

Artilleriyskaya ul.

Institut teatra, muziki i kinematografii

Muzey-kvartira Nekrasova (Nekrasova Apartment Museum)

ul. Nekrasova

Bolsoy teatr kukol

Simeonievskaya tserkov

ul. Belinskovo

V.V. Mayakovskomy

Chekhova ul.

Sheremetyevykh Dvorets (Sheremetev Palace)

Muzey Akhmatovoy (Akhmatova Museum)

ul. Zhukovskovo

Liteyny prospekt

Gorodskaya Bolnitsa

Novotel

Mayakovskovo ul.

Dom Zhurnalista

Muzey Okyabrskoy zheleznoy dorogi

Dom Akterov

Beloselsky-Belozersky dvorets (Beloselsky-Belozersky Palace)

Radisson SAS Royal Hotel

Apricot Hostel

Nevsky prospekt

Corinthia Nevskij Palace

Nevsky Forum

Maliy dramaticheskey teatr

Vladimirsky prospekt

Stremyannaya ul.

MAYAKOVSKAYA

Teatr im. Lensoveta

Dmitrovsky pereulok

Povarsky pereulok

Nevskiye Bani

ul. Marata

Hotel Dostoevsky

Kolokanaya ul.

Vladimirskaya ploshchad

DOSTOEVSKAYA

Vladimirskaya sobor

VLADIMIRSKAYA

Muzey Dostoevskovo

Kuznechny pereulok

Muzey Arktiki i Antarktiki

Pushkinskaya ul.

Bolsh. Moskovskaya ul.

Dostoevskovo ul.

Kolomenskaya ul.

pereulok Svechnoy

Razyezzhaya ul.

ul. Marata

Kolomenskaya ul.

Ibis

Dostoevskovo ul.

Ligovsky prospekt

0 — 400 m

0 — 400 yards

4

B

Grodnensky pereulok

Saperny pereulok

ul. Vosstaniya

Baskov pereulok

Radishcheva ul.

Krasnoy Svyazi

ul. Nekrasova

Maltsevsky rynok

ul. Nekrasova

Ozernoy pereulok

Radishcheva ul.

Ligovsky prospekt

pereulok

N.A. Nekrasov (Nekrasov Monument)

Kovensky pereulok

Kostel

ul. Zhukovskovo

Kontsertny zal Oktyabrsky (Oktyabrsky Concert Hall)

Grechesky prospekt

Bolnitsa im. Rauhfusa

Ulyany Gromovoy pereulok

Oktyabrsky Hotel

Ligovsky prospekt

Orlovsky pereulok

2 Sovetskaya ul.

1 Sovetskaya ul.

Apricot Hostel

PL. VOSSTANIYA

PLOSHCHAD VOSSTANIYA

Ploshchad Vosstaniya

PL. VOSSTANIYA

Nevsky prospekt

Moskovsky vokzal (Moscow Station)

Goncharnaya ul.

Ligovsky prospekt

Pushkinskaya ul.

Poltavskaya ul.

Mirgorodskaya ul.

Ibis

Ligovsky prospekt

LIGOVSKY PROSPEKT

C

9 Sovetskaya ul.

8 Sovetskaya ul.

Suvorovsky prospekt

Paradnaya ul.

7 Sovetskaya ul.

6 Sovetskaya ul.

7 Sovetskaya ul.

Grand Hotel Emerald

5 Sovetskaya ul.

4 Sovetskaya ul.

Degtiarnaya ul.

International Youth Hostel

4 Sovetskaya ul.

3 Sovetskaya ul.

Suvorovsky prospekt

2 Sovetskaya ul.

Degtiarnaya ul.

Poltavskaya ul.

Konnaya ul.

Nevsky

Pottavskaya ul.

Kharkovskaya ul.

Telezhnaya ul.

Mirgorodskaya ul.

Kremenchugskaya ul.

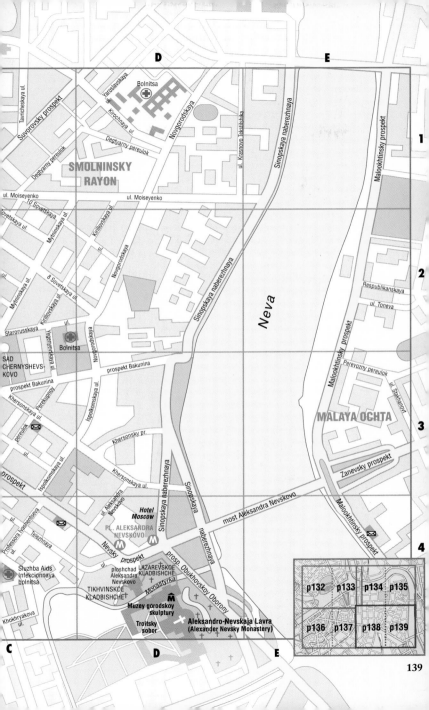

Admiralteyskaya naberezhnaya 136 B2–B1
Admiralteysky prospekt 136 B2
Admiralteysky proyezd 136 B2
Admiralteystvo (Admiralty) 136 B1
Akademichesky pereulok 136 A1
Akademika Lebedeva 134 A2–A1
Akademiya khudozhestv 136 A1
Akademiya Nakhimova 133 D2
Akademiya nauk 132 B4
Aleksandra Nevskovo, most 139 D4
Aleksandra Nevskovo, ploshchad 139 D4
Aleksandra Nevskovo, ulitsa 139 D4
Aleksandrovskaya kolonna 136 C1
Aleksandro-Nevskaya lavra 139 D4
Anglyskaya naberezhnaya 136 A2
Anichkov dvorets 137 E2
Anichkov most 137 E2
Antonenko, pereulok 136 B3
Apraksin dvor 137 D3
Apraksin pereulok 137 C3
Aptekarsky pereulok 133 C4–D4
Arsenalnaya naberezhnaya 134 A2–B2
Arsenalnaya ulitsa 134 C1
Artilleriyskaya ulitsa 134 A4
Astrakhanskaya ulitsa 133 E1
Bakunina, prospekt 139 C3–D3
Baltiyskii Dom (Baltic Hall) 132 B2
Bankovsky pereulok 137 C3
Baskov pereulok 138 A1
Belinskovo, ulitsa 137 E1
Beloselsky-Belozersky dvorets 137 E2
Biblioteka Akademii nauk 132 A4
Biblioteka im. Mayakovskovo 137 E2
Birzhevaya liniya 132 A4
Birzhevaya ploshchad 132 B4
Birzhevoy most 132 B3
Birzhevoy pereulok 132 A3
Birzhevoy proezd 132 B4
Blagoveva 132 B2
Blokhina, ulitsa 132 A2
Bol. Zelenina, ulitsa 132 A1
Bolnitsa im. Rauhfusa 138 B2
Bolnitsa 139 C2, D1
Bolshaya Konyushennaya 137 C1
Bolshaya Monetnaya ulitsa 132 B1
Bolshaya Morskaya ulitsa 136 A3–B2
Bolshaya Moskovskaya ulitsa 137 E4–E3
Bolshaya Posadskaya 133 C1
Bolshaya Pushkarskaya 132 A2
Bolshaya Raznocinnaya ulitsa 132 A1
Bolshaya Sampsonievsky prospekt 133 E2
Bolshoi Bom 134 A3
Bolshoy Ermitazh 136 C1
Bolshoy prospekt 132 A2–A1
Bolsoy teatr kukol 138 A1
Bonch-Bruev ulitsa 138 A2
Borodinskaya ulitsa 137 D4
Borovaya ulitsa 137 E4
Bortsam revolutsii 133 D4
Botkinskaya ulitsa 133 E1
Boytsova, pereulok 136 B4
Byv. Nikolaevsky dvorets 136 A2

Chapaeva, ulitsa 133 D1
Chekhova ulitsa 138 A2
Chernomorsky pereulok 136 B1
Chernyshevskovo prospekt 134 B4–B3
Chesmenskaya ulitsa 135 D3–D2
Chyzhik Pyzhik 137 D1
Degtyarnaya ulitsa 138 C2
Degtyarny pereulok 139 C1–D1
Dekabristov, ul. 136 A4–A3–B3
Dekabristov, ploshchad 136 B2
Diktatury ulitsa 135 D3
Dimitrovsky pereulok 138 A3
Divenskaya ulitsa 133 C1
Dobrolyubova, pr. 132 B3
Dom Akterov 138 A2
Dom arkhitekhtorov 136 B3
Dom Druzhby i Mira 137 E2
Dom Knigi 137 C2
Dom kompositorov 136 B2
Dom Kultury 136 B3
Dom Kultury Progress 134 B1
Dom pisatelya im. Mayakovskovo 133 E3
Dom Zhurnalista 137 E2
Dostoyevskaya ulitsa 137 E4–E3
Dumskaya ulitsa 137 D2
Dvenadtsat kollegy 132 A4
Dvorets Sheremetyevykh 137 E2
Dvorets sporta Yubileyny 132 A3
Dvortsovaya naberezhnaya 132 B4–C4, 133 C4–D3
Dvortsovaya ploshchad 136 B1
Dvortsovy most 136 B1
Dvortsovy prospekt 136 B1
Dzhambula, pereulok 137 D4
Egyptian Sphinxes 136 A1
Ermitazh (Hermitage) 132 C4
Ermitazhny teatr 132 C4
F. Engels statue 135 D3
Feodosiyskaya ulitsa 135 D3
Filologichesky pereulok 136 A1
Finlyandsky prospekt 133 E1
Finlyandsky vokzal (Finland Station) 134 B1
Finskiy pereulok 134 A1
Fonarny pereulok 136 B3
Fontannaya ulitsa 138 B1
Furshtadtskaya ulitsa 134 A3–B4
Gagarina, ulitsa 133 E3–E4
Galernaya ulitsa 136 A2
Gangutskaya ulitsa 133 E4
Gatchinskaya ulitsa 132 B1
Generalny shtab 136 C1
Glavny Pochtant 136 A2
Glinki, ulitsa 136 A4
Goncharnaya ulitsa 138 B3
Gorodskaya bolnitsa 135 E1, 138 A2
Gorokhovaya ulitsa 136 B2–C2, 137 C3–D4
Gostiny dvor 137 D2
Gosudarstvenny universitet 132 A4
Grafsky pereulok 137 E3
Grazhdanskaya ulitsa 136 B3
Grechesky prospekt 138 B2
Grivtsova, pereulok 136 B3–C3
Grodnensky pereulok 134 B4
Hermitage (Ermitazh) 132 C4
Horovaya kapella im. Glinki 136 B1
I.A. Kryllov 133 D3
Institut Kultury im. Krupskoy 133 D3
Institut Tochnoy mehaniki optiki 132 B1
Inzhenernaya ulitsa 137 D1–E1
Ioannovsky vorota 133 C2
Isaakiyevskaya ploshchad 136 B2

Isaakiyevsky sobor 136 B2
Iskusstv, ploshchad 137 D1
Ispolkomskaya ulitsa 139 C3–D3
Italianskaya ulitsa 137 D2
Kabinet 137 E2
Kaluzhsky pereulok 135 C4
Kamennoostrovsky prospekt 132 C1, 133 C2
Kanala Griboedova, naberezhnaya 136 B4–B3–C3, 137 D1
Kanala Kryukova, naberezhnaya 136 A3–A4
Karavannaya ulitsa 137 E2–E1
Karl Marks statue 135 D3
Kavalergardskaya ulitsa 135 D4–D3
Kazachy pereulok 137 D4
Kazanskaya ploshchad 137 C2
Kazanskaya ulitsa 136 B3, 137 C2
Kazansky sobor 137 C2
Kharkovskaya ulitsa 138 C3
Khersonskaya ulitsa 139 C3–D3
Khersonsky pr. 139 D3
Khokhryakova ulitsa 139 C4
Khram Spas-na-krovi (Church of the Saviour on the Spilled Blood) 137 D1
Kirillovskaya ulitsa 139 C2–D2
Kirochnaya ulitsa 134 A4–B4–C4, 135 D4
Kirpichny pereulok 136 C2
Klenovaya 137 E1
Klinicheskaya bolnitsa 134 C2
Klinicheskaya ulitsa 133 E1
Kolokolnaya ulitsa 138 A3
Kolomenskaya ulitsa 138 A4
Kolpinskaya ulitsa 132 A1
Komsomola, ul. 134 A2–B2–C2
Kontsertno-Vystavochny kompleks 135 D3
Kondratyevsky prospect 134 C1
Konnaya ulitsa 138 C3, 139 C3
Konnogvardeysky bulvar 136 A2
Konnogvardeysky p. 136 A2
Konnogvardeysky manezh 136 A2
Konny pereulok 133 C2
Konservatoriya im. Rimskovo-Korsakova 136 A3
Kontsertny zal Oktyabrsky 138 B2
Korolenko ulitsa 133 E4
Kostel 138 B2
Kovensky pereulok 138 A1
Krasnovo Kurssanta, ulitsa 132 A1
Krasnovo Tekstilshika 135 D4
Krasnovo Tekstilshika, ul. 139 D1
Krasnoy Svyazi, ulitsa 134 A3
Kremenchugskaya ulitsa 138 C4
Krestyansky 133 C1
Kresty Prison 134 B2
Kreyser Avrora 133 E2
Kronverkskaya naberezhnaya 132 B3–B2–C2
Kronverkskaya ulitsa 132 B1
Kronverksky prospekt 132 B1–C1, 133 C2
Kropotkina, ulitsa 132 B1
Krylova, pereulok 137 D2
Kunstkamera (Muzey Antropologii im. Petra Velikovo) 132 B4
Kutuzova, naberezhnaya 133 D3–E3
Kuybysheva, ulitsa 133 C2–D1
Kuznechny pereulok 138 A3
Kuznechny rynok 138 A3
Kvarengi, pereulok 135 D3–E3
Lebyazhyevo Kanala, naberezhnaya 133 D3–D4
Lenfilm 132 C1
Lenin statue 134 A2

Lenina, ploshchad 134 A2
Lenina, ulitsa 132 B1
Leonova pereulok 136 A2
Lesnoy prospekt 134 A1
Letny dvorets-muzey Petra I 133 D3
Leytenanta Shmidta, most 136 A2
Ligovsky prospekt 138 A4–B3–B2
Literatorny muzey (Pushkinsky dom) 132 B4
Liteyny most 133 E2
Liteyny prospekt 133 E4–E3, 137 E2–E1
Lobanov-Rostovsky dvorets 136 B2
Lomonosova, ploshchad 137 D3
Lomonosova, ul. 137 D2–D3–E3
M.V. Frunze statue 134 B1
M.V. Lomonosov statue 136 A1, 137 D3
Makarova, naberezhnaya 132 A3
Mal. Grebeckaya ulitsa 132 A1
Mal. Konyushennaya 137 C1
Mal. Raznocinnaya ulitsa 132 A1
Malaya Monetnaya 133 C1
Malaya Morskaya ulitsa 136 B2–C2
Malaya Posadskaya ulitsa 133 C1–D1
Malaya Pushkarskaya ulitsa 132 B1
Malookhtinsky prospekt 139 E4–E3–E2–E1
Maltsevsky rynok 138 B1
Maly dramaticheskiy teatr 137 E3
Maly Ermitazh 136 C1
Maliy prospekt 132 A2–A1
Manezhnaya ploshchad 137 E2
Manezhny pereulok 138 A1
Marata, ulitsa 138 A4–A3
Mariinsky dvorets 136 B3
Mariinsky teatr (Teatr im. Kirova) 136 A3
Markina, ulitsa 132 B1
Martinsky proezd 135 C4
Matveeva, pereulok 136 A3
Mayakovskovo, ulitsa 138 A2–A1
Medny Vsadnik, Pyotr I 136 B2
Memorialny muzey A.V. Suvorova 135 C4
Mendeleyevskaya ulitsa 132 A4
Menshikovsky dvorets-muzey 136 A1
Michurinskaya 133 C1
Mikhailovskaya ul. 137 D2
Mikhailovsky zamok 133 D4
Mikhaylova ulitsa 134 B2
Millionnaya ulitsa 132 C4, 133 C4–D4
Minsky pereulok 136 A4
Mira, ulitsa 132 C1, 133 C1
Mirgorodskaya ulitsa 138 C4
Moiseyenko, ulitsa 139 C1–D1
Mokhovaya ulitsa 133 E4
Monchegorskaya ul. 132 A1
Monetny dvor 132 C3
Moskalelny pereulok 137 C3
Moskovsky prospekt 136 C4
Moskovsky vokzal (Moscow Station) 138 B3
Mramorny dvorets 133 C3
Muchnoy pereulok 137 C3
Mussorgsky teatr 137 D1
Muzey Akhmatovoy 137 E2
Muzey Arktiki i Antarktiki 138 A3
Muzey dmmk Petra I 133 D2
Muzey Dostoevskovo 138 A3
Muzey gorodskoy skulptury 139 D4

Muzey istorii St Petersburga
136 A2
Muzey Okyabrskoy zheleznoy
dorogi 138 A2
Muzey Politicheskoi Istorii Rossii
133 C2
Muzey Revolutsionno dvizheniya
137 D4
Muzey SM Kirova 132 B1
Muzey vodki 136 A2
Muzey zdravookhraneniya
137 D2
Muzey zheleznovodorozhnovo
(Railway Museum) 136 C4
Muzeyètnografii 137 D1
Muzey-kvartira Kozlova 135 D3
Muzey-kvartira Nekrasova
138 A1
Muzey-kvartira Pushkina 133 C4
Muzey-kvartira Rimskovo-
Korsakovo 137 E4
Muzey-svyazi 136 B2
Mytninskaya naberezhnaya
132 A2
Mytninskaya ulitsa 139 C2
Mytninsky pereulok 132 B2
N.A. Nekrasov
(Nekrasov Monument) 138 B1
Nabokov muzey (nabakov
Museum) 136 B2
Nekrasova, ulitsa 138 A1–B1
Nevskiye Bani 138 A3
Nevsky prospekt 136 C2,
137 C2, 138 A2–B3–C3,
139 C3–D4
Nikolai i 136 B2
Nikolskaya ploshchad 136 B4
Nikolsky sobor 136 A4
Novaya Gollandiya 136 A3
Novgorodskaya 139 D2–D1
Obelisk Rumyanceva pobedam
136 A1
Obukhovskoy Oborony, prospekt
139 D4–E4
Ochakovskaya ulitsa 135 D3
Odesskaya ulitsa 135 D3
Oranienbaumskaya ulitsa
132 A1
Orenburgskaya ulitsa 133 E1
Orlovskaya ulitsa 135 C2–C3
Orlovsky pereulok 138 B2
Oruzheynike Fedorova ulitsa
133 E3
Ostrovskovo, ploshchad 137 D2
Ozernoy pereulok 138 B1
Panteleymonskaya tserkov
133 D4
Paradnaya ulitsa 134 C4
Passazh 137 D2
Penkovaya ulitsa 133 D2
Perekupnoy, pereulok 139 C3
Perevozny pereulok 139 E3
Pestelya ulitsa 133 D4–E4
Pestelya ulitsa 137 D1
Petra Alekseyeva ulitsa 136 C3
Petra Velikova, most 135 E4
Petrogradskaya naberezhnaya
133 D1
Petropavlovky sobor 132 C3
Petrovskaya naberezhnaya
133 C2–D2
Pevchesky per. 133 C1
Philarmoniya 137 D2
Pinsky per. 133 D1
Pionerskaya ulitsa 132 A1
Pirogova, pereulok 136 B3
Pirogovskaya naberezhnaya
133 E1–E2
Piskarevsky prospekt 135 E1
Planetary 132 B2

Pochtamtskaya pereulok 136 B2
Pochtamtskaya ulitsa 136 A3
Podyacheskaya Bolshaya 136 B4
Podyacheskaya M. 136 B4
Podyacheskaya Srednyaya
136 B4
Poltavskaya ulitsa 138 C3
Popov Museum of
Communications 136 B2
Potemkinskaya ulitsa 134 B4
Povarskoy pereulok 138 A3
Prachechny pereulok 136 A3
Pravdy, ulitsa 137 E4
Preobrazhenskaya, ploshchad
134 A4
Professora Ivashentseva ulitsa
139 C4
Proletarskoy Diktatury, ploshchad
135 D3
Proletarskoy 135 D4
Przhevalskovo, ulitsa 136 B3
Pushkinskaya ulitsa 138 A3–B3
Pyotr I 132 C3
Radishcheva ulitsa 138 B2–B1
Rastrelli, ploshchad 135 D3
Razyezzhaya ulitsa 137 E4
Reki Fontanki, naberezhnaya
137 C4–D3–E3–E2–E1
Reki Moika, naberezhnaya
136 A3–B3–B2–C2–C1,
137 C1–D1
Repina, ulitsa 136 A1
Respublikanskaya 139 E2
Rimskovo-Korsakova, ulitsa
136 A4–B4
Robespyera, naberezhnaya
134 A3–B3, 135 C2
Ropsinkaya ulitsa 132 A1
Rossiskaya Natsionalnaya
Biblioteka 137 D2
Rostralnye kolonny
(Rostral Columns) 132 B4
Rubinshteyna, ulitsa 137 E3
Russky muzey 137 D1
Rybakskaya ulitsa 138 C4
Ryleyeva, ulitsa 134 A4–B4
S.P. Botkin 133 E1
Sablinskaya ulitsa 132 B1–B2
Sadovaya ulitsa
136 B4–C4, 137 C3–D2–D1
Sakharny pereulok 133 E1
Sampsonievsky most 133 D1
Saperny pereulok 134 B4
Saratovskaya ulitsa 133 E1
Senat 136 A2
Sennaya ploshchad 136 C3
Sennoy rynok 136 C4
Shamsheva, ulitsa 132 A1
Shcherbakov pereulok 137 E3
Shevchenko ploshchad 136 A1
Shpalernaya ulitsa
134 A3–B3, 135 D3
Shvedsky pereulok 137 C1
Simeonievskaya tserkov 137 E1
Sinopskaya naberezhnaya
139 D4–D3–D2–E1
Siny most 136 B2
Skulpturniye gruppy na
Anichkovom mostu 137 E2
Sluzhba Aids Infekcionnaya
bolnitsa 139 C4
Smolnaya naberezhnaya
135 D2–E2–E3
Smolnovo alleya 135 D3
Smolnovo ulitsa 135 D3-E2
Smolny Insitut 135 E3
Smolny monastyr 135 E3
Smolny prospekt 135 D4
Smolny proyezd 135 E3
Smolny sobor 135 E3

Sobornaya Mechet 133 C2
Solyanoy pereulok 133 E4
Sotsialisticheskaya ulitsa
137 E4
Sovetskaya ulitsa, 1 138 B2
Sovetskaya ulitsa, 2 138 B2–C3
Sovetskaya ulitsa, 3 138 B2–C2
Sovetskaya ulitsa, 4 138 B2–C2
Sovetskaya ulitsa, 5 138 B2
Sovetskaya ulitsa, 6 138 B2–C2
Sovetskaya ulitsa, 7 138 C2
Sovetskaya ulitsa, 8 138 C1,
139 C2
Sovetskaya ulitsa, 9 138 C1,
139 C2
Sovetskaya ulitsa, 10 139 C1
Soyuza Pechatnikov, ulitsa
136 A4
Spaso–Preobrazhensky sobor
134 A4
St Petersburg Kontsertny zal
134 B2
Stakhanovt, ulitsa 139 E3
Starorusskaya ulitsa 139 C2
Stavropolskaya ulitsa 135 D2–D3
Stremyannaya ulitsa 138 A3
Stroganovsky dvorets 137 C2
Suvorovsky prospekt
135 C4–D4–D3, 138 B3–C2,
139 C1
Svechnoy, pereulok 138 A4
Sverdlovskaya naberezhnaya
135 C1–D1–E1, E4–E3
Syezzhinskaya ulitsa 132 A2
Synod 136 B2
Sytninskaya ploshchad
132 B1
Sytninskaya ulitsa 132 B1
Sytny rynok 132 B1
Tatarsky pereulok 132 B2
Tavricheskaya ulitsa 135 C4–C3
Tavricheskiy pereulok 135 D3
Tavricheskiy dvorets 134 C3
Tchaikinnoy Lizi, ulitsa 132 B2
Tchaikovskovo, ulitsa
133 E3, 134 A3–A4
Teatr dramy im. Pushkina 137 D2
Teatr im. Gorkovo 137 D3
Teatr im. Leninskovo Komsomola
132 B2
Teatr im. Lensoveta 137 E3
Teatr kokol-marionetok 137 D2
Teatr marodn. tvorchestva
137 E3
Teatr muzykalnoy komedii
137 D2
Teatr na Liteyny 137 E1
Teatralnaya ploshchad 136 A4
Teatralny muzey 137 D3
Teatr Éstrady 137 C1
Telezhnaya 138 ulitsa C3
Telezhnaya ulitsa 139 C4
Tiflisskaya ulitsa 132 A4
Toneva, ulitsa 139 E2
Torgovy pereulok 137 D3
Troitskaya ploshchad 133 C2
Troitsky most 133 D3
Troitsky sobor 139 D4
Truda, ploshchad 136 A2
Truda, ulitsa 136 A2
Tsirk (Circus) 137 E1
Tuchkov pereulok 132 A4
Tulskaya ulitsa 135 D4–E4
Tverskaya ulitsa 135 C3–D3
Tyulenina, pereulok 137 C2
Uchebny teatr 133 E4
Ulyany Gromovoy pereulok
138 B2
Universitetskaya naberezhnaya
136 A1

V.I. Lenin 135 E3
V.V. Mayakovskomy 138 A1
Vatutina, ulitsa 135 C1–D1
Vedenskovo Kanala,
naberezhnaya 137 C4
Vladimirskaya ploshchad 137 E3
Vladimirskaya sobor 137 E3
Vladimirsky prospekt 137 E3–E2
Vodoprovodny pereulok 134 C3
Voenno-istorichesky muzey
Artillerii 132 C2
Voenno-Morskoy muzey 132 B4
Volkhovsky pereulok 132 A4
Volynsky pereulok 137 C1
Vorontsovsky dvorets 137 D3
Voskova, ulitsa 132 B1
Vosstaniya, ploshchad 138 B3
Vosstaniya, ulitsa
138 B2–B1, 134 B4
Voznesensky prospekt
136 B4–B3–B2
Vvedenskaya ulitsa 132 B1
Ya. V. Villie statue 133 E1
Yablochkova, ulitsa 132 A2
Yakubovicha, ulitsa 136 A2
Yaroslavskaya ulitsa 135 D4
Yefimova, ulitsa 137 C4
Yegenyevskaya ulitsa 139 C2
Yekaterine Velikoi 137 D2
Yunym geroyam oborony 134 C3
Yusupovsky dvorets 136 A3
Zagorodny prospekt 137 D4–E3
Zakharyevskaya ulitsa
134 A3–B3
Zamkovaya ulitsa 137 D1
Zanevsky prospekt 139 E3
Zhukovskovo, ulitsa 138 A2–B2
Zimny stadion 138 E2
Zodchevo Rossi, ulitsa
137 D3
Zoologichesky muzey 132 B4
Zvenigorodskaya ulitsa
137 D4
Zverinskaya ulitsa 132 A2

HOTELS

Ambassador 136 B4
Angleterre 136 B2
Apricot Hostel 138 A2
Astoria 136 B2
Casa Leto 136 B2
Comfort Hotel 136 B2
Corinthia Nevskij Palace 138 A2
Cuba Hostel 137 C2
Ermitage Hotel 133 C4
Grand Hotel Emerald 138 C2
Grand Hotel Europe 137 D2
Herzen House 136 B2
Hotel Dostoevsky 137 E3
Hotel Moscow 139 D4
Ibis 138 B3
International Youth Hostel
138 C2
Iskra 133 E1
Kempinski Moika 22 137 C1
Kristoff Hotel 137 E3
Nevsky Forum 138 A2
Nevsky Grand Hotel 137 C1
Nevsky Inn 136 C2
Northern Lights 136 B2
Novotel 138 A3
Oktyabrsky Hotel 138 B2
Petro Palace Hotel 136 B2
Pushka Inn 137 C1
Radisson SAS Royal Hotel
138 A2
Renaissance St Petersburg
Baltic Hotel 136 B2
Smolninskaya Hotel 135 D3

Index

A

Academy of Fine Arts **17, 29, 85**
Academy of Sciences **17, 30**
Admiralty **10, 30, 37, 40–41, 46–7**
Akhmatova, Anna **4, 9, 25, 76, 84, 86**
Alexander Column **8, 82**
Alexander Nevsky Monastery **6, 7, 28, 44, 45**
Alexander Palace **24, 30, 107–8**
Alexandriinsky Theatre **7, 30, 32**
Alexandrovsky Garden **10, 111**
Alexandrovsky Park **14, 111**
Alexandrovsky Park, Pushkin **110**
alternative / rock clubs **102–3**
Amber Room **24**
Andreevsky Rynok **17**
Anichkov Bridge **7, 38, 39**
Anichkov Palace **7**
Anna Akhmatova Museum **9, 86**
apartments to rent **73**
Aptekarsky Island **15**
Arch of New Holland Island **11, 29**
Arctic and Antarctic Museum **18, 42, 97**
Armenian Apostles' Church **7, 44–5**
arrival in St Petersburg **126**
Artillery Museum **14, 94**
Arts Square **8–9**
audioguides **98**
Avrora **14, 94**

B

ballet **32**
Bankovsky Bridge **39**
Beloselsky-Belozersky Palace **7, 31**
Blagoveshensky Bridge **39**
Blok, Alexander **76–7, 92**
Blok Museum **92**
boat tours **129**
Bolshoy Dom **18, 19**
Bolshoy Prospekt **15, 17**
bookshops **81, 123**
Botanical Gardens **15, 111–12**

Bread Museum **97**
Bronze Horseman **10, 80, 82**
Buddhist Temple **15, 48**
buses **127**
business lunches **60**

C

Cabin of Peter I **14, 87, 95**
Canal Griboedova **6, 10, 39**
carbon emissions **126**
Cathedral of the Transfiguration of Our Saviour **18, 45, 48**
Catherine Garden **7, 82–3, 112**
Catherine Palace **24, 29, 108**
Catherine Park **110–11**
Caucasian cuisine **60**
central heating **51**
Central Naval Museum **16, 30, 96**
Central Park of Culture and Leisure (TsPKO) **15, 112, 124**
Chaliapin Memorial Apartment **15**
Chesma Church **21, 49**
Church of St John the Baptist **15**
Church on the Spilled Blood **5, 8, 44, 45–6**
Chyzhik Pyzhik monument **9, 83**
cinemas **59**
Circus **9, 42**
classical music **100, 107**
credit cards **117**
cycling **50, 128–9**

D

dance clubs **103–5**
Dolphinarium **42**
Dom Knigi bookshop **6, 31, 81, 122–3**
Dostoevsky, Fyodor **18, 21, 76, 77–8, 97**
Dostoevsky Museum **18, 97**
Duma **7**
Dvortsovy Bridge **16, 38**

E

Egipetsky Bridge **39**
Egyptian Sphinxes **17**
embassies and consulates **52**
emergency numbers **52**
Ethnography Museum **8, 87–8**

F

fashion designers, local **54**

fashion designers, Western **54–5**
Field of Mars **9, 112**
film locations **58**
Finland Station **19**
flooding **50**
Fontanka, River **7, 9, 37, 39**
food shopping **62–3**
football **125**
further reading **80–81**

G

Gatchina **25, 108–9, 110**
gay and lesbian St Petersburg **52**
General Staff Building **8**
Gogol, Nikolai **6, 10, 76, 78**
gorodki **125**
Gostiny Dvor **7, 29, 123**
Great Choral Synagogue **11, 46**
Great Mosque **14, 48**
Green Bridge **39**
Gulf of Finland **25, 50, 112**

H

health **52**
Hermitage Museum **5, 8, 87, 89**
Hermitage Theatre **8, 30, 33**
History of the Peter and Paul Fortress Museum **12–13**
Holy Prince Vladimir Cathedral **15, 48**
hotel packages **68**
House of the Soviets **21**

I

ice hockey **125**
ice fishing **124**
ice-skating **124**
ice swimming **124**
internet cafés **53**

J

jazz **100–101**

K

Kamennoostrovsky Prospekt **14–15**
Kamenny Island **15**
Kamenny Island Palace **15**
Karpovka, River **15**
Kazan Cathedral **6, 30, 39, 45, 48**
Kirov Islands **14, 15**
Kirov Museum **14–15, 87, 95**

Komarova **25, 112**
Krasin **17**
Krestovsky Island **15**
Kresty Prison **19, 76, 84**
Kronverk **14**
Krylov monument **83**
Kshessinskaya Mansion **14,
    95–6**
Kunstkamera **16–17, 96**
Kuznechny Rynok **18, 63**

L

Lenexpo **17**
Lenfilm Studios **14, 59**
Leningrad Zoo **14, 42–3**
Lensoviet Palace of Culture **15**
Liteiny **18–19**
Literary Café **6, 40**
Lviny Bridge **39**

M

Mandelshtam, Osip **79**
Marble Palace **8, 29–30,
    82, 88**
Mariinsky Palace **10, 31**
Mariinsky Theatre **10, 11,
    33, 39**
media **53**
metro system **127**
Menshikovsky Palace **17, 106**
Mikhailovsky Castle **9, 85, 88**
Mikhailovsky Gardens **8,
    112–13**
Mikhailovsky Palace **8, 31**
Mikhailovsky Theatre **9, 33**
Millionaya Ulitsa **8**
Mining Institute **17, 30**
Moika, River **9, 38–9, 80**
money **4, 53**
Monument to Nicholas I **10,
    84–5**
Monument to Peter the
    Great **85**
Monument to Pushkin **85**
Monument to Suvorov **85**
Monument to the Heroic
    Defenders of Leningrad
    21, 99
Monument to Victims of Political
    Repression **84**
Monument to Victims of the
    Revolution on the Field of
    Mars **84**
Moscow Triumphal Arch
    21, 84
Moskovsky Prospekt **20–21,
    99, 121**

Museum of Decorative and
    Applied Arts **9, 86–7**
Museum of Old St Petersburg
    12, 93–4
Museum of Political History **14,
    87, 95–6**
Museum of Space Exploration
    and Rocket Technology
    13, 94
Museum of the Defence of
    Leningrad **9, 87**
Museum of the History of St
    Petersburg and Petrograd
    1703–1918 **12, 93**
museum tickets **93**
music stores **101**

N

Nabokov, Vladimir **10, 79,
    92–3**
Narva Triumphal Arch **21, 84**
Nekrasov Apartment Museum
    18, 97
Neva, River **4, 11, 16, 38, 39,
    50, 103**
Nevsky Prospekt **5, 6–7, 36, 40,
    44–5, 66–7, 86, 114**
Nevsky Vorota **13**
New Holland Island **11, 39**
Nikolaevsky Palace **31, 33**
Novodevichy Monastyr **20**

O

Obukhovsky Bridge **39**
Oceanarium **43**

P

Palace Square **5, 8, 36, 40,
    67–9, 86–92, 114–16**
pampering **35**
Park of the Aviators **21**
Pavlovsk **24–5, 109, 110**
Peace Tower **20**
Penaty **25, 99**
Peter and Paul Cathedral **12,
    28, 47–8**
Peter and Paul Fortress **5,
    12–13, 78, 93–4, 113, 118**
Peterhof **5, 22–3, 109, 110, 121**
Petrograd Side **14–15, 48,
    70–71, 94–6, 118–19**
Petrovskie Vorota **13**
Petrovsky Stadium **15, 125**
petty crime **53**
Pevchesky Bridge **38**
Ploshchad Alexandra
    Nevskovo **7**

Ploshchad Dekabristov **10**
Ploshchad Pobedy **21**
Popov Memorial Apartment
    Museum **15**
Popov Museum of
    Communications **11, 87, 93**
popular music **101**
population **4**
Potseluev Bridge **39**
Printing Museum **13**
prosushka **113**
Puppet Theatre **43**
Pushkin, Alexander **6, 80–81**
Pushkin, town, **24, 25**
Pushkin Memorial Apartment
    Museum **8, 80, 89**
Putin, Vladimir, dines out **121**
Pyat Uglov **18**

R

Rasputin, Grigory **11, 107, 111**
recycling **51**
Red Bridge **39**
Repino **25, 112**
Rimsky-Korsakov, Nikolai
    11, 98
Rimsky-Korsakov Conservatory
    11, 100
Rimsky-Korsakov Museum
    18, 98
Rossi Ulitsa **31**
Rostral Columns **16, 30, 85**
Russian cuisine **30–31**
Russian National Library **7,
    21, 30**
Russkaya Antrepriza
    Theatre **15**

S

St Andrew's Cathedral **17, 48**
St Catherine's Roman Catholic
    Church **7, 45**
St Isaac's Cathedral **5, 10,
    31, 46–7**
St Isaac's Square **10**
St Nicholas's Cathedral **11,
    45, 47**
St Petersburg Philharmonic
    9, 100
SS Peter and Paul Lutheran
    Church **45**
Seaside Victory Park **15, 113**
Senate **10, 30**
Sennaya Loshchad **20**
Sennoy Rynok **20**
Shemiakin's Sphinxes **19**
Sheremetev Palace **9**

143

Shostakovich, Dmitry **11, 100**
skiing **124**
Singer Building **6, 31**
Siny Bridge **39**
Smolensk Lutheran
  Cemetery **17**
Smolensk Orthodox
  Cemetery **17**
Smolny **19**
Smolny Cathedral **19, 29, 49**
Smolny Institute **19, 113**
Solnechnoye **25, 112**
Solyanoi Pereulok **9**
souvenirs **122–3**
State Russian Museum **8, 87,
  91–2**
Strelka **16, 17**
Stroganov Palace **5, 29, 86**
Summer Gardens **9, 106, 113**
Summer Palace **106**
Suvorov Museum **19, 98**
Synod **10, 30**
Sytny Rynok **14, 63**

T

tapochki **97**
Tauride Gardens **19, 113**
Tauride Palace **19**
taxis **105**
Tchaikovsky, Pyotr **6, 10**
tennis **125**

theatre etiquette **32**
Theatre Museum **7**
Theatre Square **11**
theatre tickets **32**
time zone **4**
tipping **114**
Tourist Angels **53**
Tourist Information **52**
traffic **51**
Trinity Cathedral **20, 49**
trolleybuses **127**
Trubetskoi Bastion **12**
Tsarskoe Selo **24**
TV Tower **15**
Twelve Colleges **17, 28**

V

Varshavsky Express **20,
  55, 123**
Vasilievsky Island **16–17, 48,
  71, 96–7, 119–20**
vegetarians **119**
Victory Park **21, 113**
visas **53, 72**
Vitebsky Voksal **20**
Vladimir Cathedral **18, 49**
Vladimir Nabokov Museum
  10, 79
Vladimirskaya **18, 37, 48–9,
  71–3**
vodka **61–2**

W

walking **50, 128**
water quality **50**
water taxis **127**
Waterville Aqua Park **43**
White Nights **9, 38, 57, 77,
  99, 103**
Winter Palace **8, 29, 89** *see
  also Hermitage Museum*
World of Water museum **98–9**

Y

Yelagin Island **15**
Yelaginsky Dvorets **15**
Yeliseevsky shop **31**
Yubileiny Sports Palace
  15, 124
Yusupov Palace **11, 30, 106–7**
Yusupovsky Sad **20**

Z

Zhyolty Bridge **38**
Zoology Museum **16, 97**

Insight SmartGuide: St Petersburg
Written by: **Shura Collinson**
Edited by: **Jason Mitchell**
Proofread and indexed by: **Neil Titman**
All Pics © APA/Nick Bonetti and Anna
Mockford except:
4Corners 76/77; **Alamy** 75, 77B, 117T,
127B; **AKG London** 4T; **Casa Leto** 69;
Corinthia Nevskij Palace 66B; **Fotolibra**
2B; **Getty** 56B; **Ibis** 70/71; **Istockphoto,**
36/37, 103B, 105B, 118B, 119T,
120TL; **Kempinski** 66/67, 68BL, 68BM,
68BR, 114/115, 115B; **Kobal** 58/59;
Laif/Camera Press 117; **Novotel** 72T;
PA Photos 58B; **Photolibrary.com** 52B;
Rezidor Hotel Group 67B, 73B, 73R,
73T; **RIA Novosti/Topfoto** 56T, 76B, 78T,
79B, 80, 81BR, 87B; **Robert Harding**
61BR, 119B, 120L; **Sokos Hotel Group**
70T, 72L, 72R; **Stockfood** 120TR
TASS 32/33, 33B, 35B, 36, 37B, 41B,
42/43, 42B, 50B, 52/53, 54/55, 55BL,
55BM, 5BR, 60/61, 60B, 62B, 62M,
62T, 63B, 63T, 78B, 79T, 84B, 84T, 88T,

92L, 92R, 98B, 98T, 102/103, 102B,
104M, 105T, 118M, 118T, 121, 128B
Picture Manager: **Steven Lawrence**
Maps: **James Macdonald**
Series Editor: **Jason Mitchell**

First Edition 2009
© 2009 Apa Publications GmbH & Co. Verlag KG Singapore Branch, Singapore.

Printed in Singapore by Insight Print
Services (Pte) Ltd

Worldwide distribution enquiries:
**Apa Publications GmbH & Co. Verlag KG
(Singapore Branch)** 38 Joo Koon Road, Singapore 628990; tel: (65) 6865 1600; fax:
(65) 6861 6438

Distributed in the UK and Ireland by:
GeoCenter International Ltd
Meridian House, Churchill Way West, Bas-
ingstoke, Hampshire RG21 6YR; tel: (44
1256) 817 987; fax: (44 1256) 817 988

Distributed in the United States by:
Langenscheidt Publishers, Inc.
36–36 33rd Street 4th Floor, Long Island
City, New York 11106; tel: (1 718) 784
0055; fax: (1 718) 784 0640l
Contacting the Editors
We would appreciate it if readers would
alert us to errors or outdated information
by writing to:
Apa Publications, PO Box 7910, London SE1
1WE, UK; fax: (44 20) 7403 0290;
e-mail: insight@apaguide.co.uk
No part of this book may be reproduced,
stored in a retrieval system or transmitted
in any form or by any means (electronic,
mechanical, photocopying, recording or
otherwise), without prior written permission
of Apa Publications. Brief text quotations
with use of photographs are exempted for
book review purposes only. Information has
been obtained from sources believed to be
reliable, but its accuracy and complete-
ness, and the opinions based thereon, are
not guaranteed.